# Ideas of Human Nature

# Ideas of Human Nature

*An Historical Introduction*

## Second Edition

Roger Trigg

**Blackwell**
Publishing

© 1988, 1999 by Roger Trigg

BLACKWELL PUBLISHING
350 Main Street, Malden, MA 02148-5020, USA
9600 Garsington Road, Oxford OX4 2DQ, UK
550 Swanston Street, Carlton, Victoria 3053, Australia

First published 1988
Second edition published 1999
10   2007

*Library of Congress Cataloging-in-Publication Data*

Trigg, Roger.
   Ideas of human nature: an historical introduction /Roger Trigg. —2nd ed.
      p.   cm.
   Includes bibliographical references and index.
   ISBN 978–0–631–21405–4 (alk. paper)—ISBN 978–0–631–21406–2 (pbk. : alk.paper)
   1. Philosophical anthropology—History. I. Title.
BD450.T668   1999
128—dc21                                             99–30907
                                                         CIP

ISBN: 978–0–631–21405–2 (alk. paper)—ISBN: 978–0–631–21406–9
(pbk. : alk.paper)

A catalogue record for this title is available from the British Library.

Set in 10 on 12.5 pt Photina
by Kolam Information Services, Pvt. Ltd, Pondicherry, India
Printed and bound in Singapore
by Fabulous Printers Pte Ltd

The publisher's policy is to use permanent paper from mills that operate a
sustainable forestry policy, and which has been manufactured from pulp
processed using acid-free and elementary chlorine-free practices. Furthermore,
the publisher ensures that the text paper and cover board used have met
acceptable environmental accreditation standards.

For further information on
Blackwell Publishing, visit our website:
www.blackwellpublishing.com

# Contents

# Preface to the Second Edition

It is over a decade since the first edition of this book appeared in 1988. In that time there have been major political and intellectual changes. No topic is more fought over than that of human nature, and I have added a new concluding chapter dealing with some of the more recent fashions in thought, particularly that of postmodernism, which has reinforced scepticism about the possibility of a human nature that transcends history and culture. Since the postmodernist attacks on the whole Enlightenment project has focused attention on the nature of Enlightenment thinking, I have also added two new chapters on Locke and Kant, as two Enlightenment thinkers, though each very different from the other. I have left the other chapters almost untouched, so as not to cause confusion between the editions.

Some obvious candidates have still had to be left out of this book, but each of the twelve thinkers considered have been vastly influential in the history of western thought. It is no exaggeration to say that the history of the whole world would have been different but for some of the writings of those included. The views people have of themselves, and of their nature, guide their actions. A recent example is that of the influence of Marx. When this book first came out, his ideas were still a major political force. Now, with the collapse of Communism in Eastern Europe, it seems to many that his theories have been discredited, if not even disproved. Yet his views will have to be replaced by an alternative vision of what constitutes humanity.

There is no philosophical subject that is more appropriate than that of human nature for consideration in different countries and indeed different continents. As I remarked in a foreword to the Korean edition of the book, by definition it is something we all share, and arguments about it are relevant to everyone. Whatever society we belong to and whatever culture has nurtured us, the most important fact about us is that we are human. We all have far more in common with those of other races and civilisations than might first appear. Indeed it is because of this that works such as this book can be translated from one language to another and still be relevant to the reader. It is because of this that the subject of this book is of perennial importance.

I am grateful to the many people with whom I have discussed the topics of this book over the years. In particular, however, I must express my thanks to my daughter, Alison, for her help.

April 1999
Stratford-upon-Avon

# Introduction

There can be no single, simple definition of human nature. Many intertwining ideas in the history of philosophy have helped us to form our understanding of ourselves. Yet there can be no more important question than who we think we are, unless it is who I think I am, and who you think you are. The twin questions of the character of humanity and the nature of the individual person are always linked. If I think that humans are indeed a little lower than the angels, and may live on beyond this life, then I shall view myself differently from the person who accepts that the species *Homo sapiens* is one animal species amongst many, characterized only by a particular evolutionary history. The tug between seeing humans as packages of genes, existing without purpose, and as the special creation of a loving God is the modern version of a perennial debate amongst philosophers. Is human life exclusively moulded by physical forces of which we may be totally unconscious?

Human reason appears to have the power of raising itself at times beyond the constraints of its time and place. Some philosophers have even seen in it the spark of the divine. In more recent times, the ability of our reason to control our destiny has been doubted, and all kinds of unconscious forces, both social and psychological, have been alleged to be the real masters. The free, autonomous individual has suddenly seemed to be a mere puppet dancing to a tune that often cannot be heard. The self – what makes me the person I am – has seemed progressively to vanish under onslaughts from every direction. Whereas it once appeared that I was an immortal soul with an eternal destiny, and that my reason could grasp in part the true nature of things, it has over the last century or so seemed as if I cannot even be fully aware of my own nature. 'I' am the product of my genes, my society, my earliest experiences or a combination of these. In any case 'I' do not apparently exist apart from the influences that have undoubtedly been at work, shaping me and moulding me. Human reason is not what it seems, and the truth it tried to grasp may be purely illusory too. So at least, some, like Nietzsche, have concluded.

At the back of those reflections, there is one unsettling fact that all philosophers worthy of the name must at some time confront. We are all mortal. It may sound trivially true, but it becomes a problem for each of us, when we realize that each must die. How can I reconcile the fact that I am going to die with the meaning I give my life? Philosophers from Plato onwards have strenuously argued for the immortality of part at least of the human person. The Christian religion made the issue one of central importance. Without the possibility of a life beyond this one, Christ could not have been raised from the dead. Many thinkers have, however, preferred to concentrate their attention on this life, denying anything beyond. Yet without some kind of transcendental guarantee of the importance and worthwhileness of human life, it is easy to slip into despair. Certainly questions about the meaning of life cannot finally be denied from issues concerning the nature of humanity and our place in the world.

Ideas of human nature are not merely of importance to the individual, but radically affect the kind of society we live in and the kind we would like to live in. How far do we need society? Is it feasible to imagine living in splendid isolation? Linked to this is the question as to whether we are all naturally only concerned for ourselves, and only willing to co-operate with others when it is in our interests to do so. Are we, on the other hand, social beings by nature, eager to co-operate with others for the common good? Our political views may be influenced by our answers. There is also the problem about whether our natural inclinations and desires have to be restrained in society or whether they find their proper expression in it. Does the 'beast' in us need restraining, and is civilization the result of curbing some of the strongest of human impulses? Freud certainly thought so, although he regretted the fact.

Might it, therefore, be possible to change human nature through political means? Anyone who believes this will be likely to have greater faith in the effectiveness of political change, and may even be tempted by a doctrine of revolution. Those who consider human nature to be fixed, perhaps biologically, may well be more cynical about the likely effects of political action, and perhaps be more ready to acquiesce in the existing state of affairs. Conservatism, as a political philosophy, however, may also thrive when the central role of custom and tradition in human life is experienced. If they have made us what we are, by striking at them, we may seem to be striking at ourselves.

Ideas about human nature are of their essence philosophical. They are not simply the result of scientifically established facts, but are general conceptions arrived at through rational argument. They are inevitably often controversial, but the theories produced determine our vision of ourselves. Indeed the fact that human reason is capable of such reflection about itself already tells us something of human nature. Most writing on the subject is explicitly philosophical. Since, though, philosophical assumptions about our nature lie at the root of any discipline concerned with the activities of men and women, it is not surprising that some thinkers have written primarily from the standpoint of another intellectual discipline. Aquinas could perhaps be classified as primarily as theologian, Darwin a biologist, Marx a political economist and Freud a psychologist. Yet all of them were unable to be confined by the artificial constraints of one discipline. Their thinking went to the very root of human existence and had to become philosophical. Without a conception of what it is to be human, no one can say much about human societies or human practices. All too often, such assumptions are merely implicit in the work of various intellectual disciplines. Only the greatest thinkers are able to make them explicit. Yet history, social anthropology, sociology and politics, to name only the most obvious, all proceed with some view about human nature.

The largest assumption of all, which should never be taken for granted, is that there is such a thing as 'human nature'. The concept has implications, particularly that we can assume similarities merely on the basis of membership of one biological species. We will then all have some tendencies, and some likes and dislikes, in common simply because of our common humanity. That notion of humanity would not be an empty one. It is in fact controversial to hold that saying someone is human already tells us a lot about him or her. Many assert that belonging to a society is far more significant, because we are moulded by our society. If, however, this view is pressed very far, it becomes clear that we cannot assume any point of contact between members of one society and those of another. Neither set would then be able to understand the other. As a consequence, any discipline depending on the comparison of people in different societies would find its very existence threatened.

History is impossible if we cannot attribute similar motives to inhabitants of the past as to ourselves. Politics cannot compare the effects of different political systems if the members of one are not fundamentally similar to those of another. Social anthropology cannot hope to grasp the strange customs of those who, on this view, would be as alien to us as the inhabitants of some distant planet in science fiction.

The idea that it is possible to select twelve thinkers from a period of nearly two and a half millennia and from a wide variety of countries and political systems, and to consider that they are arguing about the same issues when they write about humanity, suggests that there must be such a thing as human nature. Plato and Aristotle are recognizably concerned with the same problems as philosophers writing in a world transformed by scientific and technological advance. People have remained the same. Asserting anything different is to admit that the history of philosophy is an impossible subject, particularly when it surveys issues about the essential character of humanity.

Some years ago I was visiting Pompeii, the Roman city buried by the volcanic ash of Vesuvius nineteen hundred years ago. I was looking at some of the wall paintings, while two American matrons were being shown round by an Italian guide. They were most anxious to see a painting hidden in an especially constructed cupboard. Its subject matter was pornographic, and the guide did not think it decorous for them to see it. Despite their loud complaints, he led them away saying, 'life has always been the same'. It is in the conviction that human life has remained the same in its essentials through recorded history that I make no apology for beginning a book on human nature with an ancient Greek philosopher. What he said is no less likely to be relevant to our present concerns than something written yesterday.

# CHAPTER ONE

# Plato

## *c.429–347* BC

## Context

Modern western philosophy, and the foundations of modern science, began in the Greek world of the eastern Mediterranean in the sixth century BC. The first philosophers looked for the reality behind the never-ending variety and change of the world we live in, saying that everything was really water, or air, or fire, or perhaps a combination of these. They showed that they were not content to trust in appearance: the real nature of things may well be hidden. They did assume however that human nature was subject to the same type of explanation as the physical world. The soul which gave human life was, for instance, regarded as breath, and hence air, or even as fire. It is perhaps anachronistic to call such philosophers 'materialists' even though they believed that only what was made of matter exists. The concept of the non-material had not yet been developed. Nevertheless a concentration on physical explanation left no room for talk of purpose. Everything, even human life, had occurred through a series of mechanical causes. Even when Anaxagoras, one of the philosophers before Socrates, talked of the existence of Mind as the origin of all motion, he explicitly referred to it in material terms. It was just finer and purer than other things. Plato and Aristotle were later to criticize this view, precisely because it did not make Mind the source of any purpose.

As philosophical speculation progressed, it became more obvious that we cannot rely on our senses to tell us the truth about the world. The Atomists, who believed that everything was composed of indivisible atoms and the void between them, taught that only atoms and void were real. Even taste, temperature and colour were only

matters of convention or *nomos*. This distrust of our senses led people
to wonder if anything could be true. Nihilism, the self-defeating belief
that nothing is true, seemed to beckon. A contrast was increasingly
drawn during the fifth century BC between what was true in nature,
or *physis* (from which the word 'physics' is derived), and what was a
matter of human custom or convention, *nomos*. At that time, the
Greeks were becoming more conscious of the great diversity that
existed between the customs of different places. The more contact
that was made with non-Greeks, such as Persians and Egyptians, the
more it was realized that laws and customs are human creations and
can vary from one country to another. What had previously been
taken for granted as a fixed part of human life came to appear even
arbitrary, depending on where one lived.

The historian Herodotus drew attention both to the diversity of
ways of life and to the fact that each society thinks its own actions
best.[1] He told the story of how the Persian king, Darius, asked the
Greeks of his court what price they would accept for eating their
fathers' bodies. They protested that they would never do such a
thing. When, though, he summoned people from India, whose custom was to eat their parents, and asked them how much they would
take to burn their parents' bodies, they were tremendously upset and
begged him not to speak of it. Herodotus then quoted with approval
a saying that *nomos* is lord of all.

There was also considerable diversity in customs between the
different city-states of Greece. It was pointed out that it was acceptable for females to exercise naked in the militarist state of Sparta, but
not elsewhere. Knowledge of such diversity in culture can often be
unsettling and so it proved in fifth-century Athens. Professional
teachers, called 'sophists' turned from wider speculation and concentrated on teaching practical skills such as rhetoric. Relativism
became a favoured doctrine. At its most extreme, that was the view
that whatever someone judges to be true *is* true for that person, but
it was more plausible when coupled with the distinction between
*physis* and *nomos*. Law, or convention, could be understood as having only a local validity. Just as it is nowadays right to drive on the
left in England, but wrong in the United States, so it was thought
that even moral principles could only be related to a particular time
and place. What was right in Sparta may be wrong in Athens. The
way we ought to live could only be traced back to particular political
arrangements, with no basis in the natural order of the world. There

was no ultimate purpose in life, and much that we took for granted was even illusory.

Some Greeks thought their laws were sanctioned by the gods but the spread of scepticism meant that sophists exploited the distinction between *nomos* and *physis* to advocate the abandonment of convention. We should follow our natural inclinations, doing what we want without worrying about moral constraints. It was inevitable that this stress on the validity of an individual's judgements should have been made in a democracy. Athens was a ferment of ideas, and a citizen with the gift of persuasion could quickly rise to prominence. The man who could sway the assembly of his fellow citizens could control Athens. As in all large gatherings, a powerful orator could sway people's emotions quickly. Decisions were made in haste and later regretted. At the end of the fifth century BC the Athenian democracy came to grief.

Demagogues led the people astray because they themselves lacked any real wisdom. That was how Plato saw the situation. He had seen the decline of the Athenian democracy and its defeat at the hands of Sparta. He had seen his beloved teacher, Socrates, condemned to death in 399 BC by the democracy for alleged corruption of the young. It was hardly surprising that the whole of Plato's thought represented a reaction to the view that everyone should rely on the validity of their own judgements. He wrote in dialogue form, and the hero of most of the dialogues is Socrates. It is difficult, therefore, in his earlier dialogues to be sure how far Plato is reporting the views of the historical Socrates. There is, afterwards, a gradual development of position. The early dialogues typically deal with such questions as the nature of virtue or holiness, while the middle period, exemplified by the *Republic*, shows the views normally associated with Plato. In later works like the *Theaetetus* and *Sophist*, his attention seems more taken up with technical philosophical issues, such as the question of the way words get their meaning. Even in these dialogues, his opposition to relativism is explicit.

Socrates was well known for asking for the definition of words. For instance, at the start of the *Meno* he wants to know what virtue is. Meno answers confidently by giving a whole list of virtues.[2] He says that a man should know how to administer the State in a way that would benefit his friends and harm his enemies, while a woman's job is to order her household properly and obey her husband. Socrates, however, is not interested in the list of examples, but wants to know what they have in common. He considered that all have a common 'Form' or 'essence' in virtue of which they are all virtues. Plato developed this technique of looking for the definition of general words, and considered that they were all names of things such as holiness or goodness. With this assumption he built a whole metaphysical system.

## Our Place in the World

Plato followed the example of pre-Socratic philosophers in looking for stability and permanence, but he knew that he could never find it in the constantly changing world of material objects. He turned from the implicit materialism of some of his predecessors and looked instead to another world which would provide the standards for all our judgements. This worked particularly well in the case of moral and mathematical concepts. Plato agreed that we only ever see approximate equality. We judge two sticks as more or less the same length by appealing to an absolute standard of equality, which must exist over and above the world we see. Similarly our moral standards are derived from another world beyond that of sights and sounds in which we live. Goodness is the name of a 'Form' which exists separately. It is what all good things have in common, because they share in it, and, in some way, reflect it. 'Goodness in itself' does not depend on the nature of our familiar world, and is certainly not dependent for its validity on human judgements. Like other Forms, it is objectively real, unaffected by human belief about it.

By postulating a world of Forms as absolute standards, Plato was able to draw an important distinction between knowledge and belief. The Forms could be the objects of knowledge. Most people have beliefs which are of their very nature unstable. We change our minds and are often wrong. Plato thought, though, that genuine knowledge must be tied down and linked in some fashion to the true nature of things. Anyone who possesses knowledge will, by definition, always act correctly, and hence Plato based his moral and political philosophy on his metaphysics. Democracy was not the best form of government because it depended on the fickle beliefs of the multitude. Instead he believed that any ruler should have knowledge of reality, and in the *Republic* he laid down a programme of education through which an elite of 'philosopher-kings' could be produced. They would then govern in the common interest because they alone *knew* what justice was and could judge everything by the right standard.

Plato's system is dualist. He believed there were two worlds, the perceptual world, and the real world of Forms which provides the guarantee of unchanging objective truth. This emphasis on the transcendent and immaterial world of Forms is somewhat mystical, and makes our own familiar world seem tawdry. Plato compares the soul to the eye, and truth to light. He says:

> When resting upon that on which truth and being shine, the soul perceives and understands and is radiant with intelligence; but when turned towards the twilight and to those things which come into being and perish, then he has opinions only, and goes blinking about, and is first of one opinion and then of another, and seems to have no intelligence.[3]

Plato likens the Form of Good to the sun, and in Book 7 of the *Republic* likens the human condition to the position of people who have been trapped from childhood in an underground cave. The passage is a famous and influential one. Plato tells of how they cannot turn round but can only look at a wall. Behind them a fire blazes and, between them and the fire, men pass along behind a parapet, carrying objects including statues and figures of animals. The objects cast shadows on the wall, just like puppets in a puppet show which are illuminated from behind. The prisoners also hear echoes of the voices of those carrying the objects. The point is that reality for them is constituted by shadows and echoes, even though they are merely copies of copies. As a result, they can only have a vague idea of, say, what a horse was like, since they would only have seen the flickering shadow of a crude model, and not a horse itself.

Plato shows how difficult it would be for a prisoner who was released. If he turned and looked at the fire, the glare would distress him and he would not at first be able to make out the images which cast the shadows. Thus he will be even more dazzled if he is dragged out of the cave into the sunlight. He could, to begin with, only bear to look at reflections in the water before looking at what cast them. In the end, however, he will be able to look at the sun itself, as the source of light. This is to Plato the equivalent in the everyday world of the Form of the Good in the intelligible world. Plato then points out that if the ex-prisoner returned to the cave, he would be a figure of fun, because his eyes would take a time to adjust to the darkness again. Everyone would say his eyes had been ruined and it was better not to think of ascending. Such, Plato says, is the state of anyone who passes 'from divine contemplation to the evil state of man'. If he is compelled to fight in courts of law he has to stumble amongst the images or the shadows of the images of justice with those 'who have never yet seen the true justice'. Plato is clearly remembering the fate of Socrates.

Enlightenment comes through knowledge of the eternal Forms. The vision of the Forms is the height of human aspiration, and all education must aim at producing it. Any doctrine positing another transcendent world has to explain how contact with it is possible. Plato's solution to the problem was that we regain knowledge we have already possessed. This is his theory of recollection, or *anamnesis*, according to which all learning is the recall to consciousness of innate knowledge. Plato illustrates the process in a cross-examination of a slave-boy by Socrates in the *Meno*.[4] The episode shows in miniature Socrates' usual method of arguing. The slave-boy is confronted with a geometric problem and at first answers confidently. Yet after sustained questioning he is reduced to confusion and realizes his ignorance. Finally after more questioning he can reach the right answer. Socrates' questions are leading ones and the boy understands each stage and agrees with what seems reasonable to him. Resources for gaining new knowledge seem to come from within him, and to be based on his current beliefs. Socrates maintains that the boy has recovered knowledge that he already had. The conclusion has to be that he was born with it, as he had never acquired it in this life. Socrates concludes that 'if the truth of all things always exists in the soul, then the soul is immortal.'[5] The soul must have been in contact with the Forms before it entered this life.

The process of recollection has been likened to a brass-rubbing that gradually reproduces the image of the brass beneath the paper laid on it. The image is at first hard to discern, but it finally becomes nearly as clear and detailed as the original. The distinction between knowledge at the forefront of our minds and latent knowledge that we do not realize we possess also points out the importance of the unconscious aspects of the human mind. Some have made connections between Plato's insight and Freud's doctrine of the unconscious. Certainly Plato's issues have been vastly influential in many respects. Not many in the history of western thought have followed Plato in his notion of the pre-existence of the souls, but the contention that we can rise above the constraints of the material world has exercised a perennial attraction.

Plato was so scathing about the impermanence of this world that he refused in the *Republic* to accept that it possesses genuine existence.[6] Only the Forms are genuinely real and can be proper objects of knowledge. Most people can only have beliefs, which can be easily changed, and they can only be about things that are themselves unstable, inhabiting a region between 'being' and 'non-being'. Plato drew back from completely denying reality to the ordinary world, but he certainly held that it was of considerably less worth than the eternal, unchanging world of Forms. A corollary of this is that the human soul is worth more than the body which imprisons it. In the *Phaedo* Plato maintains that the body holds the soul back in its search for truth.[7] The characteristic of the philosopher shall be to despise the body, since the soul, free of bodily sense and desire, can then aspire to knowledge of the truth.

In his later dialogues, Plato himself begins to question some of these doctrines. He is no longer so reluctant to admit that we can have knowledge of the world around us, or that we can attribute reality to it. He saw the difficulties of showing how the Forms are related to this world, and of deciding what should count as a Form. Nonetheless, his theory of Forms epitomizes 'Platonism', and his passionate commitment to objective truth against the contemporary threat of scepticism and relativism was never in doubt. The pursuit of knowledge remained the only proper role for humans.

## What is it to be Human?

Plato may have seemed to place a premium on intellectual knowledge, but for Socrates and himself knowledge encompassed everything. Socrates identified virtue with knowledge, since he optimistically thought that we will always do what we know is right. All that prevents us, then, from acting as we might is ignorance. One of Plato's major reasons for his theory of Forms was his desire to provide us with objective moral standards. Absolute

standards of justice and goodness may be imperfectly reflected in
the world, but we have to regain our knowledge of them. Plato's
rejection of the physical world as genuine reality means that our
attention must be switched to another realm. If we wish to live in
accordance with the way things are, we must become morally and
intellectually attuned to that reality.

Plato realized that human reason often conflicted with other parts
of our personality. We find the pursuit of virtue difficult, and in
explanation he divided the human psyche, or soul, into three parts,
each with its own distinctive desires. Reason should care for the
whole soul and control the emotional elements, which Plato divides
into two. Alongside the desires of reason, therefore, there are bodily
desires, for food, drink and sex, and also what is termed the 'spirited'
element which covers passions such as anger and ambition. Reason
has its own desires (for knowledge, for example) and can stir us to
action, but there is in all this the beginnings of a crucial distinction
between reason and desire. Plato exalts the characteristically human
possession of reason at the expense of the more animal parts of our
nature.

In a compelling image in the *Phaedrus*, Plato compares the three
parts of the soul to a character trying to control two ill-matched
horses.[8] One, corresponding to the spirited element, is of noble breed,
and relatively amenable, while the other, representing bodily desire,
is badly bred and poor looking 'hardly yielding to whip and spur'.
Reason is the charioteer and has a hard job controlling both, particularly the one representing bodily desire. Plato believes that reason
must dominate, but equally each part of the human personality is
essential. Reason cannot cut the horses loose but must keep on
guiding them. The aim should be harmony and integration, not
just the pursuit of reason at the expense of everything else.

The relationship of rational and irrational elements in human
character is always going to be a problem for views like Plato's.
Exalting reason and locating truth in a different realm, makes it
tempting to dismiss this world and its desires. Plato does recognize
that this hardly does justice to the facts of human psychology. He
recognizes that sexual desire is the 'chief officer' of our appetites, and
the image of the charioteer shows how difficult it is to control it. Yet
Plato sometimes associates reason and purity, and imagines their
true home is in the world of Forms. The rational part of the soul then
seems not just the guide for the other parts but actually to *be* the

soul. There is indeed a problem about the immortality of the soul if part of it is only content with the satisfaction of bodily desires. The part we share with animals may appear expendable if the soul is to be separated from the body.

Plato insists on the immortality of the soul, saying that its inherent vice or evil has not the power to destroy it. He does realize that 'it is not easy for that thing to be immortal which is composed of many elements not perfectly adapted to each other, as the soul has appeared to us to be.'[9] He argues that the soul in this life does not correspond to its true nature, because it is corrupted by association with the body, the needs of which reach into the soul. Its character is to some extent altered through association with the body. He likens the soul to a sea-god, who was not recognized because his limbs were damaged by the waves and he was covered with seaweed and encrustations. So the soul is disfigured in this life, but could be seen as it truly is if only it were to give itself to the love of wisdom. The tripartite division may give a fair view of the embodied soul, but Plato recognizes its deficiencies when the soul's ultimate destiny is remembered.

There is a recurring image derived from Plato of the body imprisoning the soul. Plato's dualism certainly opposes the immaterial and the material, and it seems natural to link the latter with all that is evil. Its impermanence and changing character was reason enough for Plato to look elsewhere for the source of truth. Yet although the soul could not be destroyed, it was not for that reason naturally good. It may seem odd to think of an immaterial soul literally having 'parts', but Plato's division draws attention to the inner conflict that so often occurs. Our choices are not necessarily going to be morally right and the whole point of what Plato says is that we are only going to be right by accident without a proper education to enable us to see what is really good and just. Often we will be hopelessly wrong. The human soul is not insulated from evil but may be the source of it if it does not possess knowledge. We have to be judged in accordance with a standard external to ourselves. Just because we happen to believe something right or good does not mean that it is.

Plato takes the conflicts that arise in us seriously, but his eyes are on distant horizons. Our true nature resides in the life of reason, derived from knowledge of ultimate reality. Christians have been tempted to see something of the Christian God in the Form of

Goodness, but it is an impersonal pattern and standard, and not a personal Creator. The Forms are 'universals' in that many different objects can share in them. We can all be good and that means we each share in that Form. The more we can aspire to a personal acquaintance with the Forms, the more we fulfil our real nature. As with all mysticism, however, there comes a point when the individual seems to be swallowed in a wider whole. Reality is possessed by the universals and not the particulars reflecting them. This poses the question of the nature of our individuality. Plato was influenced by the Pythagorean belief in the transmigration of souls. The more he thought of a soul as an impersonal spark of reason trying to recover its intimate relationship with the source of all knowledge, the easier it was to discount the particular features of a person's individuality. Philosophical contemplation could then appear as the highest and most noble way of life open to us.

## Human Society

Plato's concerns were not merely other-worldly, since the *Republic* is intended as a blueprint for the perfect State. He wanted to educate a whole class in his ideal city who would govern wisely in the interests of everyone. They would *know* what was just because their souls had grasped the true nature of justice. He asserts boldly:

> Until philosophers are kings in their cities, or the kings and princes of this world have the spirit and power of philosophy ... cities will never have the rest from their evils – no, nor the human race, as I believe, and then only will this our ideal State have a possibility of life and behold the light of day.[10]

One objection to Plato's vision is encapsulated in the Latin tag: *Quin custodiet custodes ipsos?* (Who will guard the guardians?) i.e. what guarantee is there that the elite of 'philosopher-kings' or guardians will not be corrupted by their power? If humans can never become perfect, this is an insuperable objection. Plato, however, believed that a class of rulers could be produced, given the right education, who would be governed by reason and not by the more unruly parts of their souls. That is why much of the *Republic* is devoted to education. Plato thought it more important to produce the right kind of person than to lay down detailed regulations governing the life of the State. He thought that if only the citizens were well educated they would find out for themselves what regulations were necessary. A good State would be produced by good men.

Corresponding to the three parts of the human soul, Plato believed that there were three classes in a state, the guardians, auxiliaries and traders. Just as a just man had to achieve harmony between the different parts of his soul, so justice in a city entails the removal of discord between the classes. Plato does not merely draw an analogy between the State and the individual. He believed that the various classes gained their character from the types of individual making them up. Plato says very firmly that 'in each of us there are the same principles and habits which there are in the State: for it is from the individual that the State derives them.'[11] He goes on to say that the character of a country derives from individuals, whether it be the love of knowledge, which Socrates complacently asserts, 'may be claimed as the special characteristic of our part of the world' or the love of money, which he ascribes to Phoenicians and Egyptians.

In the same spirit, he tells a story to be told to future generations of the ideal city. Some are made of gold and are to have the power of command, others made of silver are to be 'auxiliaries', while others composed of brass and iron are to be craftsmen and husbandmen.[12] A golden parent will normally have a golden child, but Plato recognizes that this will not always happen. Sometimes the guardians will have children with brass or iron in their souls, and will have to send them down to the artisans. Similarly the child of an artisan could be promoted. Merit is to be given precedence over birth for the good of the State. Plato considered that there were limits on what education could achieve. People were not infinitely malleable, and his rigid class structure was intended to reflect, and not create, differences between individuals. He was the first to put forward the influential doctrine that education must identify and produce an elite as leaders of the country. Because he thought there was considerable variation in natural ability and inclination, he believed that this had to be reflected in the nature of society.

The problem was to ensure that the different classes lived together in harmony, avoiding the strife which was a familiar feature of Greek city-states. Just as moral virtue in the individual was to be achieved by the control of one part of its soul, justice was to be reached through the dominance of one class. Plato believed that only a minority could acquire knowledge of the Good and proposed to trust them with authority. Yet to ensure their identification with the State, he ruled that they should not have any private property, and not even be tempted to put loyalty to a family before the State. Wives and children were to be held in common. Temporary marriages would be arranged, but parents were not to know who their children were.

Plato has been accused of totalitarianism, and it looks as if he was prepared to sacrifice the welfare of individuals for that of the community. The aims of the State as a whole took precedence over the needs of particular members. Plato viewed this city as an organic unity, although it is by no means obvious how far the well-being of the community can be judged apart from the well-being of its members. Certainly Plato was prepared to show a surprising ruthlessness in the pursuit of ends he considered desirable. He even maintained that the rulers would find 'a considerable dose of falsehood and deceit necessary for the good of their subjects'.[13] He was, for instance, prepared to countenance a rigged lottery in order that some would not realize why they were not being allowed an arranged marriage.

The connection between the individual and the State is still a vexed problem. Plato's 'organic' conception of the State still left room for a stress on the importance of the individual. He did not believe that individuals gained their identity merely because of their role in the State. Despite his advocacy of a fairly rigid class system, he did not think that membership of a class was the most significant fact about a person. On the contrary he considered that they belonged to a class because of the kind of people they were. Similarly the State was only going to be as good as those that belong to it. Everything in the end has to be traced back to the state of an individual's soul. However important it is that everyone work together harmoniously for the good of the whole, this reinforces rather than removes the need for personal morality. Plato was no democrat, and was cynical, or realistic, enough to believe that only a few could achieve the moral virtue necessary for the guardianship of the State. Nevertheless the State is not an end in itself. There is a higher authority, the objective standards, or Forms, which are reflected in the fabric of the world.

Plato's whole view of justice stems from his stress on the importance of morality. Plato, and Socrates, believed that people's virtue comes from inside themselves, and should not rely on external contingencies. They have to set in order their own inner life, be in control of themselves and have an inward peace.[14] Plato was fond of musical metaphors and likened the three components of a person's soul with different notes on a scale. The aim should be harmony and the removal of discordance, issuing in just and good action. His belief in the immortality of the soul makes its inner state of more than transitory interest. His wish is that we regain contact with what is of eternal value. Only when we live in accordance with the true nature of things will we as individuals, and the State as a whole, be able to flourish.

Plato's answer to those who sought to oppose nature and custom, *physis* and *nomos*, is that all our customs, both the way we live as individuals and the laws instituted in a State, must reflect reality. 'Nature' is not just the physical world, but must include purpose and value. Plato would not have made any distinction between the world of science and that of morality, or between 'facts' and 'values'. In his view what ought to be the case can never be separated from what is the case. The State and its citizens have to recognize their place in a world where goodness is not a matter of individual taste or custom. It is to be found at the heart of the way things are.

## Contemporary Relevance

It has sometimes been said that all western philosophy since Plato has been merely a series of footnotes to his work. Certainly it is hard to come to any conclusion about human nature without making a stand on most of the issues Plato cared deeply about. The most basic one is whether humans are autonomous creators of value, or whether we live in a world so imbued with value that we choose to achieve happiness by living in accord with it and reap nothing but misery by going against the grain of our nature. For Plato the creation of injustice was 'the production of a state of things at variance with the natural order'.[15] Justice is to the individual soul and the body politic what health is to the human body. Deviation from it is corruption. Moral judgements are true or false and should be properly grounded in our understanding of the nature of the world and our place in it. Plato had no room for relativists whose denial of truth led them perilously close to the incoherent position of saying it was true that there was no such thing as truth. Yet his dispute with such philosophers is mirrored time and time again in contemporary arguments.

It is far from clear that he possessed a conception of the individual like the modern one. He did not regard the soul as being a unique particular, of ultimate value in itself. At the heart of the universe lay abstractions such as Goodness and not personality. The light of eternal reason may be locked inside me, but it is hard to see that as truly *me*. What controls my interests and emotions turns out to an impersonal principle. The contribution of an individual to the city lay in the knowledge of the Forms it could recover. Knowledge and truth should permeate the organic unity of the State. Nevertheless the stress on the moral qualities of individuals as the way in which this should be achieved puts the focus on the responsibilities of each person. A State will only be as good as its members. Plato's prejudice against democracy meant that he considered some members had a more vital role than others to play. Truth cannot necessarily be gained by majority votes. Yet a doctrine which places a high value on truth is always going to find it difficult to allow individuals to make their own wrong decisions. The desire for toleration and the love of truth sometimes pull in opposite directions.

Because Plato placed such importance on the individual as a moral agent, he was particularly concerned with the conflict that all too often occurs in the human soul. The fight between reason and desire is a perennial issue in philosophy, and many would be more sympathetic than Plato to the role of non-rational desire. The question remains whether inner conflict is an inevitable part of human life, and the same issue arises at the level of the community. By drawing clear demarcations between classes, Plato seemed to make major conflict within a community more likely. Yet this was precisely what he wanted to avoid. It was because he saw the dangers, that he proposed an authoritarian solution. In so doing, he dealt with at least two sources of conflict. In any society, first of all, there are conflicting conceptions of what is good. A so-called 'liberal' society might not attempt to adjudicate between them, but merely provide mechanisms to enable each person as far as possible to live according to his or her own ideals. Plato would have none of that. There is one Good, and the life of the State should reflect that. The guardians' knowledge must direct the government of the city.

Another political source of conflict lies in the egoism of individuals who pursue their own interests ruthlessly at the expense of everyone else. This inevitably means that the powerful will always win, and it was the view which lay behind Thrasymachus' cynical belief, stated at the beginning of the *Republic*, that justice was merely 'the interest of the stronger'. Plato believed the human nature could resist the temptations of power. With their own souls under rational control, his rulers would control the city without any regard for personal gain. Yet their personal identification with the city was bought at great cost. Without family life and private property, their individuality was submerged. Their way of life would seem thoroughly unnatural.

The problem of egoism, or selfishness, raises the question of the nature of the self. What is the self that wants to further its own interests at the expense, perhaps, of other selves? Any view of human nature cannot be content with looking at humanity in general. It must also look at the differences between humans, and the conflict within each, to see if these influence the way they interact with each other. Plato's work demonstrates that the nature of human personality is a central part of the problem of human nature.

# CHAPTER TWO

# Aristotle
## 384–322 BC

## Context

The world of Plato was also that of Aristotle. Born in 384 BC he was Plato's pupil in the Academy, the school of philosophy which Plato founded in Athens. He stayed there for some twenty years, only leaving when Plato died. He eventually returned to found a new school of his own, called the Lyceum or *Peripatos*. For some of the intervening period he acted as tutor to the teenage son of King Philip of Macedon. Since the boy was to become Alexander the Great, one of the great figures of history, this was a not insignificant appointment. More important from a philosophical point of view, Aristotle's views matured and came to diverge in crucial respects from those of Plato.

Aristotle left a wide variety of works, perhaps meant to be summaries of his courses at the Lyceum rather than polished literary works. He wrote on scientific subjects and comparative politics as well as more theoretical topics. Divisions between subjects that we take for granted owe much to Aristotle. His book the *Metaphysics* was so called merely because it came after the *Physics* (*meta* means after). Yet its subject matter is still known as 'metaphysics'. Basic categories of thought that seem a matter of common sense often owe their origin to Aristotle. The very notion of such a category is Aristotle's, and it was he who emphasized the importance of 'substance'. Faced with the problem of a changing world, which had so concerned his predecessors, he carefully distinguished between the subject of a change and the manner in which it could change while still remaining the same thing. Something could change colour, for example, but it did not thereby go out of existence. The substance remained.

Aristotle's approach was more down to earth and less mystical than Plato's. He denied that 'Forms' could be separated in a higher realm of being, and located them within the world, rather than alongside it. The Form of a statue does not reside in some transcendental world, but is *in* the statue and is the way in which the matter of a thing is structured. A Form is still a universal in that there can be different instances, as when there can be several copies of one statue. The Form makes the statue what it is, and without it there would be just a shapeless lump of, say, bronze. Aristotle allows that forms can be superimposed on each other. He recognizes that bronze, itself, is already structured. At bottom, though, in principle, lies prime matter which is totally unstructured. Everything we see is a combination of matter and form. Each substance is a product of the two.

Central to Aristotle's thought is his theory of causation,[1] which is broader than the modern conception of causation. He was looking at the reason for a thing's nature, the necessary conditions for it being what it is. He emphasized both the material cause – what something is made out of, and the formal cause – the way it is structured. He also posited an efficient cause, which was more in line with what we would term causation, referring to the source of change. A craftsman is the efficient cause of what is made, and Aristotle maintained that the father is the cause of the child in this sense. The most significant cause for Aristotle is the 'final' cause. This referred to that for the sake of which something is done. Aristotle gives an example of walking to be healthy, where health is the final cause of walking. With this notion of a purpose or *telos*, Aristotle showed his commitment to a teleological view, looking for purpose is everything and not just in people's intentional actions. Aristotle thought it appropriate to ask for the *telos* or end of human beings. In this he was in agreement with the campaign of Socrates and Plato against the sophists' views. Mind and purpose were as important to Aristotle as to Plato, despite his rejection of Plato's two worlds.

Aristotle was ready to welcome the fact of diversity and individuality in a way well illustrated by his criticism of Plato's idea of the State as organic, on the grounds that it is too undifferentiated. He points out that a population is made of many different kinds of people, and says: 'There is a point at which a State may attain such a degree of unity as to be no longer a State, or at which, without actually ceasing to exist, it will become an inferior state, like har-

mony passing into unison' (Aristotle, *Politics*, 1263b, trans. Ross)
The State is in fact a plurality, 'which should be united and made
into a community by education'.

Aristotle's vision was set much more than Plato's on this world,
which he thought had neither beginning nor end. It was neither
created, nor progressing towards some perfect state, although he
accepted the notion of an ultimate final cause, the Unmoved Mover,
who is 'eternal and unmovable, and separate from sensible things'.[2]
He argued explicitly against the notion of a Form of the Good,
arguing in particular for its irrelevance to the practical concerns of
this life.[3] A doctor, he suggests, will not be helped by having a vision
of 'good itself'. He does not even study health on its own, but is
concerned with human, and, in particular individual health. After
all, a doctor heals individuals. Certainly the vision of eternity stirs
Aristotle less than Plato. Plato had linked what was most worth
while with what lasted. Aristotle however dismisses this and says of
the 'good' that it will not be any more good for being eternal. He
adds that something is no whiter for lasting a long time than what
perishes in a day.

The yearning for eternity and the feeling that what does not last is
not worth much is nevertheless very pervasive in human beings.
The idea that living a human life is like writing in the sand on a
beach, while the tide is coming in fast has always terrified many
people. All traces of our existence will soon be wiped away. The
ensuing sense of impermanence and future bereavement and extinction has often been too much for some people to bear. The knowledge of our own future death and the consequent belief that
everything must be ultimately meaningless is a basic human experience. All theories of human nature should take it seriously. Yet on
this issue, despite their strong sense of the centrality of purpose,
Plato and Aristotle parted company. Aristotle dealt with the problem
of change within this world without feeling the need to point to
eternal standards as the sources of meaning and value. For him
truth did not require permanence.

## Our Place in the World

Aristotle's awareness of the importance of differences in the world,
whether between people in a State, or between States, did not lead

him to relativism. He looked for purpose in everything. He recounts how the family first arose, to be followed by an association of families in a village. The several villages unite in one community (a *koinonia*) which is large enough to be self-sufficient. Aristotle then argues that if the earlier forms of society are natural, so is the State, as it is their 'end'. He adds that the nature of a thing is its end (the *physis* is its *telos*.) He continues:

> For what each thing is when fully developed we call its nature, whether we are speaking of a man, or home, or a family. Besides, the final cause and end of a thing is best, and to be self-sufficing is the end and the best. Hence it is evident that the State is a creation of nature, and that man is by nature a political animal.[4]

Aristotle emphasizes this last point by distinguishing between humanity and bees as gregarious animals. He draws attention to the vital fact that philosophers constantly return to, namely, that alone of the animals, we possess the power of speech. This is particularly important, in Aristotle's view, as it means that we do not just make noises in response to pleasure and pain, as some animals do. It allows us to talk the language of morality, of what is just and unjust, good and evil. This is, for Aristotle, crucial in any community, whether the family or the State. He linked the purpose or function of an organism, or of an institution, with what was good for it. Nature had made it in that way, and reason could discover what was right for it. Thus the study of politics and law could not be separated from an understanding of their moral purpose. He begins his famous treatise on morality, the *Nicomachean Ethics*, by saying that his inquiry is a branch of political science, since the aim of politics is human good. Aristotle would never have been able to comprehend the modern desire to separate 'facts' from 'values', so as to cleanse political science, and indeed social science generally, of the taint of moral commitment. For him the nature of a community was inextricably bound up with what was good for it.

The individual cannot exist on his or her own, and nature has therefore created political organizations in which there is a division of labour, and hence classes. Anyone who cannot live in society, says Aristotle, is a god or an animal. An instinct for living in a community is implanted in us, although that does not mean that people will always associate together. Aristotle distinguished between what something could be potentially from what it was actually. An acorn is a potential oak tree, although it is not yet one. It is a part of a thing's nature to be one thing potentially but not another. An acorn is not a potential apple tree, for example, let alone a horse or a cow. Nevertheless it will not automatically grow into a large and flourishing tree. It needs the right conditions. Similarly, just because humans are sociable by nature does not mean that they will always be so. They need the right conditions in which to flourish. It is for this reason that Aristotle remarks that 'he who first founded the State was the greatest of benefactors.' The State provides the right environment for people to fulfil their nature. Aristotle says more than once that 'nature makes nothing in vain.' There is a proper end for humanity and for the communities in which humans live, but it is up to us to pursue this end by means of our reason. Aristotle says that humans are the best of animals, if they fulfil their proper purpose, but are the worst of all when separated from law and justice. History has all too often proved the truth of this.

The juxtaposition of the notions of nature (*physis*), and law (*nomos*) shows that Aristotle is intent on repudiating the sophists' separation of the two. His emphasis on the social instincts implanted in us shows that he does not accept that law, or custom, is in any sense unnatural or arbitrary. Its function is to complete our nature, rather than to go against it. Our nature needs it. He considered that three things made men good and virtuous (and only males were going to be citizens.)[5] They are nature, custom and reason. He insisted that each must be in harmony with the others, and it followed that citizens should be educated to care for the common interest. For Aristotle a city could be virtuous only when its citizens, sharing in the government, were virtuous. That is why he linked politics and ethics.

Aristotle thought it necessary for a city-state to rely on habit or custom to help create the right environment. An individual must have had proper character training through education, so as to be habituated to a life of virtue, while a State must ensure it has the right laws, proceeding from a rational basis. Aristotle was in no doubt of the importance of the rule of law. He remarks that people may hate being thwarted by other people but the law is not burdensome in laying down what is right.[6] An impersonal system of rules will work better than the imposition of a particular person's will, which will only rouse resentment.

Aristotle recognized a subtle interplay between natural justice and the law. He was well aware of the great divergence in practice between different constitutions, with different laws in different places. He therefore drew a distinction between natural and legal justice, so that laws need not be identical everywhere.[7] There could be variations in the light of particular circumstances, and in some matters the actual form of the law need not matter. In one case a regulation may require the sacrifice of two sheep, in another the sacrifice a goat. To take again the modern example of which side of the road to drive on, it is important that everyone follows the same rule, but nonsense to say it is more correct or just to drive on the left than the right. Yet Aristotle himself realizes that variation is enough to make some believe that *all* law is mere convention, like the rule of the road. He gives the example of physical laws, according to which 'fire burns both here and in Persia'. They have the same force everywhere, in a way in which laws of justice do not appear to. We cannot change the nature of fire, but we do seem to be free to go against what Aristotle claims is human nature. Yet he still wants to uphold what is natural, and therefore good, for each organism and each institution. Constitutions vary, but Aristotle insists that there is 'but one which is everywhere by nature the best'. People can act individually and collectively in an irrational and unprincipled way. Aristotle would claim that such random behaviour is typical of the slave mentality and of animals. It is not the way humans should act. Anyone can act in a degenerate way, but nature did not mean them to. Going against nature can only harm the agent, while going with it will be conducive to human well-being, or happiness.

Our place in the world is dominated by our role in human society. For Aristotle, human beings find their existence conditioned by their political context. That is not to say that they are moulded by society, but rather that the well-being of each individual cannot be separated from the well-being of the *polis*, or city. The political environment is a moral one too. Each city is a community with a common purpose and a shared moral end. Whilst allowing for considerable differences between individuals, Aristotle did not share the modern liberal ideal of letting each person decide his or her own ends. Such radical individual freedom would not only have seemed to Aristotle to be destructive of the very idea of community but also to have gone against reason itself. Each community must have a shared conception of what is good. 'The good life' could not be achieved by individuals in isolation.

## What is it to be Human?

Aristotle believed that slaves and animals were unfitted by nature to form a State, since they did not have the power of free, rational choice. Some humans are free by nature and those who are able to understand reason but not to exercise it themselves are slaves by nature.[8] The latter are still to be contrasted with animals, because Aristotle thought that even domesticated ones could not apprehend reason, but merely followed their instincts. The power of reason, which is as much a moral as an intellectual faculty, is what distinguishes the human from the animal. It makes civilization possible, and indeed the idea that the political is of primary importance is really just the view that humanity needs civilisation. We need to co-operate with one another, each contributing to the common good. It was perhaps inevitable that a Greek should associate a city so closely with what is good for humans. Its free association of citizens submitting gladly to the rule of law, and all aiming for the common good would seem to provide the very essence of what marked off humanity from the animals.

Reason could keep the uglier passions in check, and the results would be balance and harmony. For Aristotle, moderation was everything. The virtues were, for instance, means between extremes. A courageous person would avoid, for example, the twin extremes of cowardice and undue rashness. For similar reasons, Aristotle favoured the existence of a large middle class in a city. Yet he was a man of his time, willing to countenance slavery, and unwilling to give any but a subordinate place to women. For all that, his vision of a State whose citizens are fired by civic virtue as well as self-interest still has much to teach us. He was writing of comparatively small communities, compared with the vast nations that constitute the world today, but the emphasis on the need for citizens to aim at justice and the common good may still be relevant.

Aristotle's views were not based on vague aspirations or pious hopes, because his whole philosophy led him to believe that humans must behave in a rational manner if they were to follow their nature.

To be properly human, one had to use the powers that are distinctive of humans. He asked what plants and animals lack that humans possess. Even plants are nourished and grow. Animals can perceive things and act in accordance with decisions. Only humans possess reason. The conclusion drawn is that 'the function of man is an activity of soul which follows or implies reason.'[9] In particular, human good is the activity of the soul in accordance with virtue. Reason and moral goodness can never be properly separated.

The different faculties apparent in different creatures were related by Aristotle to the nature of the soul. Plants had a soul, he thought, which was concerned with nutrition. The soul of animals is related to their appetites and desires as well. The human soul, in turn, includes the nature of the plant and animal souls but in addition possesses the rational faculty. For all full-grown living things, plants, animals and humans, Aristotle recognized that 'the most natural act is the production of another like itself'. This would be a function of the nutritive soul, while perception is a matter for the appetitive faculty belonging to animals. He points out that if animals possess sensation and can feel pleasure and pain, they are bound also to desire to obtain what is pleasant and to avoid what is painful. Thought and calculation, however, are reserved for humans because of their reason. Talking of the soul of something is thus to refer to some ability of an organism, and not to a 'thing' hiding in the body. Aristotle would not imagine he could separate a plant's soul from the rest of the plant. The soul is the final cause of the body, in that it gives it its purpose, thus making it what it is. He uses the analogy of an eye, arguing that if an eye were an animal, its soul would be its sight.[10]

There is obviously great difficulty in thinking of a soul as separable from the body. This may not seem to matter in the case of plants, but it is of vital importance in that of humans. Plato had laid great stress on the immortality of the soul. Yet just as Aristotle made the forms present in things, instead of separated from them, he also made the soul, which he said was the form of the body, inextricably linked with the body. The result is a psychosomatic unity, which would find favour with many philosophers of mind today. All the faculties of soul are, Aristotle recognizes, linked to the complex of body and soul. The abilities of plants and animals are indissolubly linked with their material presence in the world. As Aristotle points out, though, even anger, courage, joy, loving and hating and all other 'affectations of the soul' have to be expressed through the body. Only if there is a way of acting, appropriate to the soul, which does not need a body, can the soul be envisaged as capable of separate existence.

Aristotle does wonder whether thinking might not provide an example of a capacity divorced from the body, but he mentions it tentatively.[11] His main emphasis is on embodiment, although he is no materialist. He does not believe that descriptions of the soul can be reduced to material terms. Nevertheless he is no dualist, separating mind from matter. To him a person is an embodied soul, or a 'souled' body. In so far as the soul is a form, it is reckoned a 'substance' by Aristotle, real enough, but not 'substantial' in a modern sense. It is the organizing principle in an organism, but he says firmly that it is unnecessary even to ask whether the soul and the body are one.[12] That is like asking whether wax and the shape given it by a stamp are one. We can, he believes, no more detach the soul from the body than separate the crest from the sealing-wax it has been pressed on.

There remains a tension in Aristotle's work despite his stress on the world we experience and his dismissal of other-worldly metaphysics, as well as his stress on the way humans find their proper existence within a city's civilization and the consequent emphasis on the role of practical wisdom and virtue. Involvement in the practical affairs of the city may be all very well, but Aristotle harks back to his definition of what is special about humanity. He says:

> That which is proper to each thing is by nature best and most pleasant for each thing: for man, therefore, the life according to reason is best and pleasantest, since reason more than anything else is man. This life therefore is also the happiest.[13]

The self-sufficient life of philosophic contemplation still holds the most attraction for Aristotle, and he felt it important to try to rise to the level of divine reason. He was not content to think merely of human things, but we must, he says, 'make ourselves immortal, and strain every nerve to live in accordance with the best thing in us'. Although Aristotle could not conceive of a creation of the world out of nothing, he did allow that there was an 'Unmoved Mover', the ultimate object of all thought and desire. The only possible object of divine thought was itself, and he aspired to grasp such divinity himself. Perhaps the influence of Plato lived on, since there is a difficulty, acknowledged by Aristotle, of making human good dependent on human nature, just as the good of everything else resulted from its own nature. It then seems somewhat contradictory to reach out beyond the human and attempt to grasp the divine. Either the 'Good' is independent of humanity and can be shared by us and God, or it is simply the outcome of human nature. In that case, the good for us could not also be the good for God.

Certainly the spark of reason within us, whether ultimately divine or not, is very much an impersonal matter. If the highest end for humans is theoretical contemplation, all that makes *me* up must be ultimately discarded. Absorption into the life of reason available to God leaves little room for self. An Aristotelian soul is very impersonal. What makes *me* the person I am is not explained by his doctrine of the soul. The body seems to have to provide the means of individuation. Yet an important part of being human is being a distinctive and unique individual. Being *me* and being human cannot be totally separated from each other. The nature of human personality is part of the problem of human nature.

## Human Society

Any State, not held together by force, requires some form of commitment from its citizens. An obvious reason for living in a community is self-interest, but a State based on the single-minded pursuit of self-interest by its citizens is very insecurely based. No one in such a State is really concerned for others or for the common good. Each tries to manipulate others for his or her own ends. The link between the existence of communities and the concern for self-interest is an issue of the utmost importance in any consideration of human nature, and most theories of human nature have to deal with it. A connected issue is the role and function of morality. Some would imagine that morality is merely a form of enlightened self-interest, as the maxim 'honesty is the best policy' suggests. One road safety slogan proclaims 'Drive carefully: the life you save may be your own.' That also appeals to prudential considerations.

Aristotle recognized the need for us to band together in communities larger than families or small villages, to provide the basic necessities of life and the context in which a good life can be lived. As well as regarding morality as a branch of politics, he also saw that citizens must be banded together by something other than appeals to justice and honour. Separate individuals cannot live together without ties of affection and concern for each other, such as the natural links between members of a family. The State is made up of families. He believed that even a master and a slave should be friends, with a common interest. Because of this conviction that family affection was important for the State, Aristotle attacked Plato's notion of wives and children being held in common, at least for the class of guardians. He complained that Plato deprives the guardians of happiness, holding this to be a serious matter on the grounds that the whole cannot be happy unless its parts enjoy happiness. He says: 'If the guardians are not happy, who are?'[14] He says that 'love will be watery' if women and children are held in common.[15] Affection distributed over a wide range of people becomes diffuse, and the intimate character of human relationships will be lost. As Aristotle observes, the father will not be able to say 'my son' or the son 'my father'. He continues: 'Of the two qualities which chiefly inspire regard and affection, that a thing is your own, and that it is your only one – neither can exist in such a state as this.'

Aristotle takes up a similar position over private property. He points out that everyone takes delight in their own possessions, and that people are far more devoted to what concerns them individually than to what is held in common. He wisely remarks that 'that which is common to the greatest number has the least care bestowed upon it'. He is therefore in favour of the institution of private property, but he insists that we should share our possessions with others, particularly our friends. 'Property', he says, 'should be private, but the use of it common.'[16] At root, he realizes that we all love ourselves, and he admits, 'love of self is a feeling implanted by nature and not given in vain'. He distinguishes, however, from the love of self which results in our obeying the most authoritative element in us, namely reason, and the selfishness that merely craves for the satisfaction of desire.[17] The common interest would be served if all were to strain for what is noblest within them.

Aristotle devotes, perhaps remarkably, two whole books of the *Nicomachean Ethics* to the topic of friendship. Austere philosophies of moral obligation have tended to concentrate on the importance of abstract principles, and have sometimes ignored the ties of blood and friendship which bind people together in a community. Indeed we are often told that favouring others merely because they are family or friends is morally questionable. No doubt it can be in some circumstances, but Aristotle did not doubt the moral importance of such basic associations between individuals. Friendship (*philia*), or affection, is, he believed the greatest good in a State. Far from being a threat to the common interest, it helps to bind people together and preserve States from revolution.[18]

Aristotle's concern for the common interest also led him to insist that education should be the business of the State, regulated by law.[19] Because the whole city had one end, each citizen must learn the same things through training and habit. The path of virtue was not a matter of private concern alone, and was too important to be left to individual whim. Yet Aristotle was under no illusion about the difficulty of acquiring virtue. The different faculties of the soul were always in potential conflict with each other. Nature may mean reason to have the authority, but it does not follow that it always will. We can only become virtuous by becoming accustomed to doing virtuous things. The courageous man, for instance, will learn courage by first performing courageous actions. A virtue is a state of character which has to be acquired. It is perhaps something of a paradox that we have to learn to act in the way that is most in accord with our true nature. What is natural is not necessarily what we find easiest to do or even what we most desire. It is, though, what will contribute most to our well-being. A State should help us to fulfil our nature, and Aristotle never underestimates the power of habit and tradition. Unless the State provides the right background, humans will never be able to flourish.

For Aristotle, reason, and not desire, decides the ends we are to pursue. What we want is not the same as what we need. His teleological approach means that he cannot allow as a serious possibility that we may each have different ultimate ends. Human nature is given to us and not chosen by us. We can act against it but we cannot abolish it. It is the function of society, he believes, to help us to act in accordance with our true nature, and, for this reason, the purpose of the State must be a moral one.

## Contemporary Relevance

It is sometimes said that, following Darwin, evolutionary biology has shown the truth of what Aristotle tried to demonstrate with his metaphysical teleology. Biology can, so it is claimed, show how humans have evolved with a moral sense. The demands of biological fitness have ensured that humans have a moral nature. This is in itself controversial, and we shall consider the claim in connection with Darwin's work. Although it may be attractive to couple the names of Aristotle and Darwin, on the grounds that they both link morality with human nature, it is also wrong. Even if evolution through natural selection has produced some kind of human 'moral sense', this would count as efficient causation, in Aristotle's terminology. It has produced our nature, but is not our end, or that for sake of which we exist. Aristotle does not believe we are naturally virtuous, since we have to learn how to acquire virtues. The path of evolution may have resulted in beings like us, but that says nothing about purpose or a final cause. Neo-Darwinian biology would have little room for such talk, holding that Aristotle's views were unscientific precisely because they were teleogical. The notions that organisms should be viewed as wholes and possess intrinsic goods, and that their development is linked to an appropriate end seems alien to much scientific thought. Yet the idea that the overall good of an organism can have a role even in the scientific explanation of its nature may be a fruitful one.

Aristotle's moral theory placed great emphasis on free, rational choice. Although he was well aware of the complexities of human psychology, human nature should be, he considered, firmly subordinated to reason. In the long line of philosophers who have opposed reason and desire, none has championed the role of reason more strongly. For him reason could not be merely the sorting out of different priorities and of inconsistencies between different preferences, as it is for many modern economists. The nature of the preference must itself be called into question, so that the harmful ones are discarded and the beneficial ones retained.

Aristotle's view of the State is different from many modern views. He does not think it should be an impartial referee trying to reconcile opposing interests and desires. He does not accept individual desire as basic, as though we are just a motley collection of private individuals with no shared interest. Private interest and public good may never be completely reconcilable, but Aristotle's vision was of citizens combining naturally to achieve the common good. He was aware of the significance of tradition, but he refused to adopt the 'organic' conception of the State, which he accused Plato of holding.

He gave much more notice to individuality and difference in a society, recognizing the reality of economic, social and cultural differences, and stressing that each person should obtain happiness. This was, however, in a basically moral context, in which the interests of one individual should not be pursued at the expense of others. Aristotle's world was a moral world, where there was no fundamental distinction between what is the case and what ought to be the case. We do not have to live in accordance with our true nature, but we will not find fulfilment or happiness unless we do. We incur a cost if we go against the grain of nature. We will flourish if we fulfil our natural potential. 'Value' is not chosen and created by isolated individuals, but is to be discovered woven into the fabric of the universe. With Aristotle a conception of natural law combining *physis* and *nomos* begins to be elaborated, which has had enormous influence and is still a live issue.

Aristotle avoids the excesses of rampant individualism by emphasizing community and custom. His stress on law and morality shows that he is still concerned for the freedom of the individual. His State depends on the moral responsibility of each person, and not collective force. Underlying everything will be the bonds of natural affection in families and friendship between citizens. When the alternatives seem to be totalitarian rule, or the struggle of each person to get his or her way at the expense of others, Aristotle might seem to be offering an attractive middle course. There are, though, obvious difficulties in transferring his vision from the context of a Greek city-state, with thousands of citizens, to a modern nation composed of many millions.

Despite, however, Aristotle's general policy of looking at the particular, rather than the general, the individual rather than the universal, and despite his determination not to let the State destroy the real differences between individuals, his treatment of the individual person raises difficulties. What is the nature of the self? The notion of an Aristotian soul may seem inadequate to those who believe they are more than their bodies. It seems to be merely a general principle of reason and of the other faculties, which does not in itself seem to account for what 'I' am. 'I', many would say, am unique. Moreover, Aristotle did not even think that humans are of special importance. He denied that the art of politics is the highest form of knowledge, since, he says, 'man is not the best thing in the world.'[20] He considered there were other things more divine in their nature than humanity, and he gives as an example 'the bodies of which the heavens are framed'. They had to be as they were, possessing necessary, rather than contingent, existence. For Aristotle personality is not at the heart of the universe. Abstract reason and its objects are of greater importance. In some matters, he has not moved as far from Plato as might first appear.

# CHAPTER THREE

# Aquinas

## 1225–1274 AD

## Context

A medieval Christian saint may seem a peculiar figure to deal with immediately after Plato and Aristotle. St Thomas Aquinas was born near Naples in 1225, and so we are stepping forward over fifteen hundred years. Yet the oddity, if that is what it is, lies in the history of western philosophy. The thirteenth century was a time of considerable intellectual vigour, when philosophers were looking back to the works of the Greek philosophers, and, in particular, Aristotle. His books were becoming available in new Latin translations, and his themes being put in a Christian context. Indeed Aquinas could follow Aristotle so closely that he sometimes appears to be writing merely a Latin paraphrase of the Greek original. Aristotle's influence went beyond the Christian world of the time. Islamic scholars, such as Averroës, interpreted him and were in their turn discussed by Christian philosophers.

Great universities were being founded. Paris was the most important of the age, but the first colleges at Oxford were founded in Aquinas' lifetime. Europe, through the medium of the Latin language and under the influence of the Church, was still a unified civilization. Aquinas, who became a Dominican friar, despite an aristocratic background, was able to leave Italy and teach at Paris. After a prolific life, pouring out large works of philosophy and theology, he died in 1274. He was canonized fifty years later, but the canonization of his works took longer. The encyclical of Pope Leo XIII in 1879, *Aeterni Patris*, completed what had been a long process. Thomism eventually became the official philosophy of the Roman Catholic Church, although it is a moot point whether that has helped Aquinas' reputation. It is undeniable, however, that he was a great thinker in his own right.

Despite the Aristotelian framework of his philosophy, there were limits to how far Aquinas could accept Aristotle's views. Distinctions between actuality and potentiality (what something is and what it could be), matter and form, substance and the four causes are much in evidence. These gave Aquinas the equipment with which to set out doctrines, which harmonized with those of the Bible and the Church. Aristotle's works were the catalyst which stimulated Aquinas to make an original contribution to Christian theology. How far his philosophy can be separated from his theology is a difficult question. He believed that the existence of God could be rationally demonstrated, but much of what he says is coloured by his theological assumptions.

As a Christian, Aquinas could not accept that the cosmos had never had a beginning, as Aristotle had believed. Aquinas did not think that philosophy could demonstrate a creation from nothing, but accepted that it could only be known through revelation. He adhered firmly to the Christian view that the world was created by God. He thought of the earth as the centre of the universe, with the celestial bodies moving around it in a uniformly circular motion. Echoing Aristotle, though, he thought they were 'incorruptible'. Yet Aquinas was dissatisfied with the kind of teleology found in Aristotle. A Christian could not expect to discover the true purpose of creatures in the world merely by reference to their natural tendencies and inclinations. Reference had to be made to the will and providence of a personal God, a Creator. Ultimately purpose had to be seen as given to the world and, in particular, to humanity. Natural ends and inclinations were relevant, but not on their own account. They had been implanted by God, and so the world had to be judged in terms of eternal standards that came from outside it. In many ways, such a picture is derived more easily from Plato's philosophy than Aristotle's.

Aquinas changed Aristotle's view of the importance of contemplation to the notion that the highest good is the beatific vision of God. The understanding of God is the goal for every intellect, but that is impossible in this life. Like Aristotle, Aquinas believed that the distinctiveness of human beings lay in the intellect. In true Aristotelian fashion, he declared that 'each thing's nature declares itself through its activity'.[1] 'The activity', he continues, 'peculiar to man is understanding'. Ultimate happiness will come when that understanding finds its fulfilment in the knowledge of God. Aquinas has been criticized for being too 'intellectual', and perhaps implying that human nature can only be truly exercised in philosophical understanding. Yet since it is impossible to love God without knowledge of Him and since the vision of God will satisfy our deepest longing, it is perhaps wrong to think of knowledge and love as easily separable.

Human destiny is put by Aquinas on an altogether different plane from Aristotle. Life after death is essential to his whole outlook. We cannot know God through the nature of material things, and we have to wait until the constraints of this life are removed. There is also the ethical demand that evil-doers be punished, and those who are virtuous rewarded. Aquinas was well aware that justice was not necessarily done in this life. Evil people flourish, and without action by divine providence beyond the confines of this life, evil would have triumphed. Moral virtue and vice take on a greater significance than they would otherwise have, if this life is part of something greater. The kind of people we become here and now determines our eternal destiny. Aquinas talks of the tortures of the damned in a thoroughly medieval fashion, but the link between our lives on earth and a life beyond death is crucial. A Christian would believe that people matter more as individuals when they are viewed as possessors of immortal souls. It is no coincidence that Aristotle was able to contemplate infanticide with equanimity, while no Christian could. For Aquinas, the meaningfulness and the importance of this life is bound up with belief in a life to come. One of his greatest departures from Aristotle lay precisely in the question of the survival of the human soul beyond death.

## Our Place in the World

A Christian conception of human nature will always be coloured by the doctrines of the Incarnation and the Resurrection. According to the first, Jesus was not just a very holy man, or an outstanding prophet, He was actually the Son of God, showing human nature as God intended it to be, and the divine nature in a form intelligible to humans. According to the second, Jesus rose from the dead, and showed himself to the disciples in bodily form after the Crucifixion. Indeed, St Paul considered that the whole Christian gospel rested on the question of resurrection, saying: 'If it is for this life only that Christ has given us hope, we of all men are most to be pitied.'[2]

The Incarnation seemed to sanctify matter and the human body, in particular. It seemed inappropriate to denigrate matter in favour of spirit, if the Word could become flesh. Christians, though, have often been tempted to do just that, especially those influenced by Plato. Similarly, the Resurrection of Jesus, although in a radically transformed and glorified body, could appear to be a glorification of matter and not of spirit. It is not surprising that some Christians, like Aquinas, distrusted the Platonic doctrine of the immortality of the soul, and have been more attracted by Aristotle's conception of the human person as a unity, an embodied form, rather than as a soul trapped temporarily within a body. It is easy, on the latter view, to slip into thinking of the soul as the source of good and the body as the source of evil. Yet Aristotle's idea of a substance as matter structured by a form makes the problem of personal immortality acute. If it is our nature to be embodied, what happens when we die? To use Aquinas' word, our bodies are 'corruptible'.

Aquinas tried to steer a middle course between Plato and Aristotle over the nature of the human person. He maintained that sensation was not just an activity of the soul, but a body was needed as well. He said that 'man [homo] is not only a soul, but is something composed of soul and body.'[3] He pointed out that it was because Plato thought that sensation belonged to the soul that he was able to hold that man was 'a soul using a body'. Aquinas emphasizes that a soul cannot be a person any more than a hand or foot can be, since it is only part of human nature. He could not, however, leave the argument there, since he wanted to say that the soul was incorruptible, and could not die. He also wanted to draw a contrast between animals and humans. Following Aristotle, he accepted that understanding, alone among the acts of the soul, could take place without a physical organ. That was what distinguished the human race from animals. The sensitive soul, which depended on the union of body and soul for its ability to perceive, would not survive death. Animals' souls would not exist apart from the body, although Aquinas did accept that to some extent humans and animals shared the same kind of mental life, at least as far as perception and sensation are concerned.

The human soul is the form of the body, but has to exist apart from the body. This was Aquinas' dilemma. He maintained that 'the human soul continues in its mode of existence, even when the body is destroyed, whereas other forms do not.'[4] Its ability to understand shows that it does not need the body, but 'it has a natural aptitude and inclination for union with the body'. One difficulty for Aquinas, given his Aristotelian framework, is that the different powers of the soul, nutritive (as in plants), sensitive (as in animals) and 'intellective' (as in humans) appear in danger of being separated at death. Might there even be different souls in the one body? Certainly Aquinas accepted that the human embryo does not at first possess the faculty of the soul devoted to understanding. This is of course relevant to the vexed issue of abortion, although Aquinas himself would not have approved of that, on the grounds that it was killing a potential human being, if not an actual one.

Aquinas refused to start talking of different souls. The soul gives unity to the body and can only be single. His solution was to say that a soul is corruptible if it is merely a 'sensitive' soul and that the power of sensation does not involve incorruptibility.[5] If, however, it is at the same time a soul with understanding it takes on incorruptibility in a way that the soul of an animal cannot. Another point Aquinas wished to emphasize was that human understanding is an individual matter. Some interpreters of Aristotle, particularly Islamic ones, had wanted to say that there was one rational principle or intellect in all humans. The more it is emphasized that form is a 'universal', the more tempting it is to conclude that humans share the same form. If the form is the soul, perhaps there is one human soul. As Aquinas points out, however, 'if the intellect is one, however diverse its instruments, then Socrates and Plato have to be called one man understanding.'[6] It is essential to distinguish between the individual possessing knowledge and the knowledge that is possessed.

How, though, can a separated soul be individuated if it is without its body? Aquinas cannot shake off the belief that it is really the body which makes a person this or that particular individual. He says: 'There are many souls because there are many bodies, yet when the bodies disappear, the many souls continue to exist.'[7] A soul is capable of a life of understanding on its own, and is therefore to be compared to an angel. Aquinas has a lot to say about angels, who, for him, are pure intellects, incorporeal, and with an immediate understanding of truth. His treatment of their existence, and of God's, shows that Aquinas is ready to accept the possibility of thought without a body, and of existence without matter. However much he sometimes gives the impression that a soul without a body is like the grin without the Cheshire Cat, individuals can, he believes, exist in a disembodied state, engaged in a life of understanding.

It is perhaps all the more surprising, therefore, that Aquinas emphasizes that the disembodied state is temporary, and that human nature requires a body to achieve wholeness. He could not shake off the conviction that he was not his soul. He says:

> Now the soul when separated from the body is in a way imperfect: even as any part is when severed from its whole: and the soul is naturally part of human nature. Therefore man cannot obtain ultimate happiness, unless his soul be reunited to his body: and this is all the more true, seeing that, as we have shown, man cannot reach ultimate happiness in this life.[8]

Aquinas holds that there will be a resurrection on this earth, when separated souls will be reunited with their bodies. Although in one sense the reunion is natural, since the soul needs the body for a full and proper life, he does acknowledge that it is brought about by the power of God. Aquinas asserts: 'The same man will be restored as a result of the union of the same identical matter with the same identical form.'[9] This very literal understanding of everlasting life on this earth, clothed in flesh and blood, carries with it obvious difficulties. Aquinas is much exercised by considerations such as cannibalism, which might result in different bodies claiming the same matter. It soon becomes apparent, however, that the glorified body in the resurrected life will not function as our present bodies do. There will be no use for eating or sexual intercourse, and each will be occupied with the life of contemplation.

Aquinas has emphasized the wholeness of the human being, our psychosomatic unity by paying a great price. It is often said that Christianity holds a belief in the resurrection of the body, rather than a Greek belief in the immortality of the soul. It is certainly vital for Christian doctrine that persons retain their identity and individuality beyond death, in a way that was not always guaranteed by the Greek notion of the soul. Yet too much stress on the importance of the physical characteristics of the body can produce odd results. Aquinas seems to have ended by endorsing both bodily resurrection and the immortality of the soul. Once he had conceded that incor-

poreal existence was intelligible, and that individuals can retain
their identity without a body, he had made the crucial concessions.
He was dissatisfied, however because of his Aristotelian stress on the
importance of the integrity of the person, with body and soul united.
Yet the more the centrality of the body and its perceptions is emphasized, the more unclear it is that humans can exist beyond death.
Aquinas never resolves the tension between his view of the mental
life of the disembodied soul, and the position that souls are only
individuated by matter.

Many visions of the resurrection of the dead have suffered from
over-literal embroidery. Although the constant danger is that the
idea lapses into unintelligibility, we have to recognize that we are
talking of things which by definition are beyond our experience and
understanding. Even Aquinas envisages our corporeal state, after a
general resurrection, as so transformed as to make its connection
with our present life extremely tenuous. There will not even be any
spatio-temporal continuity, if corpses had totally disintegrated. Ultimately the question whether it is *I* who survive, as opposed to, say,
somebody with a body like mine, depends on the question of the
continued identity of the soul or whatever constitutes the self apart
from the body. However much Aquinas may wish it otherwise, the
immortality of the soul seems to be the central issue.

Christians have tended to take the Resurrection of Jesus as their
model, and it is a central part of the Christian faith that Christ
demonstrated that individuals are recognizably still themselves
beyond death. Aquinas accepted that the risen Christ's behaviour
was governed by the need for Him to demonstrate His reality to His
disciples on this earth. Once though this is conceded, talking of the
nature of Christ's resurrected body as the pattern for all human
existence after death becomes a dubious exercise. This type of question may seem to be merely a matter for theological speculation, but
it is impossible to separate the problem of personal immortality from
the most fundamental issues concerning human nature. The value
of the individual person, the purpose of human existence, our moral
responsibility, our distinctiveness from animals – all these issues are
bound up with the question of our eternal destiny, if any. Yet our
experience in this life suggests the crucial importance of embodiment. Aquinas was only able to allow for a temporary existence in a
disembodied state because he could not conceive of a genuinely
human existence beyond the confines of our own familiar world.

## What is it to be Human?

Human rationality sets us apart from animals. Aquinas was as concerned with our moral understanding as with other aspects. He believed firmly in the responsibility we have to take before God for the life we live. We can be rewarded or punished beyond this life, both as separated souls and after the general resurrection, precisely because the choices we made and the decisions we took were ours. We cannot claim that we were in the grip of forces beyond our control. We possess free will. Aquinas says that 'otherwise advice, percepts, prohibition, rewards and punishment would all be in vain.'[10] We need knowledge of what we are doing, and this must be controlled by reason. A stone falling to the ground does not know what it is doing, while a lamb fleeing from a wolf might have some understanding. Nevertheless it is acting through its natural instincts and not through deliberation.

Human free will can be given the possibility of various courses of action. Aquinas says: 'The judgement of reason is open to various possibilities, and not determined on one course.' Human freedom follows from human rationality, although Aquinas recognizes that reason and desire may conflict on occasion. He also accepts that people can be endowed with different temperaments and have special inclinations.[11] Whatever our particular preferences may be, they are subject to the judgement of reason. Yet if freedom consists in the operation of reason, and if we can sometimes succumb to irrational desire, are we still free when we act against reason and in accordance with the desire? If we are, freedom and rationality seem to have separated. If we are not, we cannot be blamed for our actions since we are not responsible for our actions. One answer Aquinas would give to this type of problem, particularly familiar in cases of weakness of will, is that habits, traits of character and passions can be dealt with indirectly by reason. We can judge them and set about acquiring or eliminating them. I can train myself not to want certain things and to want others.

Christianity has always emphasized the role of free will, and its connection with human responsibility. Determinism, holding that any event, even human decisions, has a cause, challenges the claim that we are ultimately responsible for what we do. It is not fatalism, because it does not suggest that events occur whatever we decide.

Our decisions and choices, it is admitted, do help to explain our actions. We are not like the drivers of trams destined, whatever they might wish, to travel in pre-ordained routes on rails laid down long ago. Determinism would hold that our position is more like that of a driver of a diesel bus, with no overhead wires or rails to constrain it. In one sense, the driver is free to take the bus wherever he pleases. He could take his passengers for a trip to the seaside if he chose, but he is not really free if he is employed to take the bus along a fixed route. Once questions of external constraint are removed, the problem is how far our choices are really ours and how far they are the product of forces which may be outside our control and sometimes even our knowledge.

Determinists would say that there is still room for praise and blame in a determinist system as causal factors influencing an agent's decision. Like the carrot or the stick for a donkey they can affect behaviour. They are only administered to produce certain actions in the future and not because anyone deserves them. Reward and punishment cannot be justified, since each one, according to the determinist, is the product of a long chain of causes, whether social, psychological or biological, which stretches back beyond that person's own reasoning about the situation. Aquinas could never accept any version of determinism, or accept, as some would argue, that determinism and free will are compatible. There is a fundamental divergence between those who regard causal explanation as the only proper explanation of action, and those, like Aquinas, who regard reason as sovereign. My reason may cause my actions, but to anyone believing in genuine free will it must itself be produced by only rational considerations. In that way I am never merely the sum total of the causal influences on me. In particular, I must myself be the source of my moral judgments and be held responsible for them.

One reason for the Christian emphasis on free will is the awareness of the large amount of evil in what is claimed as God's world. Much of it is the result of human selfishness and wickedness, or 'sin'. Sin seems to infect the whole of human existence, and we even appear to be born with a predisposition to it. It is easy to imagine sin 'enslaving' us and the doctrine of original sin has perhaps been a response to this kind of human experience. Sometimes Christians have talked of the total depravity of humans. The corruption has seemed so great that only the grace of God could offer hope. Yet it is easy to overstate this so that it seems impossible for the warped human mind to grasp any truth or recognize any divine revelation. Aquinas did not go this far, because of his high regard for the power of reason, which he believed could reach out to God. He further thought that we all actually have a natural inclination to virtue. Aquinas identified the working of reason with the path of virtue, and so it would follow that a human without an inclination to virtue would also lack the power of reason and not be human at all.

Sin cannot destroy our natural capacities, but, Aquinas says 'that good of virtue which is the inclination to virtue is lessened by the fact of a person's sinning'.[12] The more we do what is wrong, the more we are accustomed to that kind of action. 'An inclination towards one of two contraries', he says, 'necessarily diminishes any inclination towards the other'. The more we sin, the more we are likely to. Yet, as he points out, sin cannot stop us being rational, since then we would no longer be capable of sinning. Animals cannot sin, since it must be the result of a choice freely made. We can make it more difficult for ourselves, but never impossible, to avoid sin. We are, though, all in the grip of 'original sin' which Aquinas viewed as an illness of the soul. It involved the disruption of an original state of justice, when the will was subject to God. As a consequence, all the parts of the human personality, or the powers of the soul, are no longer kept in balance and harmony. Each battles with the rest as it strains for what it wants.[13] When reason is defeated by desire, we go against our nature, because what is natural follows the 'order of reason'. The paradox, then, is that although we are free to go against our true nature, there is a sense in which for Aquinas 'human nature' can never be corrupt. It shows what humans ought to aim at, rather than the ways they actually do behave.

## Human Society

Given the view that human nature sets the standards for us, Aquinas' view of natural law is far from simple. He is not thinking of laws of nature, such as those supplied in modern physics or chemistry. He would not think that everyone will in fact live in accordance with natural law. He believes they ought to. He accepts the necessity of human law in addition, but does not expect it to reflect everything laid down as natural law by the providence of God. He remarks that law has to be laid down for a great number of people, the majority of whom do not have high standards of morality.[14] He continues:

> Therefore it does not forbid all the vices, from which upright men can keep away, but only those grave ones which the majority can avoid, and chiefly those which do harm to others, and have to be stopped if human society is to be maintained, such as murder and theft and so on.

Morality and the law will not coincide for Aquinas, since morality is more demanding. Law does have a moral function. Its purpose should be the common good, although laws can be unjust when they are not derived from the natural law. Aquinas follows Aristotle in denying that the law should take a neutral stance between differing moral outlooks. He, too, would have rejected many aspects of modern liberalism. Indeed he believes that laws should provide a context in which people's moral impulses can be strengthened and their immoral ones restrained. He considers that some young people need the threat of legal sanctions to restrain them, saying: 'Becoming so habituated, they may come to do of their own accord what earlier they did from fear, and become virtuous. This kind of discipline, compelling through the fear of punishment is the discipline of the laws.'[15]

Human law must be derived from natural law, and Aquinas' view of the latter can only be understood in the context of his belief in a providential God who has ordered all things for their own good. He says that 'under God their law giver, all created things have various natural inclinations.'[16] All things obey the eternal law in so far as they follow their inclinations, and in our case that involves acting in accordance with reason. When we are carried along by irrational desire, we are going against our true inclinations, and thus against our nature. Aquinas says of humanity after the Fall:

> When it turned from God, it fell into a condition when it could be carried away by sensuality. This befalls each individual to the extent that he falls from reason: in effect he becomes like the beasts who are borne along by their sense-appetites.[17]

Sensuality must be subordinated to reason, and yet, as a purely animal tendency, sexual desire was, he accepts, ordained for the common good, for the conservation of the species.

We are as free to break the natural law, as any law of the land, provided we are willing to accept the consequences. Only actions in accordance with the natural law, and hence God's eternal law, will bring humans any good. When they go against the purposes for humanity revealed in God's creation, they are bound to produce heartache and misery for themselves and others. Aquinas believes that while natural law does not compel us, it sets guide-lines for us to live fulfilled lives in accordance with the will of the Creator.

The commands of the law of nature, according to Aquinas, correspond to the ranking of our natural inclinations.[18] First we want to preserve ourselves and natural law helps us maintain the necessities of life. Secondly, we hold certain inclinations in common with other animals at the level of the basic instincts of sex and bringing up offspring. Thirdly, Aquinas believes we have an inclination towards the good, at the level of our rational nature. He gives as instances that we should know the truth about God, and should be able to live together in society. Then we should avoid ignorance and not offend those with whom we ought to co-operate.

Aquinas believes that human nature is still essentially good despite the effects of sin. 'Natural law', he says, 'cannot be cancelled in the human heart'. He was aware that reason could be blocked, and also that wrong customs could be established in whole societies. An example he gives is that robbery was not reputed to be wrong amongst some peoples. Nevertheless the aim should be for natural law to be reflected in the way society is ordered. Yet applying general principles, which link human nature to what is good, to give guides for conduct can be difficult. Presumably the natural law never changes if human nature does not. The circumstances of life, though, may alter, and our understanding may progress. There are many modern controversies, for instance about contraception, or even genetic engineering, which illustrate how difficult it is to apply intuitions of what is 'natural' to human behaviour.

One of Aquinas' own examples shows the problem. He points out that something can agree with natural right in two ways.[19] Nature can be inclined in a particular direction, so that, for example, it is wrong that any harm be done to another. The second way is that nature does not bid the contrary. We have to be clothed, though it could be said that we are naturally naked. Aquinas then gives the further examples of private property and slavery, which, he alleges, exist 'through human reason for the convenience of human life, and not by natural law'.[20] He seems to be saying that the principles of natural law are indifferent to the question of slavery. It is an issue on a par with wearing clothes, not a natural state, but justifiable rationally to meet human needs. Yet human slavery would appear to be as much against natural law and natural right as anything could be. It is legitimate to consider how useful from a moral point of view is a theory of natural law which can condone slavery. Even granted that social conditions are different in our day, we may have to conclude that our understanding has, in this area at least, improved on that of Aquinas. The conclusion that cannot be drawn, without making nonsense of the doctrine of natural law, is that what was right for Aquinas may not be right for us, merely because of our membership of a different society. Natural law cannot be changed in its basic principles, when human nature has not changed, although the way it is applied may depend on circumstances. There is clearly room here for argument about what is and is not basic. Aquinas, of all people, however, would not wish to dissuade us from using our reason to discuss the proper nature of human societies.

## Contemporary Relevance

St Thomas Aquinas wrote at a time when theology was pre-eminent. It was as important to him to establish the relative positions of humans and angels as to discuss the similarities and dissimilarities between humans and animals. He sharply distinguished the mode of existence of heavenly bodies from that of terrestrial objects. His work could easily be dismissed as the product of a pre-scientific age, but this is too superficial a reaction. Many of his philosophical beliefs, concerning, say, free will or natural law, are still widely influential. The question of the relationship of the mind and the body is one of the most enduring and controversial of philosophical problems. The most basic divergence is between those who wish to identify the two in some way, and those who wish to say that there are two entities interacting. Monists would say the mind and body are ultimately one. Some have claimed everything is really mental, but the success of modern science has led many to reduce the mental to what is physical. They then insist that the workings of the mind, whether beliefs and desires, or sensations and emotions, just *are* the workings of the body, and perhaps more particularly of the brain. As such they are in principle brought within the scope of scientific study. They are opposed by dualists who would argue that the mind is distinct from the body and that just as it can be affected by the body, so too can it act on the body.

There are many who are unhappy about thinking that there is a self that is somehow distinct from the body. They find it attractive to try to find a middle path that suggests that persons are not just bodies, but are not separate from them. They are more than lumps of matter but are necessarily embodied, so that they form a psycho-physical unity and are not made up of two different parts uneasily living together. Anyone holding this would be more attracted by the metaphysics of Aristotle than of Plato, so that Forms are present in matter rather than existing in a separate world. The charm of Aquinas for many modern thinkers is his emphasis on the unitary nature of the person. We are then not imprisoned in our bodies, but are our bodies, or more accurately are composed of a body and soul, each of which needs the other. His views seem to provide an alternative to Descartes' later separation (in the seventeenth century) of the mind and body in what became the classic dualist position.

A modern conception of mind cannot be simply identified with Aquinas' notion of a soul. He thought plants had souls. There are, however, connections and some have seen affinities between the views of Aquinas and those of the later Wittgenstein. Both would be opposed to Descartes' (or Cartesian) dualism. Any discussion of the nature of the human person, though, cannot avoid the question of whether we can survive death. This issue is particularly acute for Christianity, where the question of our future destiny is given much prominence. Are we, as Aquinas thought, a little lower than the angels, or are we merely complicated animals? The issue is related to the question of the relationship of mind and body, and for all his talk of embodied souls, Aquinas has in the end to accept that souls can exist apart from the body. Once he has made this concession, it would seem that he has shown himself a dualist at heart. Certainly a monist, holding that only the physical is real, cannot allow for the possibility of life after death.

The question is whether a middle course between monism and dualism is possible. Aquinas himself had to contend that a dead body, without its soul as form, was not a body in the same sense as a living one. This seems an odd claim, but only goes to bolster those who would claim that something is then missing from the body. Yet having made a major concession to dualism, Aquinas feels the need to recover his position by positing a bodily resurrection on this earth. This was in accord with the Christian doctrine of his time, but it leaves him uneasily poised between monism and dualism. We are left with the question as to whether human personality can only be expressed through a physical body. The answer to this affects our view of ordinary embodied people, as well as being relevant to questions about our eternal destiny. Aquinas confronted the issue, but it is difficult to see that he resolved it.

# CHAPTER FOUR

# Hobbes
## *1588–1679*

## Context

The world of Thomas Hobbes was strikingly different from that of
Aquinas. The Reformation, with its continuing struggles between
Catholic and Protestant, produced a greater emphasis on the role of
the individual. This resulted in different visions of the nature of a
community, be it Church or State. Hobbes came from Malmesbury in
Wiltshire, and was born in 1588, the year of the Spanish Armada.
He was at Oxford University when the Catholic- inspired gunpowder
plot of Guy Fawkes and his associates was discovered. He lived
through the turbulent age of the English Civil War, prudently spend-
ing some years in France, and eventually died at a ripe old age in
1679. The age of modern science and scientific method was dawn-
ing. The microscope and telescope had been invented. It was the age
of Galileo and of Descartes.

All these influences are apparent in Hobbes' work. He is best
known for his *Leviathan*, or *The Matter, Form and Power of a Commonwealth*, of 1651. That work tried to establish the nature of
political obligation, but his writings extend far beyond this, and
show his interest in scientific matters. Indeed the scientific outlook
colours his whole view of humanity. Just as seventeenth-century
physics viewed matter as made up of small atoms, Hobbes took
an atomistic view of human society. It could, he believed, only be
explained in terms of the individuals comprising it. The nature of
politics could only be understood if we understand humanity.
He says: 'For the knowledge of the properties of a commonwealth,
it is necessary first to know the dispositions, affections, and
manners of men.'[1] Humans should not be understood first in

the context of society, since society itself has to be explained in terms of the way people behave. The point is illustrated well by the picture on the title page of *Leviathan*.[2] The monarch is portrayed looming over his kingdom, but on closer inspection, his figure can be seen to be made up in turn by lots of tiny people. The State, and its power, is merely the sum total of its citizens.

We are, therefore, by nature, atoms, existing independently outside society, and we have to learn to co-operate. Yet this view turns human sociability into a problem. It is something to be justified. There has to be an answer to the question about why we should be sociable or care for each other. This strongly individualist stance was opposed to the position that humans were political by nature. Aristotle had thought it was natural for us to form communities, but this was partly because he attributed certain essential properties to us which make us human. Hobbes would have none of that. He criticized those who believe that because there is one name applied to many different things, that means the name picks out something special, that each thing shares in. He denies that such general names actually name anything, arguing against those who 'seriously contend that beside Peter and John, and all the rest of the men, that are, have been, or shall be in the world, there is yet something else that we call *man*, viz *man in* general.'[3] He concludes that 'there is nothing universal but names'. Such a view is called 'nominalism' and is in direct opposition to any emphasis on common properties, such as Plato's theory of Forms. A paradoxical consequence of Hobbes' view is that there should, strictly speaking, be no such thing as 'human nature'. There are only individuals who may or may not resemble each other. The more the resemblances are emphasized, the more nominalism risks lapsing into talk of common properties. Hobbes, however, begins with the motivation of the individual, and with that as the starting point, we must expect collisions and strife as much as helpfulness and co-operation.

Hobbes' divergence from Aristotle is no coincidence, since he speaks most bitterly of him. His dislike was fuelled by the fact of Aristotle's influence on the Roman Catholic Church through Aquinas and others. Like many Englishmen of his time, Hobbes was distrustful of the power of the Church of Rome, and delighted in listing the pagan influences in it. He clearly thought Aristotle one such heathen influence and says:

There is nothing so absurd that the old Philosophers ... have not some of them maintained. And I believe that scarce any thing can be more absurdly said in natural philosophy than that which now is called *Aristotle's Metaphysics*: nor more repugnant to Government, than much of that he hath said in his *Politics*: nor more ignorantly, than a great part of his *Ethics*.[4]

Hobbes criticized the notion of an incorporeal soul which could exist separated from the body. Since he attacked the very idea of an essence, he would not tolerate any notion of a separated essence. To him 'a man is a living body'.[5] 'Body' and 'man' name the same thing. Hobbes' materialist outlook is very apparent, and he was certainly no dualist. He was, instead, much influenced by the progress of the science of his day, and his distrust of Rome was deepened by its opposition to new scientific theories. He writes: 'Our own navigations made manifest, and all men learned in humane societies now acknowledge, there are antipodes. And every day it appeareth more and more that years and days are determined by motions of the earth.'[6] Yet, he grumbles, ecclesiastical authority had punished some who had entertained such doctrines.

The English Church was being faced with new disagreements in Hobbes' time. The Civil War had a religious dimension in that for a time episcopacy was suppressed in England and other forms of church government introduced. At stake was the doctrine of the Church. The Church of Rome had insisted on the mystical nature of Christ's Church on earth, transcending individuals. The Church of England, as the established Church, found it hard to distinguish between nation and Church, or village and parish. New doctrines of church government, however, held that churches were gathered communities of believers, who covenanted together under God to live lives of holiness. The Church was no longer regarded as universal, but local, composed of like-minded individuals banding together. Independents, such as Congregationalists, insisted on the independence of the individual church and the sovereignty of the congregation. After the Restoration these arguments became solidified in different denominational structures. Echoes of the controversies still remain. The disagreements, though, illustrate how important, at the time of Hobbes' writing, were questions of the relationship of an individual to a community. Are we parts of wider whole, or does the existence of the community depend on our voluntary allegiance? Can we by our decisions actually bring a community into being?

Whatever the issues paramount in the Civil War, Hobbes was deeply affected by the mere fact of its taking place. His writing tries to set out a basis for political obligation that can gain the assent of everyone, whatever their beliefs. Indeed for him the threat of anarchy was a worse prospect even than tyranny. Plato and Aristotle had assumed general agreement about the nature of the good life, so that only ignorance could make anyone unaware of what was good and bad. Hobbes, however, was a subjectivist about ethics. Just as beauty is sometimes held to be in the eye of the beholder, he held that moral judgements were only valid for the person making them. He believed that words such as 'good', 'evil' and 'contemptible', 'are ever used with relation to the person that useth them'.[7] He stresses that 'there being nothing simply and absolutely so', judgements of good and bad are either an individual matter or depend on the decision of whoever represents the State. It follows that no political theory could be based on a moral outlook. Instead there must be an appeal to something that would gain the agreement, or at least the acquiescence, of everyone. The absolute priority was a framework within which civil peace could be guaranteed.

## Our Place in the World

Hobbes' materialist presuppositions are made explicit in the introduction to *Leviathan*. He claims that 'life is but a motion of limbs', and continues:

> Why may we not say that all automata (engines that move themselves by springs and wheels as doth a watch) have an artificial life? For what is the *heart*, but a *spring*: and the *nerves* but so many *strings*; and the *joints* but so many *wheels*, giving motion to the whole body?[8]

Humans are, it seems, examples of 'engines'. Above all they are self-seeking and self-maintaining ones. Hobbes' enthusiasm for portraying human life in terms of the technology of his day should serve as a warning to those who try to do something similar in our own day, perhaps drawing comparisons with computers. Hobbes' mechanistic materialism, coupled with his nominalism and individualism, provides a heady mixture. Human action must, he believes, be explained in terms of the behaviour of individual bodies and the causes operating on them. Even human society had to be understood in terms of the influences on individuals, and for that reason human biology became relevant.

Hobbes was a determinist, and made no sharp distinction between us and animals. He says firmly that the freedom of willing or not willing is not greater in man than in other living creatures.[9] Hobbes did not deny we are free, but defined freedom, as some modern philosophers have, as the ability to do what we want, or to act in accordance with what we will. However, merely being free to put decisions or choices into action is not the same as being free to choose in the first place. A dog that is not tied up can get what it wants, but it does not possess the freedom to deliberate, emphasized by Aquinas. For Hobbes human freedom was merely lack of constraint. A stone rolling freely down a hill would be as free as he supposed us to be.

Hobbes was strongly criticized by his contemporaries for his determinism. Punishment could not be justified, it seemed, if everyone was caused to want and choose things by forces beyond their control. What, too, could be the point of worrying what to do, or of seeking and giving advice, if everything is determined? Hobbes had answers, though he could not leave room for any idea that people *deserve* punishment. All he could do was to point out that punishment, or at least the fear of it, is itself a potent cause, affecting people's behaviour. He asks of the case where someone is 'necessitated to steal' and is then put to death: 'Does not this punishment deter others from theft? Is it not a cause that others steal not?'[10] He concludes that the law is 'a cause of justice', and insists that deliberation or consultation can themselves be causes of choice. Determinism does not make deliberation pointless, though the deliberation will in its turn be caused.

Considering the importance of free will for Aquinas, Hobbes' determinism may seem at odds with the Christian faith. Yet Hobbes quotes freely from the Bible and insists that his political theory does not conflict with the Word of God. On the other hand, he does hold that God is 'incomprehensible', and although he uses the term 'natural law', it is very far removed from Aquinas' moral conception. His attack on the objectivity of value is itself curious from a Christian standpoint. He deliberately puts his justification for the existence of a

State in a secular context, which does not presuppose the truth of any particular religious views. Hobbes is particularly dismissive of the relevance of a life after death, and will have nothing to do with those who rate the attaining of 'an eternal felicity after death' above 'the preservation of man's life on earth'. No doubt his experience of the Civil War led him to add that 'such are they that think it a work of merit to kill, or depose, or rebel against the Sovereign Power constituted over them by their own consent'. His reason for discounting life after death is significant. He says, with barely concealed contempt: 'There is no natural knowledge of man's estate after death: but only a belief grounded upon other men's saying that they know it supernaturally, or that they know those that knew them that knew others that knew it supernaturally.'[11]

It is easy to see why Hobbes was called an atheist by some of his contemporaries. His scientific emphasis seemed to restrict 'the world' to the material world and humans to elaborate machines. He was indeed even named in Parliament as the author of blasphemous and profane works. 'Hobbism' became a word of abuse, but his work still gained considerable popularity. Samuel Pepys even had to pay three times the proper price to get hold of a copy of *Leviathan*. Hobbes' understanding of human nature was clearly in tune with that of many of his time.

## What is it to be Human?

Hobbes could easily appeal to everyday experience to confirm his central claim about human behaviour, which is, quite simply, that we are all selfish, and willing to take advantage of others for our own gain. He asks of anyone sceptical of his position 'what opinion he has of his fellow subjects, when he rides armed: of his fellow citizens when he locks his doors: and of his children and servants, when he locks his chests.'[12] In other words, our ordinary actions show that we do not trust each other, but think that everyone will pursue their own interests, even at the expense of others. There are plenty of clichés in everyday speech, such as 'I'm all right, Jack' or 'looking after number one', which suggest that Hobbes' view of our overriding concern for ourselves coincides with much popular wisdom.

Hobbes' believes that 'in a state of nature' where humans are roughly equal and unconstrained by the laws of a particular society, they must try to survive as best they can. Self- preservation is the priority and our natural desires cannot be judged good or bad in themselves. Morality has no role. The 'natural condition of mankind' is one where each individual comes into collision with everyone else, each trying to achieve security. Hobbes uses two graphic analogies. He talks of 'war' which is 'of every man against every man'. This does not necessarily mean actual fighting but describes the constant struggle that will take place if they live without security and must be entirely dependent on their own resources. As Hobbes points out, there would then be none of the advantages of society, no industry, agriculture, navigation or scientific knowledge. There would, instead, be continual fear, and the danger of violent death. The catalogue of misery in the state of nature is ended with Hobbes' most famous phrase that 'the life of man' would be 'solitary, poor, nasty, brutish and short'.

It does not matter to Hobbes that his conjectures about the human condition outside the constraints of society may not be historically accurate. He does, though, give the concrete example of 'the savage people in many places of America', who, he alleged, had no government at all. The point he wishes to make is that there could be no society without government and without the sanctions of law. Instead there would be merely individuals who would be mutually antagonistic. This is a secular equivalent of a state of original sin, a condition from which we have to be rescued. Hobbes' solution, however, never suggests that our urge to protect ourselves and further our own interests is wrong. He never condemns the selfishness or self-absorption he depicts. That is what humans are like, he claims, and all social arrangements have to take account of the fact. Our reason for wanting to enter into social relationships must precisely be because it is in our own personal interests to do so. Hobbes' political theory is firmly grounded in the consistent pursuit of rational self-interest.

Hobbes' second illustration compares human life to a race. He says that this race 'we must suppose to have no other goal, no other garland, but being foremost'.[13] Competition is part of the very fabric of our lives, with each trying to outdo the other. We either want to gain at others' expense, or to defend the possessions we have already acquired. We also want glory and honour for ourselves. There can be great cruelty in such a race. Hobbes says that 'to see another fall is disposition to laugh', although he grants there is room for pity, and even help for others. One competitor might even carry another in the race out of charity. Nevertheless the emphasis is on an aggressive individualism, fuelled by a fear that others will deprive us of what we want. Hobbes talks of natural right, but it is not a right to justice. Instead everyone has a 'right to everything, even to one another's body'.[14] Our basic right of nature is to use our abilities as far as we can for the preservation of ourselves. Thus is born in philosophy a conception of rights which is totally divorced from any balancing notion of duty or obligation. This is bound to create an unstable basis for a society, if each person demands recognition of his or her interests without being willing to pay attention to those of others. No society can exist in such a condition, and Hobbes had to show how a sense of obligation could be generated even when it is not there naturally.

Is Hobbes right in assuming that we are each only concerned with our own interests? It is indeed unclear how far he really wished to go in expressing such egoism. A strong version is psychological egoism, the view that an individual can only want his or her own good. If I help you, according to this, I want my welfare and not yours. Perhaps I desire the satisfaction of being generous. This is a logical thesis which can degenerate into the uninteresting position that I want what I want. Yet if I want your good, the fact that it is my desire does not mean it is selfish. It is still *your* good I wish for, not mine. The question is whether Hobbes can allow that I am concerned with your good at all. We have seen that he accepts that one will help another in the race of life. He accepts that even in the state of nature people may be generous. There is still the question whether they may not be merely pursuing their own interests, if the motive is selfish.

Hobbes describes charity by saying that 'there can be no greater argument to a man of his own power than to find himself able not only to accomplish his own desires but also to assist other men in theirs'.[15] Similarly, he describes pity as the 'imagination or fiction of future calamity to ourselves, proceding from the sense of another man's calamity'.[16] The self-centred nature of this position is clear, in that concern for others is made a by-product of concern for oneself. It seems that I am not really concerned for you, except in so far as your plight triggers off a sympathetic reaction because of my concern for myself. Similarly, helping you gives me a delightful sense of power. The logical issue, however, is whether or not Hobbes can actually deny that I am at all concerned with your interests even as a means to something else. Bishop Butler, a famous moral philosopher of the eighteenth century, attacked Hobbes on this point, suggesting that a mere love of power does not distinguish between objects. I cannot just want power, but have to use it in a particular way. To exercise power over you, there must be something about your circumstances I want to change. If I want, say, to stop your pain, because it makes me feel superior, that may be basically selfish, but what I want must be the cessation of your pain, and not just my feeling superior.

Hobbes may conceivably even have agreed with Butler. His definition of pity, after all, is not simply fear of some future calamity. He is saying that seeing another's misfortune makes us imagine a similar thing happen to ourselves. Sympathy is bound up with a knowledge of what it would be to suffer the same thing oneself. There is a large element of self-absorption in this, but it does not follow that the object of my emotion is my own imagined calamity rather than another's real one. My care for others may be flawed, but it could still be, in part, care *for others* and not just myself. Hobbes recognizes that there can be the 'natural affection' of parents to children, and that we can have affection for others near us.[17] He is more sceptical about our assisting strangers, suggesting that such actions are 'to purchase friendship', or possibly through fear 'to purchase peace'. Nevertheless the suggestion remains that our self-absorption need not be total, and that we can care for at least some other people.

Perhaps Hobbes cannot be convicted of outright psychological egoism, but the way in which he concentrates on the individual outside the constraints of society leads him to emphasize our concern with our own interests. It seems that care for others, even if possible, can never be whole-hearted, but has to be linked to our own basic concerns. Hobbes believed that human society must be built on this fact. Since our most insistent drive is to self-preservation, society has to be justified on the grounds that it is conducive to our security.

## Human Society

Hobbes' view of society and our place in it is somewhat negative. Its purpose is to ward off the unpleasantness and danger of the state of nature. He says little, for instance, of the positive role of the family.

Fear drives us to co-operate with each other. We have to reach agreement with each other in a contract or covenant, so that we can remove the state of war with each other and gain peace. Reason, according to Hobbes, cannot determine our passions or appetites but it can be put to their service. A fundamental 'law of nature' is that we seek peace and follow it. Because it is not in our interest to live in insecurity, we must agree not to fight and compete with others, in so far as they make the same agreement with us. Hobbes' idea of a natural law is a rule 'by which a man is forbidden to do that which is destructive of his life, or taketh away the means of preserving the same: and to omit that by which he thinketh it may be best preserved'.[18] The emphasis on self-interest makes this very different from Aquinas' idea of natural law. Hobbes does claim that his views coincide with the 'Law of the Gospel', namely 'whatever you require that others should do to you, that do ye to them'. But the preoccupation with self and with what *I* can gain, makes it seem far from a normal Christian doctrine of love.

We might all accept that covenants or agreements to co-operate would be mutually beneficial, since most human activities depend on joint activity. The problem that faced Hobbes was that given we are all self-seekers, and that in itself was not to be condemned, there seems little guarantee that agreements will always be kept. It is always tempting to back out of a bargain after we have got what we wanted, but before it has cost us anything. Why, for instance, should I pay for goods once I have taken delivery of them? Unless we appeal to moral considerations of trustworthiness and honesty, the answer must be that we will pay because otherwise we will be punished by law.

Hobbes realized that getting people to keep agreements was a difficult matter when all are concerned with their own advantage. If I know that you are unlikely to keep to a bargain if you can avoid doing so, I am unlikely to keep my side. As Hobbes says: 'It suits not with reason that any man should perform first, if it be not likely that the other will make good his promise after.'[19] That, however, is in the state of nature, and Hobbes attempts to solve the problem by postulating the existence of a civil State which has the power to keep both parties to the terms of their agreement. It is not enough for covenants to be made, but those making them must also agree to a political framework in which they can be enforced. Indeed only when laws are made in a State, is there any question of right and wrong, according to Hobbes. Sin, for him, is voluntarily breaking a law of the land.

The situation is summed up in Hobbes' words that 'covenants, without the sword, are but words, and of no strength to secure a man at all.'[20] People may have come to an agreement but that does not mean that their basic inclinations have changed, or could be changed. Reason has to devise ways of making it in their own interests to keep their promises. It becomes imperative that a Commonwealth be erected, so that we each voluntarily hand over power to an assembly or to one person. Hobbes himself preferred monarchy, while accepting that he could not wholly justify his preference. With the power we give, the sovereign will act in our name to provide peace. This is how 'that great Leviathan', the State, is created, and obligations can be made enforceable. According to this view, 'every particular man is author of all the Sovereign doth.'[21] Citizens cannot distance themselves from the Sovereign's actions, let alone put him to death.

The Commonwealth should maintain our peace and security, but Hobbes accepts that the right we have by nature to defend ourselves is always in existence. Our loyalty to the State remains conditional. He says: 'The obligation of subjects to the Sovereign is understood to last as long, and no longer, than the power lasteth, by which he is able to protect them.'[22] Just as when an army is defeated, there comes a point at which discipline and order is forgotten, and the soldiers become a rabble, each concerned to escape, so there comes a point when the State itself collapses and each has to look only to personal security. Loyalty and fidelity are not virtues for Hobbes. It was notorious that Hobbes gave subjects leave to withdraw obedience from a government precisely at the moment it most needed their loyalty. The corollary is that we ought to obey any political power once it has been successfully established and is able to provide security. The emphasis is on *de facto* rather than *de iure* power, the brute fact of actual power, rather than any constitutional right to rule. Certainly *Leviathan* was quoted by some of Hobbes' contemporaries in defence of the *de facto* rule following the execution of Charles I.

Self-interest is the basis of all covenants and Hobbes realizes that pursuit of it may always encourage in turn the deliberate breaking of a covenant. He would agree that it is rational to do so, if the covenant cannot be enforced. Keeping one's promises when no one else does so merely makes someone 'a prey to others'. The various laws of nature, listed by Hobbes, may dispose one to seek peace and security, by for instance being grateful to others for benefits received, or by being accommodating to them. He does not think they should encourage us to do anything that is to our detriment. Everything must be subordinated to the insistent demands of self-preservation. Hobbes had to face the question as to why we should not trade on the gullibility of others by making, but then breaking, covenants. He imagines a 'fool' tempted in just this way, saying 'in his heart, there is no such thing as justice.'[23]

Hobbes holds this reasoning to be specious. The apparatus of the State exists to deal with it, and I must also take into account the opinion of others. He points out that no one 'that breaketh his covenant, and consequently declareth that he thinks he may with reason do so', can be received into society, except by error, and he holds that no one can safely count on that kind of mistake being made. The question, though, remains. What if I know I could get away with it? What if I know that others will never find out? Hobbes would find it difficult to avoid the conclusion that this made the breaking of an agreement justifiable. It is not enough to protest that one could not rely on never being found out. Hobbes' society could only exist by virtue of the vigilance of the law, and not the loyalty or trustworthiness of its citizens. By definition, it has no moral basis and is in perpetual danger of collapse.

## Contemporary Relevance

Hobbes' view of society stems directly from his view of humans as self-seeking individuals, with no predisposition to co-operate with others or help them unless it is in their own interest. His notion of a social contract is an attempt to show how a society can be constructed for everyone's benefit, even when no one has an interest in anyone else's interests. Prudence replaces morality, and reason merely implements pre-existing desires. Rationality becomes the remorseless pursuit of whatever one wants. Hobbes has drawn a picture of a competitive society which bears a marked resemblance to some people's view of a capitalist society. Indeed many economists' notion of a 'pure' market economy is precisely of one that works by means of the cumulative choices of individuals, each concerned with his or her own interest. A common definition of 'rational economic agents' is those who will always try, when they have the opportunity, to benefit themselves at the expense of everyone else. Assumptions like this, made at the level of economic theory, have much in common with those of Hobbes. Yet one does not need to be a Marxist to wonder whether it is right that the common good has to be so ignored in favour of private interest. For instance, despite Hobbes' quotations from the Bible, Christianity has never countenanced the idea of such unredeemed selfishness. Hobbes may have secularized the idea of original sin, but Christianity has recognized that humans have the ability to rise above their sin and self-centredness, at least through the grace of God. Aquinas indeed was positively optimistic about humanity's inclination to good, even granted the baleful effects of sin.

Worrying paradoxes arise if rational choice is considered to be choice of what is perceived to be most beneficial and least harmful to oneself. The connections with Hobbes' view are clear but the problems are modern. Assume I am a factory owner, tempted to save costs by letting untreated effluent flow into a river. I may want a clean river and agree that laws should clamp down on pollution. Does it therefore follow that I do not pollute the river myself? I have to measure my probable costs against the probable benefits to me. I may fear prosecution or getting my firm a bad reputation but that may merely indicate that I must take care not to get caught. What about the river? There are problems which typically arise in connection with what are called 'public goods', whether clean air, clean water, or anything for the benefit of everyone. If I can get the benefits without paying the cost of obtaining them, I am better off. My small amount of pollution may not make much difference, and perhaps does not matter. On the other hand, if everyone else is already polluting the river, again it does not matter, as the damage is already done. So, assuming I do not get caught, there seems no reason not to let the effluent into the river. Yet everyone else can, and probably will, argue in the same way and the results will be disastrous. Unless policing can be absolutely effective, and it never can be, a society of self-seeking individuals is always going to find itself in difficulties.

The plight of the commons illustrates the same problem. When everyone has a right to graze animals on the same piece of land, no one exercises the self-restraint that they would if the land was private property. Each wants to get as much grazing as possible, and there are typically too many animals let loose. The ground is over-grazed and the grass deteriorates. Each person can reason that either others will show restraint or they will not. If they do not, there is no reason for one person to restrict the number of animals, since it will not make any real difference. If, however, most are going to show restraint, then it is tempting for individuals to take advantage of the situation, and get more grazing for their stock. Everyone can reason in the same way, and again the land is over-stocked. A follower of Hobbes could at this point argue that an effective system of super-vision and control is necessary. The users of the common could agree to set up a board to take care of the grazing, and perhaps to restrict the numbers of animals. This will only work, assuming the users are wholly selfish, if the board is vigilant and has proper powers of punishment. Even then, the users will have every incen-tive to attempt to outwit the board they themselves set up, and each to gain an advantage over the other.

Arms control agreements between nations that are ruthlessly pursuing their own interests, and fishery agreements to prevent over-fishing by fishermen who remain eager to get as big catches as they can, also provide examples. The continued pursuit of self-interest which produced the agreement in the first place, can also serve to undermine it. Keeping to an agreement merely because one was a party to it seems an excessive luxury to those who are trying to steal a march on their competitors. The minute it can be broken without detection, it will be. Integrity, faithfulness, loyalty and honesty have a limited currency in a society of egoists.

There may be much within us that is self-seeking and that can only respond to incentives or the fear of punishment. Politicians may have to take account of that. Many thinkers, however, have argued that there is a nobler aspect of human character. We can be self-sacrificial as well as self-seeking. We can look to the interests of others as well as to our own. If so, a political theory, such as Hobbes', is taking an unduly cynical view of human nature. A State which cannot tap the unselfish aspects of character by inspiring the loyalty and service of its citizens is not only impoverished. Its inherent instability will eventually ensure its collapse.

# CHAPTER FIVE

# Locke

## *1632–1704*

## Context

Just as Hobbes was affected by the English Civil War, John Locke was
intimately involved with its aftermath. He was born in Somerset, not
far from Bristol, then the second city of England. His family was one
of minor gentry who supported Parliament in the Civil War. He was
educated at Westminster School through the generosity of a patron,
and went on to Christ Church, Oxford, where he remained to teach.
He was caught up in the religious disputes which simmered after the
Restoration of the Monarchy and of the Established Church, and
later became involved in political affairs at the highest level under
the aegis of the Earl of Shaftesbury. Indeed he had to go into exile in
Holland in 1683, ultimately returning to England when the Catholic
King James II was deposed. He came back on the same ship as Queen
Mary II, after she and her husband William III had jointly succeeded
to the English throne in the so-called 'Glorious Revolution'. In the
meantime his native county had witnessed an abortive uprising,
which Locke had supported, even giving money to help finance it.
The Duke of Monmouth had landed in Dorset and led a rebellion
which ended in disaster in the heart of Somerset at the Battle of
Sedgemoor in 1685. The harsh treatment meted out to the rebels by
the infamous Judge Jeffreys, Lord Chief Justice, is still remembered in
the West of England as the 'Bloody Assizes'. Men were hanged in
large numbers as a deterrent in many towns and villages, including
twelve men in Locke's own village of Pensford.

The most fundamental split in English society at that time was
between those who were willing to conform to the authority and
practices of the Church of England and those who wished to dissent

and to worship in their own way. A catalyst was the Act of Uniformity of 1662 which attempted to impose the use of the Prayer Book on all English churches. It precipitated a split in the English Church which still remains. Since Church and State were virtually synonymous, and a 'parish' was simultaneously an ecclesiastical and political unit, the political rights of 'dissenters' or 'nonconformists' became a large issue. How far could religious freedom be tolerated? How far should it extend? There were those in the Church of England, called 'latitudinarians' who wished the Church to be as comprehensive as possible, and who wished to tolerate variations of belief and practice within it. The pluralism which Locke eventually came to advocate went further than that and encouraged an official toleration of at least some of those who had placed themselves beyond the Established Church and the authority of its Bishops. Locke's advocacy of toleration had an influence even on the thinking of those who drew up the American Constitution nearly a hundred years later. His own sympathies, however, were somewhat circumscribed. He could not allow recognition of political rights for Catholics, who, he considered, owed allegiance to a foreign sovereign, the Pope, and were themselves intolerant of others. Equally significant was his refusal to recognize atheists. This was a fundamental point for him, since he believed that politics depended on morality, and morality was founded on a belief in God and in an afterlife where our conduct in this life would receive due reward or punishment.

It is impossible to understand Locke's philosophy properly without realizing something of his background. In the most famous of all his works, the *Essay concerning Human Understanding* published in 1690, he refers to 'the faculty of reason whereby Man is supposed to be distinguished from the beasts, and wherein it is evident that he much surpasses them'.[1] Later he says that it is religion that should most distinguish us from animals 'and ought most peculiarly to elevate us'.[2] Nevertheless, he adds bitterly, it is in religion that 'men often appear most irrational, and more senseless than beasts themselves'. Reason provided the antidote to violence and he is thus anxious to establish religion on a rational basis, just as he wanted to do the same for political society. He had a horror of religious 'enthusiasm', of which he reckoned that England had suffered a surfeit. Enthusiasm merely replaced reason with the 'ungrounded fancies of a man's brain'.[3] However, despite his reputation for radical thinking, John Locke was a devout Christian. One of his major works in the last decade of his life was entitled *The Reasonableness of Christianity*. Its main contention was that all that was required in Christian belief was that Jesus was the Messiah. He believed the two indispensable conditions for obtaining eternal life to be faith and repentance, or, in other words, 'believing Jesus to be the Messiah and a good life.'[4] Because of its few theological requirements, the book laid Locke open to accusations of heresy. In particular, did he believe that Jesus was the Son of God in a unique sense? Was he denying the doctrine of the Trinity? He was suspected of being a Socinian (or, in later parlance, a Unitarian). He remained, however a loyal Anglican, and it may have been that he was merely trying to be as inclusive as possible in his definition of what it is to be a Christian.

One thing is certain, and that is that Locke wished to assert the centrality of reason even in the realm of religious faith. He was as aware as anyone of the limits of reason, and saw the need of direct revelation from God. He says sadly that 'human reason unassisted failed men in its great and proper business of morality' because it was never able to make out 'an entire body of the law of nature'.[5] We therefore needed to be told our duties by one sent from God. Nevertheless anything learnt through revelation had also to be agreeable to reason. The latter has to give its vote for the truths discovered through revelation. Moreover reason is needed to recognize something as a genuine revelation in the first place.

What, then, is this 'reason'? It is easy to see Locke simply as the first great British empiricist philosopher, to be succeeded by Bishop Berkeley, and then David Hume. Certainly he identified himself very much with the newly founded Royal Society, of which he became a member. His explicit emphasis on the role of experience 'on which all our knowledge is founded'[6] appeared to value the role of observation and to underpin the new scientific method. It is well known that in the 'Epistle to the reader' at the start of the *Essay*,[7] he refers to master-builders such as Boyle or 'the incomparable Mr Newton', who were at that time advancing the sciences. Locke's own purpose was not to provide any grand metaphysical scheme, but, he surprisingly says, 'to be employed as an under-labourer in clearing ground a little and removing some of the rubbish that lies in the way to knowledge'. He thus appears to align himself firmly with those philosophers of a later age who have given priority to the empirical sciences, and have thought that the function of philosophy was merely to provide clarification of what is essentially scientific reasoning. This is part of the truth, but Locke had a wider vision of reason, which was also central to his understanding of human nature. Just because reason is opposed to force, he felt that it ought to be the instrument of forging public agreement and toleration within the Church and in society at large. No doubt, because of his experiences in the turbulence of his times, he wished to appeal to a faculty which he believed was shared by all humans. If we are all reasonable creatures, in the sense of having within us a faculty of reason, perhaps in the end we can be reasonable, rather than violent, in our dealings with each other. Locke's philosophy was a stabilizing influence within a badly fractured society.

## Our Place in the World

What then was the source of this faculty of reason in human beings? Locke's answer was unequivocal. Its source lay in God as Creator. As well as the particular revelation attested to within Christianity, Locke was insistent that God had revealed His goodness and mercy generally 'by the light of reason',[8] at least to those who made use of that light. He goes on to refer to 'the same spark of the divine nature and knowledge in man, which making him a man, showed him the law he was under, as a man'. People are able to put out or neglect that light, but with it anyone could in principle grasp that law, which is the 'eternal, immutable standard of right'. They would be using a rationality, which Locke, in an evocative phrase much favoured by some English theologians in the seventeenth century, describes as 'the candle of the Lord'. This not only stresses the divine origin of human reason, but also, of course, indicates its limited nature. We cannot know everything, even though we are able to obtain a degree of knowledge which places us far above all other creatures. Locke insists at the start of the *Essay* that humans have 'light enough to lead them to the knowledge of their Maker and the sight of their own duties'.[9] Even though we have to rely on candle-light and not broad sunshine, 'the candle, that is set up in us, shines bright enough for all our purposes'.

Any rational understanding of our place in the scheme of things has to take account of the origin of that rational understanding. How is it that humans can reflect on their own position in the world? Locke's answer is unequivocally that of a theist. This is God's world ordered in a particular way, and we can only understand it (as animals cannot) because of God's gift of reason to us. Locke's major interest underlying all his philosophy concerned the foundations of morality and its relationship with the will of God. We are told that the *Essay*, despite its wide-ranging survey of the possibility of human knowledge, had its origin in conversations about morality and revealed religion. There is, indeed, a perpetual tension between Locke's stress on the role of human reason, and our continuing need for revelation. Locke did not want to disown the central importance of God's revelation in Christ, but at the same time he wanted to insist that everything has at the last resort to be approved by our reason. This meant that just as individual claims to direct inspiration should be treated with suspicion, so tradition must itself be judged by the standard of reason. Authority had to receive the rational consent of the people.

Despite, however, this stress on reason as a gift to humans by God, Locke is best known for his attack on the possibility of any innate knowledge. His empiricism is seen in sharpest relief in his insistence that we are not born with any innate ideas, of the kind championed, for instance, by Plato. We do not even have any prior understanding of God or any natural disposition to be good (or evil). There is no 'law of nature' written in our souls. We have to learn what or duties and responsibilities are. Locke firmly believed that all knowledge comes from experience, and he himself turned to anthropology for his knowledge of human nature. He found it significant that there were reports from navigators of whole nations 'among whom there was to be found no notion of a God, no religion.'[10] For Locke, the human mind was at birth a blank tablet, a white paper, on which anything written was to come from experience. This was not only a philosophical position of great significance concerning the nature of human knowledge. It had direct applications to our understanding of the character of education. He concluded long and detailed recommendations about how to bring up children, with the view that the individual 'is only a white paper or wax, to be moulded and fashioned as one pleases.'[11] In the long-running argument about the relative significance of heredity or environment for the formation of character and the teaching of skills, Locke is whole-heartedly on the side of those who ascribe everything to environment. It is experience, and experience alone that makes us what we are. It seems to follow that no one can be born with any innate talents.

Locke tended to view the process of receiving experience as being, at least to begin with, unduly passive, and says of 'bare, naked perception', that in it, 'the mind is for the most part, only passive; and what it perceives, it cannot avoid perceiving.'[12] This clearly lent itself to a very mechanistic view of the working of the mind, and it is perhaps not surprising that many found in Locke an incipient materialism. Could even the process of reason be reduced to the motions of matter? One of his most controversial suggestions, particularly in his own time, was that God could possibly have given to 'some systems of matter, fitly disposed' a power to perceive and think.[13] Locke considered that it was beyond our ability to understand how far this could happen, as opposed to thought being restricted to an immaterial substance. Since all our 'ideas', or concepts, have to be derived from experience, Locke believed that issues about the nature of the soul, and whether it could be material, had to lie beyond our knowledge. It was instead a matter of faith and probability. Although he protested that he did not in any way wish to lessen a belief in the immateriality of the soul, and although his belief in life after death clearly played a central role in his view of morality, it was hardly surprising that there was outrage in some quarters that such a notion could even be entertained. At a time when the physical sciences were in the ascendancy, anything which appeared to suggest that matter played a more central role in human life than had been traditionally thought would immediately be seen as an attack on central religious doctrines about our nature as souls with an eternal destiny.

Basically what Locke seemed to be putting forward as a possibility was a property dualism, rather than a substance dualism. Thought, and the mental generally, may not be reducible to descriptions of matter, but Locke seems to acknowledge that it need not follow that we posit an immaterial 'something' to own it. Mental properties could then be regarded as different from physical ones, without the postulation of a non-material 'self'. Indeed, his influential stress on the centrality of consciousness for personal identity explicitly made the issue of substance a secondary issue in that context. He believed that our selves are constituted by our consciousness. He claims: 'It is by the consciousness it has of its present thoughts and actions that it is self to itself now, and so will be the same self as far as the same consciousness can extend to actions past or to come.'[14]

It was, however, basic to his philosophy that we do in fact assume that there are substances, as subjects of qualities that are observable. These substances are of various kinds, not just man, but horse, gold, water and so on. It is notorious that on Locke's own admission we have no clear idea of the nature of such substances, beyond the characteristics we observe. His conclusion is that substance therefore stands for 'only an uncertain supposition of we know not what...which we take to be the substratum or support, of those Ideas we do know'.[15] Locke's empiricism is here at odds with a more metaphysical view of not only human nature, but the nature of familiar objects. His views inevitably lead to the possibility that science would be able to uncover the nature of such substances (for instance, discovering that water is composed of hydrogen and oxygen), without the need to continue positing something beyond our knowledge. The problem always in philosophy with such posits is that they can be easily discarded, without any apparent effect on our actual knowledge. This may work with ordinary physical substances. The question of the nature of the self is more complicated. Hume would later, from an empiricist standpoint, dissolve the notion into a mere bundle of experiences. Locke is much more agnostic. The question must remain, however, whether he was entitled to such empiricist qualms, given his Christian views about moral responsibility, and a continuing life beyond our present one. Can I be held responsible for my behaviour in this life, if there is no continuing self? Locke's reply was that consciousness alone was sufficient to constitute our individuality, and he saw no difficulty at all in conceiving of the same consciousness continuing in a different kind of resurrected body.

## What is it be Human?

Locke's stress on the centrality of experience for our knowledge raises the question whether there are limits to what humans can experience. Does such a philosophy, for instance, inevitably lead to a science-based outlook which builds up a picture of the world that is firmly circumscribed by what we can experience through our senses? This will inevitably lead to a materialist or 'naturalist' picture of reality, ourselves included. Whatever Locke's hesitation about the character of the self, he was adamant both that there is a God and that God cannot be conceived as a material Being. Indeed he provides a general argument against any materialist reduction of thought to matter. He holds that 'unthinking particles of matter, however put together, can have nothing thereby added to them, but a new relation of position, which 'tis impossible should give thought and knowledge to them.'[16] If thought is accounted for in terms of matter, it will follow, he thinks, that every thought must be accidental. The power of free choice is removed. Rationality becomes the 'accidental unguided motions of blind matter'. Locke thus does not just envisage the possibility of a reality beyond the material world. He is claiming that all rationality depends on a reality which transcends the physical world. This is, of course, another way of asserting the ultimate dependence of reason, as the 'candle of the Lord', on the nature of God.

According to Locke, God created us with a particular nature, because it was His freely chosen will to do so. There has been a long-running controversy since Plato as to whether things are good because God willed them to be, or whether God willed them because they are independently good. Locke felt strongly that God did not have to create a particular kind of world. As it is, we are subject to whatever He wills. In an early work, *Essays on the Law of Nature*, Locke stressed the binding nature of such natural law on all humans whether they recognize it or not. It is the result of the way that God 'in his infinite and eternal wisdom' has made us.[17] Our moral duties thus follow necessarily from our very nature. Locke was far from being a moral relativist and accepted the universal nature of the binding force of natural law. This does not mean that everyone follows it. Locke was more aware than many of the diversity of human practices. Nevertheless, many are, he believes, led astray by tradition or their passions. Like brute beasts, they follow the herd, 'since they do not allow themselves the use of their reason, but give way to appetite.'[18]

Locke maintains that 'natural law stands and falls together with the nature of man as it is at present'.[19] The point is that God could have made us differently, and then because our nature would have been different, our moral duties would also be different. Morality answers to our present nature. Locke is thus able to refer firmly to a fixed rule of morals, 'which reason itself pronounces, and which persists, being a fact so firmly rooted in the soil of human nature'. He seemed to hanker after a demonstration of the truth of moral beliefs that could be as certain as anything in mathematics. In 1681, for example, he remarked that 'I cannot but think morality as well as mathematics is capable of demonstration'.[20] The general tenor of his work, however, suggests that this was an unrealistic ambition. If human nature is the result of a particular choice by God in Creation and does not have to be as it is, it would seem to follow that only an empirical method (and perhaps revelation) will help us discover how in fact we have been made and what is good for us. The function of reason therefore is not to recover immutable and necessary truths about the human condition. Humans themselves do not have to be as they are. If we were very different, so would our be our needs and our desires. Locke remarks that God 'could have created men such that they would be without eyes and not need them'.[21] It is thus not surprising that Locke turns to anthropology, and certainly his approach might suggest that an empirical investigation into the roots of human nature may also cast light on the nature of morality. He saw a strong connection between our contingent nature and the content of morality.

Why, though, should we fulfil our moral obligations, even if we come to recognize what they are? Locke is very critical of Aristotle and his followers, who, he believes, merely introduce systems of classification of virtues and vices only. They may, he says teach us to speak their language properly, but they fail to show why we should be drawn to virtue.[22] He insists that moral actions 'depend upon the choice of an understanding and free agent'. Locke seems to think that since we naturally seek happiness and avoid misery, ethics has to be built ultimately on an appeal to our self-interest through the promise of reward and the threat of punishment. It is by this means that superiors, he says, enforce observance of their laws. Only the attraction of pleasure (understood in a wide sense) and the evil of pain, can provide 'motive or restraint to the actions of a free understanding agent'.[23] All this may go to show the necessity of human laws in human societies, but Locke's eyes are set higher. In order to set morality on a proper basis, he has to show the existence of a natural law, backed up by a law-maker, who has 'a power to reward and punish according to the tenor of the law established by him'.

This emphasis on pleasure and pain, happiness and misery, as the springs of human action may seem somewhat surprising when coupled with stress on the role of reason and a belief in God. Cannot humans be motivated by what they see is worthwhile and good, without always having to be driven by the fear of eternal punishment? Cannot I love my neighbour for his or her own sake and not just because God has told me to and I am afraid of the consequences of disobedience? The existence of God's law creates our obligations, but this apparently means that we cannot simply obey God's will because it is intrinsically good. It seems as if we are to obey because He has commanded, and has the power to require compliance. As Locke says in his earlier writing, God has created us out of nothing and can reduce us again to nothing.[24] The conclusion must be that we are subject to Him 'in perfect justice and by utmost necessity'. Even Locke's account of Christian revelation is couched in terms of God's authority as Creator, rather than God's love. Showing the need for revelation to assist natural reason, he suggested that it was a shorter way of dealing with the needs of ordinary people that 'one manifestly sent from God, and coming with visible authority from Him, should as a king and law-maker, tell them their duties; and require their obedience'.[25] Yet even in what Locke himself says, there are hints of a wider vision. His stress on the divine wisdom suggests that God's commands are far from arbitrary, and, in human societies, his emphasis on the consent of the governed suggests that the power of the government is not the only factor.

## Human Society

Locke equated the natural law (God's law for humans) with the law of reason. Our reason, he is quick to maintain, does not so much establish this law as search for and discover it.[26] This, though, inevitably produces a certain scepticism about tradition. The law of nature is everywhere the same and traditions vary, says Locke crisply, so that, if there is a law of nature, it cannot be known by means of tradition.[27] It is hardly surprising that Locke's views have been invoked by reformers and revolutionaries who have wanted to protest about the injustice of their circumstances. An appeal to reason must be impatient with those who are content with the ways things have always been done.

The American Declaration of Independence, made nearly a century after Locke was writing, and influenced by him, states that 'all men are created equal, that they are endowed by their Creator with certain inalienable rights, that among these are life, liberty and the pursuit of happiness.' This was basically Locke's position, although he would not have agreed that those truths are self-evident. Instead he appealed to a rationality that relied heavily on human experience. Through this he thought that we could see that all men are naturally in a state of freedom and equality. In his *Second Treatise of Government* he claims that reason teaches that 'being all equal and independent, no one ought to harm another in his life, liberty or possessions.' Everyone ought 'to preserve himself' and 'to preserve the rest of mankind'.[28] This holds good in what Locke terms the state of nature where it us up to the individual rather than any community to put the law of nature into effect. This differs from Hobbes' conception, in that although by definition the state of nature contains no government or civilization, it suggests that even there the interests of everyone are to be taken into account. Each person matters equally, because each was created by God. Ruthless pursuit of personal interest has no place in all this. We are allowed to punish those who offend against the law of nature, because offenders declare by their actions that they are not prepared to live according to reason. Similarly we can seek proper reparation from them. In fact, in the state of nature, humans ought to live as they are intended by God to live.

Locke is unequivocal in his assertion that in the state of nature, everyone is free and equal. It is a condition where men live together 'according to reason' but without any earthly authority to judge between them.[29] Our labour then entitles us to private property as the fruit of that labour. He remarks that this law of reason makes the deer the property of the 'Indian' who killed it. The land that had been given in common had to be cultivated, and thus through labour was handed over to the 'industrious and rational'[30]. Thus land could be appropriated and private possessions appear. This in fact provided the chief motive, Locke thinks, for the coming together in community and the founding of political society. Property has to be preserved, and men, Locke thinks, are liable to be biased in their own interest. An impartial judge is therefore necessary with the power to enforce justice. Yet all has finally to be done with the consent of the people. Power must be limited by reason. In particular, taxes cannot be levied without the consent of the majority, whether given by themselves or by their representatives. It is easy to see how the cry of 'no taxation without representation' by American colonists in the next century bore more than an accidental resemblance to Locke's theory of natural rights. Similarly, for Locke, 'the end of Government is the good of mankind',[31] and when a king or other ruler uses force and oppression, 'everyone has a right to defend himself and resist the aggressor'.[32] Locke approved of the people then taking the law into their own hands and founding a new constitution or putting the old one in new hands. It was the latter that happened in England in 1688, but Locke's views were to have an unforeseen influence in America in 1776.

In all of this, the underlying theme is that reason can make itself judge over tradition, law and custom. An examination of human nature, coupled with God's will for us, shows that we naturally have rights and that these can be used as a yardstick against which the justice of governments can be judged and challenged. Reason brought to bear upon the contingent facts of human life can draw to our attention basic rights and duties. We have responsibilities to others and they have to us, even in our 'natural' condition. These reveal God's will for us, but the human institutions which we construct gain their authority purely from their ability to further our welfare. Traditional sources of authority, whether political or religious, must all be submitted to the judgement of human reason.

Yet Locke was a man of his time. His views of natural rights were not necessarily the same as those who would passionately campaign for 'human rights' today. Nowhere was this more obvious than in the way he dealt with the native peoples of North America. America, in fact, was much in his thoughts, and he had been closely involved in the drawing up of a constitution for Carolina. For him the America of the seventeenth century was a wilderness waiting to be cleared, cultivated and civilized. It was to a large extent still in the state of nature, as were its peoples. In a striking phrase, Locke asserts that 'in the beginning all the world was America'.[33] It was a world without real political authority (since Locke regarded chieftains as not much more than generals of armies), and where the natives did not make full use of the abundance of resources available. It was a world lying open for colonists to appropriate, and by means of their labour take possession of the land. Its original inhabitants had, Locke considered, no proper political society. Moreover, colonists had the right of self-defence, and the right to seek reparations. This was significantly different from later appreciations of some similar situations in the British Empire, where treaties were entered into

between the Crown and peoples who were in effect recognized as
nations in their own right.

## Contemporary Relevance

Locke believed that those who violated the law of nature thereby lost
their natural rights. Those, for example, who use force are no longer
under what he terms 'the common law of reason' and therefore
forfeit any right to be treated as humans.[34] They may be treated as
'beasts of prey'. Human rights were not of an absolute character for
him but could only be claimed by those who behave as people with
reason. Indeed, although Locke's theory of rights has been influential, he does not in fact use the term 'natural right' very frequently. It
is controversial just what he saw the relation of rights and duties as
being. Which has priority? Do I have a right to certain treatment
because others have a duty to treat me in that way or is it the other
way round, with my duties arising because of other people's possession of rights? What is clear is that everything stems from our
common obligation to serve our Creator. All rights and duties can
only be seen in a theistic context.

Our contemporary age is much given to the rhetoric of human
rights. The idea that our own behaviour can disqualify us from any
claim to rights, so that we might even forfeit our right to life, is a
somewhat unfamiliar one. A current assumption is that we have
rights simply in virtue of our common humanity. We can make
demands on others simply because we are human. Yet this begs
both the question whether the category of being human is a meaningful one, and also why it matters anyway. An extreme relativism
cannot allow that people in different cultures do share any common,
essential character. Locke was no relativist, and his Christianity gave
the answer to the second problem. We are all equal before God and
have an eternal destiny. In effect we must matter to each
other because we matter to God. Yet one of the problems that
Locke's philosophical legacy has encountered has been a tendency
to abstract much of what he says from its theological context
and assume that it can still make sense. His strongly rational empiricism depended heavily on reason as a God-given gift, partially
reflecting both the rationality of Creation, and the wisdom of God.
Without God, the role of reason can become much more

problematic. The more sceptical empiricism of Hume is the logical outcome.

Locke's respect for science made sense when it was thought that science was investigating a rational order which reflected the mind of the Creator. He had, he felt, good reason for assuming the existence of a structure and order in the physical world which lay open to discovery by observation and experiment. A similar belief in a Creator was important to the scientists such as Newton and Boyle whom Locke was willing to serve as an 'under-labourer'. Locke's belief that the world had been created by a God who could have made everything (including human nature) very different gave a metaphysical justification for his empiricism and for his respect for science. As we have seen, God, he thought, did not have to make the world in any particular way. Just because of that contingent nature of the world, we could not discover anything about its nature nor how humans fit into the scheme of things by relying on pure thought. We had to look at how things happened to have been made, through experimental science and through the study of human beings in such subjects as anthropology. Thus at the root of Locke's approach was an assumption that although we have to look at the world to discover its nature, and although it all could have been very different, nevertheless he could rely on it having an inner order and structure, and a regularity which could warrant generalizations from the seen to the unseen. In such questions as 'the coherence and continuity of the parts of matter', Locke firmly says, 'we cannot but ascribe them to the arbitrary will and good pleasure of the Wise Architect'.[35] The contingent order of the universe made Locke's empiricism possible, but it depended on a theism which many later empiricists would find incredible. Yet it is arguable whether science can properly proceed without some such assumption.[36] Locke's philosophy certainly draws attention to the fact that modern science started with theistic assumptions.

Yet it is not only science, which in Locke needs the idea of God. His stress on 'reason' is characteristically modern, in his willingness to use it to oppose tradition and authority. Unlike many of the Enlightenment thinkers of the eighteenth century, particularly in France, he did not use it as a weapon against Christianity. He was certainly opposed to the intolerance shown by the Catholicism of his day, but he saw human reason as the ally of Christianity and not its enemy. The 'candle of the Lord' was able to cast light on the law of

God. However, in his willingness to subject even alleged revelation to the demands of reason, he was giving the right of judgement to a human faculty in a way that may seem to make humans the arbiters of what is to count as knowledge. Not just tradition, but individual claims to divine inspiration, and the authority of the Bible itself, were all subjected to searching assessment by human reason. Locke was willing to look beyond the natural world to the supernatural and to accept that some things were above reason, because they were beyond the scope of our natural faculties. Yet there is already apparent the possibility of a clash between what seems to be apparent to humans and can be established by the new methods of science, and the claims about a transcendent God, and a life after our earthly one, which Locke himself thought so important. It is perhaps not surprising that his philosophy could be seen very differently by those who tried to make use of it. In his lifetime, John Toland used Locke's position to argue that there were no 'mysteries' in Christianity. Everything lay open to human reason. This was the path to deism (the belief in a Creator who did not intervene in our world) and on to an atheism, which concentrated on the world open to human reason. Yet in the eighteenth century the great evangelist, John Wesley, was an admirer of Locke and his philosophy, and his own (very orthodox) theology was much influenced by it.

A belief in the sovereignty of human reason was to lie at the roots of Enlightenment thinking in the eighteenth century. In the seventeenth century philosophers in England, such as Locke, set in train a process which involved the extolling of human reason. With his stress on the importance of reason, liberty and toleration, and his close connection with both the rise of modern science and the establishment of modern democracy, Locke has as much claim as anyone to be one of the sources of that Enlightenment. Yet whether one thinks of human rights, of the grounding of science or of the possibility of rationality, abstracting any of them from the theistic context in which Locke firmly believed raises major questions. One of the most profound philosophic issues of our present age is whether notions such as 'reason', 'science' and even 'human nature' can survive without the belief in God which first gave life to them.

# Hume

## *1711–1776*

## Context

David Hume was born in Edinburgh in 1711 and died only a matter of weeks after the American Declaration of Independence in 1776. He lived through the comparative stability and tranquillity of the Georgian period, and his emphasis on custom and tradition perhaps reflects the philosophy of someone who had not lived through major upheavals. He has been called a 'conservative' but that term is strictly anachronistic, since conservatism was articulated as a response to the excesses of the French Revolution a few years later. Many then became frightened of attempts to sweep tradition away in the name of reason.

Hume has been considered by many to be the greatest of all British philosophers, although he was also a famous historian. His philosophy is much in tune with a scientific age, following in the British empiricist tradition of Locke and Berkeley. He stressed the central role of human experience, in the process making knowledge itself depend on the capacities given us by our human nature. His idea of human nature had to provide the basis for his philosophy. Empiricists typically hold that our knowledge is built upon the experience of our senses. Reason cannot tell us on its own what must be the case, but we have to find out through experience the way things are. What cannot be experienced is discounted, and so the 'world' becomes merely what is accessible to humans. Bishop Berkeley had equated reality with what could be perceived, but had avoided the unwelcome consequences of things going out of existence when no one perceived them by bringing to his system the perceptions of God who would know everything. Hume was far more sceptical. He was suspected of atheism, but in fact his scepticism was even more wide-ranging.

A basic purpose of science is to search for regularities in nature and to try to explain them. Hume argued that causation was merely a matter of two events always occurring together, coupled with our psychological disposition to link them. There is no necessary connection between them. He says that 'all our reasonings concerning causes and effects are derived from nothing but custom'.[1] We just happen to associate two things in our minds, with no question of any rational justification for doing so. The position emphasizes the way we associate one experience with another and forces attention to the basic springs of human nature at the level of instinct. It shows the importance of customs and traditions, built up in human society as a response to the basic traits of humanity and to human experience. Yet it cannot assure us that we are correct in our beliefs. Indeed empiricism may appear an ally of science, but it can also undermine it. What grounds have we for assuming uniformity in nature? If we do not, science becomes impossible. Hume's solution was not to rely too much on reason, but to be content with what we find it natural to expect. He remarks that 'nature breaks the force of all sceptical arguments in time.'[2]

The title of Hume's major work, *A Treatise of Human Nature*, is significant for two reasons. It demonstrates the centrality of the notion of human nature for his thinking. With reason dethroned, human passions and instincts take on greater importance, helping to explain the way we interact with the physical world and with each other. It is, however, the same title as that given by Hobbes to part of his own work.[3] Hobbes and Hume are not usually associated and Hume rarely mentions Hobbes. Yet despite obvious differences, there are clear similarities between the philosophy of the two. Hume rejected egoism, but was in no doubt of human selfishness. His views on human freedom show the influence of Hobbes. Both believe that morality and politics must be studied by the same methods as the physical sciences, and begin with the motivation of the individual. For that reason, both spend a considerable time investigating the nature of different human passions.

In his introduction, Hume claims that 'the science of man is the only foundation for the other sciences' and he stresses the importance of experience and observation even in the study of humanity.[4] He then refers to philosophers who have 'begun to put the science of man on a new footing' (including Locke and Bishop Butler). Yet he omits the name of Hobbes, perhaps not caring to associate his own work with someone whose name was still anathema in many quarters. Hume was always conscious of how a reputation for atheism could harm him. One place where he does mention Hobbes is in the context of stressing the general uniformity we can expect in human character. Hume accepted that individual, and national, character can vary, but he also believed that 'there is a general course of nature in human actions, as well as in the operations of the sun and climate.'[5] As a result, we can be as sure that humans never could behave in certain ways as that we know that fruits will not ripen in winter in the far north. We would not believe anyone who said he had seen them, and Hume adds: 'I am apt to think a traveller would meet with as little credit, who should inform us of people exactly of the same character with those in Plato's *Republic* on the one hand, or those in Hobbes' *Leviathan* on the other.' Through our experience, we find regularities and come to expect them, both in human action and in the workings of the physical world.

Hume was not a materialist like Hobbes, and did not identify the perceptions of the human mind with the behaviour of matter. He did, though, refuse to make any distinction in principle between the regularities we observe in human action and those of physical objects. The mind associates what is constantly found together, and what we term 'human nature' is a product of what we have come to expect from our experience of our fellows. Yet, paradoxically, our propensity to connect what always happens together is itself a product of that self-same nature.

Hume's scepticism, like all scepticism, cannot be taken very far before it undermines itself. He does refer to 'the necessary and uniform principles of human nature',[6] although a little later he stresses the way in which the mind *forms* the idea of cause and effect from observation and *feels* the necessity. The emphasis is on the operation of the human mind and not the way things are. It is, seemingly, a part of our nature to react to the world as we do. If, however, it appears to be human nature to form a certain picture of human nature, there is a danger of a certain incoherence. The question is how far the associations the mind makes are merely the result of experience. Can the human mind begin to categorize the world without some initial propensities and tendencies? It is this type of consideration that leads philosophers, such as Plato, to appeal to the

notion of innate knowledge, or causes the biological notion of
instinct to be invoked. It is in fact very difficult for a consistent
empiricist to have any view of human nature, without a theory as
to how we may be born with certain predispositions. It is hard to
explain everything in terms of *our* experience, without a conception
of who *we* are.

## Our Place in the World

Hume's determination to treat the behaviour of physical objects and
human action in the same way means that he attributes the same
kind of causal necessity to human action as to the effect of one
billiard ball striking another. He talks of a prisoner who goes to the
scaffold knowing he cannot escape, as much because of the obstin-
acy of his gaoler as because of the walls and bars of the prison.
Hume refers to the train of ideas that will run through the prisoner's
head as he confronts the certainty of his death: 'The refusal of the
soldiers to consent to his escape: the action of the executioner: the
separation of the head and body: bleeding, convulsive motions and
death'.[7] Hume's point is that some are voluntary actions by people,
while others are natural causes, but the mind treats all of them in
the same way. Each is a link in a connected chain.

The predictability of other people is an essential for Hume. We
have, he points out, to think of actions as purely random, if we are
unwilling to view them as caused. He concludes that 'liberty, by
removing necessity, removes also causes, and is the very same thing
with chance'.[8] Action that is not caused will not be regular, but will
be unpredictable. Life would then be impossible, since, Hume stresses, we rely on other people behaving in ways that we can expect to
be the same. Just how much our life is governed by such assumptions is brought out in this graphic example: 'A man who at noon
leaves his purse full of gold on the pavement of Charing Cross, may
as well expect that it will fly away like a feather, as that he will find it
untouched an hour after.'[9]

Hume followed Hobbes in opposing liberty to constraint. A stone
rolling freely is as free as a human being acting freely, although both
are being caused to behave as they do. Hume thereby hoped to show
the compatibility of freedom and causation. Indeed, unusual and
unpredictable behaviour would be a threat to morality, it might

seem, since moral behaviour is not random or arbitrary. Yet, according to Hume, neither is it instigated by reason, since only desire or passion could, he believed, prompt us to act. Mere intellectual understanding, without any desire, would never cause us to act. Explicable human action, therefore, had to be caused by motives arising from what we wanted. It could not be rational while being uncaused. Hume thus rules out any proper alternative to caused action, with the type of reason- governed action described by those who believe in free will forbidden by definition.

Hume is often criticized for his ahistorical approach. He assumed that humans at all times and places will be similar in important respects. This is a crucial issue in any study of human nature. The more that society is assumed to shape people, the easier it is to relate 'human' nature to the social context in which it is found. Would people in primitive 'hunter-gatherer' societies have *anything* in common with the inhabitants of an advanced industrial nation? Are the citizens of a capitalist economy similar in all respects to those of a socialist State? Hume's answer to this type of question appears uncompromising, though he did recognize the necessity of human society, and he was quite ready to notice differences in national character. He says:

> It is universally acknowledged that there is a great uniformity among the actions of men, in all nations and ages, and that human nature remains still the same in its principles and operations... Would you know the sentiments, inclinations and course of life of the Greeks and Romans? Study well the temper and actions of the French and English.[10]

Hume bases this assertion on the general agreement to be found on the matter, but he was a little optimistic since this has become one of the most hotly debated issues concerning human nature. Without the assumption of basic similarity the study of humans becomes problematic. Understanding other societies and other periods of history becomes difficult, if not impossible. Even apparent similarities can no longer be taken at face value. The example of leaving gold at Charing Cross is no longer obviously intelligible if we exclude the assumption that the inhabitants of eighteenth-century London were not so very different in their basic impulses from us. If they were like us, the example is instantly acceptable and to the point, but if they may not have been, we have to wonder what kinds of motivation may have been true of them and not of us. There would be no guarantee that they would be intelligible. We have to assume that human beings have always been greedy. Yet greed is a vice which many have sought to eradicate through social engineering. By changing social conditions they hoped that they could change people. This is one of the theories behind revolutions. It is of fundamental importance whether one can change human nature. Hume himself was in no doubt of the risks inherent in overthrowing custom and tradition.

Hume makes human nature a matter of our common experience. We all acknowledge certain universal tendencies in human behaviour. As Hume was an individualist, deeming society constituted by the desires and needs of individuals, questions about human nature come down to issues about me and you. Who am I? What makes me the person I am, and different from you? Controversies about human nature cannot avoid arguments about the nature of the self. Just as some deny the whole notion of human nature, so there are those who dismiss the idea of there being 'selves'. Hume was a defender of the concept of human nature, but his empiricism would not let him accept the idea of a subject of experience. The difficulty is that I cannot experience myself as such, since I am having the experience. Introspection and self-examination can tell me something, but it is always I who am conducting the examination. There are limits to how far I can observe myself observing myself. I remain the subject as well as the object of the experience.

Many philosophers have felt that the nature of the self can never be fully captured by any empiricist theory, and that no experience can ever wholly reveal the intricacies of oneself. By definition such an approach must be anathema to the empiricist, and Hume insisted that the self be revealed in experience if the very idea is to be intelligible. The notion of experience trying to capture the subject of experience may seem paradoxical, but that did not prevent Hume trying to discover the self amongst his own experience. He writes: 'For my part, when I enter most intimately into what I call *myself*, I always stumble on some particular perception or other, of heat or cold, light or shade, love or hatred, pain or pleasure. I never catch myself at any time without a perception.'[11]

It thus appears that *I* am just a succession of different experiences, with nothing to hold them together. They have no owner. This is

Hume's conclusion, although it is perhaps tempting to respond by asking *who* precisely it is that never catches himself without a perception. He says of people that 'they are nothing but a bundle or collection of different perceptions, which succeed each other with an inconceivable rapidity, and are in a perpetual flux and movement.' The search for the inner nature of the person must forever prove frustrating for an empiricist. The greater importance is attached philosophically to human experience, the less importance is given to who has the experience. The self is discarded on the grounds that the notion is purely metaphysical, and as such beyond experience. Yet this has the effect of making the concept of personal identity problematic, with difficulties arising as to how the same person endures over a long period. Hume's radical solution was to give up the idea of a person beyond the continuous stream of overlapping experiences. He was, not surprisingly, sceptical about life after death. He remarks that reason alone cannot establish the immortality of the soul, and adds: 'Nothing could set in a fuller light the infinite obligation which mankind have to Divine revelation: since we find that no other medium could ascertain this great and important truth.'[12] Given Hume's other views, this remark is probably not to be taken at face value. The biting irony which arises from his scepticism is clear.

## What is it to be Human?

Hume believed that our reason merely leads us to recognize the relations between things, while our desires prompt us to act. In a memorable phrase he insisted that reason is 'the slave of the passions', because it cannot set our ends for us, but can only show us how to achieve what we already want.[13] He ruled out any idea of practical reason, and defined 'reason' more narrowly and 'passion' more widely than is normal. This view of the function of reason could not be further from that of Aristotle. Hume believed that our preferences are fixed, and cannot be influenced by reason, or indeed by social pressure. This means that politics can only be envisaged as an answer to the problems set by human nature. Politicians cannot hope to create a new world. Because of the relative powerlessness of our reason, we must use the instincts and desires we have. This involves a certain conservatism. 'Custom', Hume asserts, 'is the

great guide of human life'.[14] Just how deep-rooted this is is illustrated by the way, as Hume points out, that the mind expects heat
or cold if presented with a flame or with snow. We have no option
but to have a particular belief when placed in such circumstances.
Why is this? Hume asserts more than that it is through past experience. We have certainly found flame and heat, or snow and cold,
have always been 'conjoined together'. The expectation that this will
go on happening is not the result of reason. Hume says: 'All these
operations are a species of natural instincts, which no reasoning or
process of the thought and understanding is able either to produce or
to prevent.'[15]

This down-grading of the role of reason removes a major distinction between humans and animals, and Hume stresses the similar
role played by instinct in the lives of both animals and people. As he
says, a beast does not see any 'real connexion' between objects.
Reason is itself an instinct which enables us to move from one
phenomenon to another. Hume adds: 'This instinct, 'tis true, arises
from past observation and experience, but can any one give its
ultimate reason why past experience and observation produces
such an effect, any more than why nature alone should produce
it ?'[16]

Hume concludes that habit is 'nothing but one of the principles of
nature'. This is an interesting concession, since there is always the
danger in empiricism of placing so much emphasis on the relevance
of experience that inborn tendencies or predispositions are ruled out.
That would mean that humans could be moulded in many different
ways and that there was no such thing as human nature. The
minute, however, it is acknowledged that the workings of animal
instinct rely on 'nature', new possibilities of scientific investigation
are opened up. Hume's insistence on the role of instinct and fixed
preferences in the lives of animals and humans gives a philosophical
opening for the work of Darwin.

The effect of demoting the power of human reason is nowhere
more striking than in the context of morality. Hume wishes to base
this on fixed human preferences and says in a notorious phrase: ' 'Tis
not contrary to reason to prefer the destruction of the whole world to
the scratching of my finger.'[17] No desire or preference can be judged
irrational or changed through reason, which can merely establish
means to given ends. Reason cannot pass, Hume believes, from what
*is* the case to what *ought* to be the case, and his distinction between

the two has had a lasting impact. Many fail to quote the sentence following the one about the finger. Hume then says: ' 'Tis not contrary to reason for me to choose my total ruin, to prevent the least uneasiness of an Indian or person wholly unknown to me.' He was not an egoist, because he accepted that our preference could be for the good of others at the expense of our own. His point is simply that whatever our preference, it cannot be subjected to the judgement of reason.

Reason may be able to establish that all people should be treated with equal respect, but once the role of reason is rejected, it is necessary to face the fact that humans prefer their families and friends to the welfare of those who have no connection with them. Hume accepts this and denies that there is such a passion as the love of mankind as such.[18] He sums up what appears to be a natural human trait when he says: 'A man naturally loves his children better than his nephews, his nephews better than his cousins, his cousins better than strangers, where every thing else is equal'.[19] Once again Hume anticipated a phenomenon which was to arouse the interest of followers of Darwin. Love of kin may have genetic foundations, while love of self is an important element in ensuring that we each survive. Hume recognized that 'it is rare to meet with one, who loves any single person better than himself' but still insisted that ' 'tis as rare to meet with one to whom all the kind affections, taken together, do not over-balance all the selfish'.[20] He gives as an example the willingness of a father to spend most of his fortune on his wife and children rather than himself. This is certainly an instance of benevolence, and not selfishness, but caring for my own children is different from an altruistic concern for any, unrelated, children in need. Morality appears also to demand that, while Hume seems to suggest it may be too much to ask, on the grounds that concern for others will become more attenuated, the more remote they are from us.

This problem is bound to arise with any moral theory based on what people feel, and hence on their sympathies rather than their reason. Hume makes much of the principle of sympathy, calling it the 'chief source of moral distinctions'.[21] He means by it the tendency to see things from other people's point of view, something he admits is easier to achieve in the case of those close to us. It is indeed natural to love one's own children more than other people's, but that is a different question from whether someone needs my help.

The people I want to help and the ones I ought to help may not always coincide. There is a tension between the universal demands of morality and our particular sympathies. When Hume put the views of his *Treatise* in more popular form in his *Enquiry Concerning the Principles of Morals*, his stress is on benevolence extending to the whole of humanity rather than those we particularly favour. While distinguishing between 'reason' and 'sentiment', he defines the relevant sentiment as 'a feeling for the happiness of mankind, and a resentment of their misery'.[22] There are times when Hume seems to be appealing to some form of 'moral sense' in a way beloved of many eighteenth-century philosophers, and this is far removed from a view of morality as founded on restricted sympathies and self-interest. There is certainly an ambivalence in his work taken as a whole on how far humans can be expected to care for each other merely in virtue of their common humanity. Hume is, however, always totally consistent in supposing that morality is not established by reason. Whether our benevolence is wide-ranging or limited, it still, he thinks, springs from our human nature. Morality is, then, not something imposed on or demanded of humans, but is the outcome of a basic trait of human character. Morality, for Hume, does not merely have to take account of human nature. It is an expression of it.

## Human Society

Hume believed that society has to take account of the unalterable facts of human nature. It is in the interests of everyone to join together in a society, but people are not naturally just. It is an 'artificial' virtue, so society has to provide mechanisms through which it can be enforced. As Hume says about the frailty and perversity of human nature, 'men must endeavour to palliate what they cannot cure'.[23] Society must merely provide a framework in which the bad effects of some aspects of human nature can be minimized. We cannot change our passions but they can be channelled in a proper direction. He would have nothing to do with the idea of a social contract, regarding the notion of a state of nature as a 'mere philosophical fiction'.[24] He remarked that no one until recently had ever thought that government was founded on any compact. Believing that matters could only be settled by an appeal to 'general opinion', he regarded it as obvious enough that we have to obey a government because otherwise society could not exist. We are all dependent on society, since by joining together we can compensate for our weakness and increase our strength. The division of labour is beneficial in that different people can specialize in particular tasks. We can help each other for our mutual benefit. Hume considers that nature has given us, of all animals, the most wants and necessities, and very slender means of meeting them. He contrasts us with a lion which may need a lot of meat but has compensatory advantages because of its courage and power.[25] We have to supply our defects by banding together.

Although we need each other, we all have our own concerns, so that society is as likely to be the cause of collisions and jealousy as of happy co-operation. We will all probably grab as much as we can for ourselves and our relatives and friends. Since we are competing for limited resources, the situation is made even worse. Justice is needed because of this. As Hume says: 'Increase to a sufficient degree the benevolence of men, or the bounty of nature, and you render justice useless.'[26] Conventions arise in society for the establishment of justice and of property. Hume is well aware that although the preservation of society is in our common interest, we naturally prefer what is present to what is remote. The possibility of short-term gain may make anyone want to ignore the demands of justice. We cannot cure the 'narrowness of soul', as Hume calls it, which makes us forget our long-term advantage. He says of humans: 'They cannot change their natures. All they can do is change their situation, and render the observance of justice the immediate interest of some particular person, and its violation their more remote.'[27]

Thus government is established and the law administered, with people such as magistrates charged to act for the benefit of the whole. Disputes can be arbitrated and great public ventures undertaken. Bridges and harbours can be built, canals formed, fleets equipped and armies disciplined.[28] Hume hopes that magistrates will find an immediate interest in the interest of their subjects, since they are 'satisfied with their present condition and their part in society'. Even if this is so, they are going to find difficulties if they have to impose their will on a population that is too recalcitrant. Law can restrain a minority but cannot go against the majority without a very repressive apparatus of State.

Hume's response to this problem included reference to the importance of habit and custom. Children should be brought up

accustomed to behave in particular ways. Society may not have
been brought into being by the conscious consent of its members,
but conventions have evolved so as to deal with the problems posed
by human nature. One principle of human nature, which Hume calls
attention to is that 'men are mightily addicted to general rules'.[29]
We may even go on feeling obliged to give allegiance to a tyrannical
government, but Hume is adamant that if rulers themselves, because
of the 'irregularity of human nature' start being driven into excesses
by their own passions, we should not tolerate it. Government may,
for him, be based on common interest rather than common consent,
but in the last resort we are equally justified in withdrawing our
allegiance.

Conventions, like that of private property, arise out of a sense of
common interest, but they are neither agreed explicitly, not are they
the outcome of a promise. Indeed, for Hume, promising itself arises
from human conventions. They arise gradually, and slowly become
established as we see the disadvantage of transgressing them. Everyone comes to conform and can base their behaviour on the reasonable expectation that others will behave similarly. Our common life
in this way becomes imbued with habit and custom. Hume gives an
analogy of two men pulling the oars of a boat.[30] They may not have
explicitly promised each other to make an equal contribution, but
just got on with it, trusting that each will do what is in the interest of
both. In the same way, the most basic institutions of human society
have evolved. Gold and silver, says Hume, become the common
measure of exchange in this way. Even more important, languages
become established by this method. Mutual co-operation has come
about through slow development. We learn what is in our interest,
provided others act similarly. Our reliance on each other grows
through the ages as human customs are built up.

There is a connection between this position and the views of
Adam Smith, one of the founders of economics, and a friend of
Hume in Scotland. He held that although we may not intend consciously to promote the public interest, our separate decisions very
often have the unintended consequence of doing just that. Concerned for our own security, we are led by an 'invisible hand' to
achieve what we never intended. Unintended consequences are not
always desirable, but with the passing of time humans can gradually
adjust their behaviour to avoid unwelcome effects. Long-standing
traditions will have been built up by the gradual modification of

people's habits in the light of their effect on each other. Anyone holding this position would be uneasy about radically changing an institution. A delicate mechanism built up over many generations without ever having been deliberately planned cannot be easily supplanted. The consequences would be unforeseeable and possibly dangerous. Hume's trust in instinct, habit and custom extends through every level of his philosophy from his epistemology to his distrust of major political innovation. In each case, his justification would, he claimed, lie in the need to take account of basic facts of human nature.

## Contemporary Relevance

Hume's reliance on experience has proved congenial to modern philosophers emphasizing the centrality of scientific knowledge. Reasoning about anything beyond human experience was ruled out, and logical positivists in the years before and after the Second World War were able to see a kindred spirit in Hume. They themselves stressed the meaninglessness of any statement that could not be scientifically tested. Nevertheless his philosophy is always in danger of over-reaching itself. Too great a scepticism about the inherent orderliness and regular causal processes of the world can make the practice of science pointless. We may switch attention to the expectations we as humans bring to reality, but this is to change the subject completely. The more that human nature is emphasized as the central concept of epistemology, the less are we able to take the rest of reality seriously. The world we aim to explore through the methods of science should not be a mere reflection of our own abilities, capacities and prejudices.

Hume's stress on the universal character of human nature meant that although he accepted that we need society, he also believed that we bring our nature to it. Society has to serve pre-existing needs and desires, and does not help to create them. Society cannot change us. This marks a controversy that has become virulent during the last century. Many Marxists, for example, would hold that a different form of society can mould a new type of person. Certainly the relationship between individuals and society is highly complex. Hume's position lies at one end of a spectrum of possible views, with his belief that our central characteristics are fixed before they can be influenced by society. Contemporary economics often assume the fixed nature of human desires, and it is a view which fits well with biological understandings of human nature. Hume's references to instincts, both in animals and humans, cry out for a more scientific understanding. He was himself aware of this, commenting that we tend to call an instinct whatever we find extraordinary and inexplicable.[31] It was left to Darwin and his successors to provide a scientific theory about how instincts could be implanted in organisms.

Hume's influence has been deep and wide-ranging in modern philosophy. Perhaps nowhere is the radical nature of his thought more apparent than in his attack on the notion of a self as a substance. We each feel we are individual persons. I am me and you are you. We are more than a parade of overlapping experiences. It seems natural to think of a self as their owner, and it is important from the moral point of view that we think it. Unless I am the same person who had such and such an experience five years ago, I need accept no responsibility for what happened then. Responsibility is linked to there being persons. Morality demands that I acknowledge my actions as *mine*. If Hume is right, however, it becomes exceedingly problematic as to who 'I' am. Experiences can overlap, but without the notion of a substance as their subject, there seems no way of deciding who, if anyone, possesses them.

Philosophers are nowadays much tempted by physical criteria for personal identity, relating identity to the continuity of a body through space and time. Yet thought-experiments by philosophers can sow the seeds of doubt about the adequacy of the body in general and the brain in particular for settling disputes about who a person is. What of a case where my brain is gradually replaced? In the end there is a completely fresh brain. Does that mean that I cease to exist at a particular point? What if the brain is gradually transferred to another body? Will there be a point at which I switch bodies, or might I even be in two bodies at once? Many philosophers would refuse to accept that there has to be a definite answer to these problems. Indeed the questions still assume that there is such a thing as the self, even though it is identified, in a materialist manner with the brain.

Hume was no materialist, and there is more than a hint of Cartesian dualism in his treatment of the workings of the mind. He did however raise the issue about whether or not the difficulty which surfaces in trick cases about brain surgery is not in fact always with us. Anyone following Hume has to accept that our position in ordinary life is as bad as in any example from science fiction. There is no connecting thread linking experiences, and our survival never involves anything beyond the mere fact of a temporal succession of experiences, interwoven with each other. There is no extra ingredient that makes these experiences *mine* or *yours*. On this view, when we fear extinction at death, we fail to realize that we are wishing the continuation of something that was not there in the first place. There is little sense in wanting further experiences, even eternal ones, if they are not going to be mine or indeed anyone's.

Questions about human nature cannot be divorced from issues about the nature of the individual person. The concept of the self has been intimately linked with concepts of moral responsibility, individual freedom and rationality. It is no coincidence that Hume's idea of the freedom of the will was compatible with determinism. It is no accident that reason was given second place to the passions. Any attack on the notion of a continuing self has wide-ranging consequences. Freedom, responsibility, reason and even the idea of a person as such are all put at risk. Hume may have been conservative about changing social institutions. He could not have been more radical in his attack on some of the most basic assumptions of western civilization.

# CHAPTER SEVEN

# Kant

## (1724–1804)

## Context

When people are asked to name the philosopher who most epitomizes the European Enlightenment, Immanuel Kant is likely to be an obvious choice. Yet as we have seen, some of the principles of the Enlightenment, particularly its stress on human reason in the place of tradition and authority, had long been current. They had played their part in the rise of modern science in the work of men such as Newton. Locke had, a hundred years before, helped to give them philosophic currency. Even while Kant was writing, they were working themselves out on the political scene, in the founding of the United States, and in the cataclysmic events of the French Revolution.

Unlike Locke, Kant played no overt political role. He was content to spend his life as a professional philosopher, becoming professor of logic and metaphysics in the University of Konigsberg. He never travelled widely, and yet he soon acquired a considerable reputation in Germany and beyond. At that time Konigsberg was part of East Prussia, under the rule of Frederick the Great. Although an absolute monarch, Frederick had himself encouraged much freedom of thought, particularly in the sphere of religion. When he died in 1786, his successor Frederick William II took exception to Kant's lack of religious orthodoxy, and Kant had to promise not to write further on religious matters. Konigsberg itself was a trading city, destined to be caught up in the later problems created by the shifting national boundaries and changing politics of Eastern Europe. Called Kaliningrad, it has been part of the Soviet Union and is now stranded in an enclave of the Russian Federation, separated by the Baltic States from the rest of Russia.

Kant himself came from a home of modest means and was much influenced by his Pietist upbringing. Pietism was a movement within the Lutheranism of the eighteenth century which emphasized the importance of ethical living. It is significant that although he clearly absorbed and accepted the moral teaching of Christianity, Kant did not accept the truth of many of its doctrines, in particular the importance of revelation, and the centrality of the historical figure of Jesus. For him, religion was to be totally a matter of reason and could not be based on contingent matters to which all rational beings did not have access. He did not himself attend public worship later in his life.

In his philosophy, Kant was faced by the challenge of empiricism, and by the significance of the rise of the physical sciences. Hume had undermined the scope of human reason, in a way that Locke had not. Kant was particularly critical of Locke's readiness to 'prove the existence of God and the immortality of the soul with the same conclusiveness as any mathematical proposition – though both lie entirely outside the limits of possible experience'.[1] Yet Hume's more consistent empiricist approach, Kant believed, only led to total scepticism, leading, for instance, to a refusal to accept that there are causes. We can never say of an apparent effect that something must have preceded it. All we can do is observe the conjunction of events, and however many similar cases we come across, we can make no assumptions about what has to happen. As a result, Kant says, 'we would have to give blind chance its right, with which all use of reason ceases'.[2] Natural science itself was at risk from a philosophy which had been spawned by the development of modern science.

Kant was faced with a deep problem. On the one hand he was reluctant to allow that we could obtain knowledge of reality by the exercise of our reason alone. He did not want to return to the metaphysics, and possibly the theology, of an earlier age. Yet if he accepted the findings of modern science in an empiricist spirit, he was liable to find that even the most fundamental concepts of that science, such as cause, could be given no rational justification. It is not surprising that he names Hume's 'sceptical teaching' as the spur that drove him to write his monumental *Critique of Pure Reason*. He comments that it was Hume 'who can be said to have really begun all the assaults on the rights of pure reason which made a thorough investigation of them necessary'.[3] What then was the possible scope of human reason? Marooned between the discoveries of modern

natural science, and the apparent certainties of traditional metaphysics, Kant felt that neither gave full recognition to the central importance of rationality. One dissolved reason in the flux of experience.
The other appeared to give priority to a realm of reality which Kant
felt was inaccessible to human beings.

In his conclusion to the *Critique of Practical Reason*, Kant summed
up his dilemma. He was both an inhabitant of a world open to
science, and yet at the same time his own rationality opens up for
him a world that is not contingent. It does not just happen to be the
case, but is, in some sense, universal and necessary. In other words
the world of pure reason is not the one discovered by science. The
space of reasons is distinct from the nexus of ordinary events in the
physical world. Kant draws from this some important conclusions
about how he had to view himself. He distinguishes two things that
fill his mind with reverence 'the starry heavens above me and the
moral law within me'.[4] The first, he says, begins with the world of
his experience and extends out 'into an unbounded magnitude with
worlds upon worlds'. That view annihilates his importance as an
'animal creature'. He reflects that after it has been provided in some
unknown way with life for a short time, it 'must give back to the
planet (a mere speck in the universe) the matter from which it
came'. Yet that is not the whole story. Kant does not, as a more
conventionally religious philosopher might, then invoke God to
explain the worth of human beings. Instead he looks in on himself.
He refers to his 'invisible self', which, he claims, gives him a world to
be discovered by the understanding alone. It is this, he says, which
'infinitely raises my worth as an intelligence by my personality, in
which the moral law reveals to me a life independent of animality
and even of the whole sensible world'. Thus Kant is drawn away
from his biological make-up, and the more obvious features of
human nature. Instead, for him, the crucial heart of the matter is
a rationality which is not bound by the empirical world, and from
whose existence he derives some far-reaching conclusions. Yet at the
root of all his complicated philosophy, is a belief in the intrinsic
dignity and worth of all human beings, regardless of wealth or
position. That dignity rests simply on the fact that they are rational
beings. He thus confronts Hume's philosophical heirs with what he
regards as the logical consequences of the existence of that rationality. He neither withdraws into the mysteries of metaphysics nor
capitulates to the despair of scepticism.

## Our Place in the World

Kant had a great respect for science and its discoveries, but he had an even greater respect for the powers of human reasoning. He had the task of trying to reconcile the two, in a way which did not compromise human autonomy. Kant was very conscious that he was writing in the 'Age of Enlightenment', and it is not surprising that in an essay of 1784 he attempted to answer the question 'What is Enlightenment?'. His answer is significant in that he does not point to any particular scientific discovery, or to the necessity of a particular political arrangement. Such things were secondary to the crucial issue, which he saw as being the position of human beings. Again, this was not explained by means of a metaphysical explanation of their place in reality. Rather, he stressed the importance of realizing their autonomy. Humans have to take responsibility for themselves and not give themselves up to the direction of another.

Kant says firmly that 'enlightenment is the human being's emergence from his self-incurred minority',[5] and he defines minority as the 'inability to make use of one's own understanding without direction from another'. We must each, he proclaims, have the courage to make use of our own understanding. He does not underestimate the difficulties, or the laziness and cowardice that holds us back. All that is required is freedom, although that itself is to ask a lot, particularly when the demand is made in the public sphere. Kant is not afraid to draw conclusions about the character of an enlightened society from what he says, and grumbles that all he hears is the cry 'Do not argue'. For instance, he complains, the clergyman says, 'Do not argue but believe'. For Kant, however, we must all come of age, and not be afraid to take on the responsibilities of adults. We must be free to make our own decisions and to take responsibility for them. This clarion call for freedom has echoed down the years, and, both on an individual and political level, would seem to many to pinpoint our role in the world. We are here to be free. The nagging questions remain, however, that we are free – but to be what or to do what?

For Kant freedom is the linchpin. In his practical philosophy, for example, the autonomy of the will is regarded as the supreme principle of morality. It is distinguished from what Kant terms 'heteronomy' which means submitting oneself to the will of another, or to some objective states of affairs. In either case one is not using one's own will but is handing over responsibility to someone or something else. The obvious example is the will of God, to which Locke, for example, had given prominence in his philosophy. For Kant that involves a submission to another's authority in a way which abdicates responsibility. Yet all this is symptomatic of an even deeper strand of Kant's thought which sees human beings as set in a very complicated relationship with the wider world. He had rejected an empiricism which built up our picture of the world from experience. Yet he did not think that the way we think, using various concepts, could be explained by reference to any objective states of affairs beyond us, which may in any case be beyond our reach. He was therefore faced with the conundrum as to what was the relationship between our thoughts and reality. What has to be the case to enable us to think as we do? What are the conditions for our holding the concepts we do? How can we explain the very possibility of human reason? It was to face this issue that he wrote his *Critique of Pure Reason*.

Kant realized that he could account for the possibilities of human knowledge, not by appealing to the character of the world we know, but by examining how we can know in the first place. He says that what 'constitutes our subject-matter is not the nature of things, which is inexhaustible, but the understanding which passes judgment on the nature of things'.[6] Thus Kant is looking at what makes human understanding possible and he wished to do this not by giving a scientific or traditional metaphysical account, appealing to evolution or to God. Instead he hopes to find an answer from within the conditions necessary for us to exercise our rationality. He gives as an example the questions how either mathematics or a 'pure science of nature' is possible. He continues: 'Since these sciences actually exist, it is quite proper to ask how they are possible; for that they must be possible is proved by the fact that they exist.'[7] He appeals to what he terms 'the nature of universal human reason', and says from the very existence of that, questions arise which reason must put to itself. Knowledge about such conceptual matters Kant terms 'transcendental'.

Yet why is it that even if there is such a thing as 'universal human reason' Kant believes that knowledge of its functioning is so crucial? After all, are we not interested in the world we live in, and not just how we think about it? Kant answers this question with an illustration from the discoveries made by what for him was modern science. He pointed out that accidental observations strung together were not enough to form a necessary law. Yet while reason has to approach nature to be taught by it, it must do so not like a pupil learning what he is told, 'but of an appointed judge who compels the witnesses to answer questions which he has himself formulated'.[8] In other words, science depends as much on our understanding and the way we approach nature, as on the character of nature itself. In modern terminology, Kant is stressing the importance of theory. He himself is, however, making a much wider philosophical point, which covers the whole of our relationship with the world. What we think the world is like depends as much on the nature of human understanding and the categories we bring to bear, as on reality itself. Indeed we have no access to things as they are in themselves, but can only deal with things as they appear to us. This is Kant's famous distinction between so-called 'noumena' as opposed to 'phenomena' or appearances. Kant warns of the dangers of confusing an indeterminate concept of an intelligible entity 'beyond our sensibility' with a determinate concept of something our understanding can deal with.[9] We cannot think of what lies beyond out thought. If we can think of something, its character necessarily, at least partially, depends on the nature of the concepts we possess.

This is all an example of Kant's so-called 'Copernican revolution'. He pointed out that Copernicus failed to explain the movement of heavenly bodies on the supposition that they moved round the spectator. Instead 'he tried whether he might not have better success if he made the spectator to revolve and the stars to remain at rest'. Kant took this as an analogy for his treatment of the concepts humans use in their reasoning. He explains that before his time 'it has been assumed that all our knowledge must conform to objects'. In other words, we try to discover the nature of a reality that exists independently of us. Kant wished to reverse this procedure. He says that 'we must make trial whether we may not have more success in the tasks of metaphysics, if we suppose that objects must conform to our knowledge'.[10]

Our concepts therefore structure the way in which we can think of things. As a result, even such basic categories of thought as cause, or space and time, are to be viewed as human ways of thinking. They form the conditions under which we can deal with world. They do not describe the objective character of the world. Time, for instance, cannot be said to exist in itself, apart from the way we are in contact with the world.

Kant's view certainly enables him to investigate the conditions which make human thought possible, but they have the consequence of making the world (whatever that is) to be centred on us and our capabilities. Reality is essentially anthropocentric. This certainly helps to underline the Enlightenment stress on the central importance of the human being. It emphasizes that the world, at least as given to our understanding, inevitably reflects that understanding. There is thus no surprise that the world is intelligible to us. It is not that it has been made that way, but that we have to construct a picture of the world in terms of our own reason. Metaphysics then becomes less a search into the nature of a world beyond us, as an uncovering of what has to be the case to enable us to think as we do. Attention is redirected from a transcendent reality to the possibilities of human knowledge. We become absorbed in ourselves and our own thinking. It is not surprising that for Kant human autonomy was the key.

## What is it to be Human?

Kant's understanding of the relationship between human thought and the non-human world is subtle and complicated. His emphasis on human freedom and human rationality, however, comes into its own when he looks at the foundations of morality. He considers that our freedom as moral beings, able to use our will to determine what ought to be done, needs no further justification or explanation. We cannot go on to ask why we as humans (or any other rational beings) should exist. He says that our existence 'has the highest purpose within it', and that we 'must not be subjected to any influence of nature in opposition to that purpose'.[11] Neither theology or metaphysics can explain our worth, and we must rise above the influences of our ordinary human nature. In fact we have to be governed by our will to do what is right and not what we may happen to want.

Kant's most influential work on the nature of morality is the short *Groundwork of the Metaphysics of Morals*. In that, he sketches out the consequences for morality of his more basic views about our place in the world. From what has already been said, it is obvious that Kant wishes to regard the human ability to reason as the most fundamental feature of human nature. Indeed, in a sense he does not regard it as part of our nature at all. The rational pursuit of duty, of doing what is right simply because it is right, is not to be understood a property of human beings as such. Kant argues that only rational beings can issue commands to themselves and therefore act for reason, and not because of impulse. He therefore talks of human beings as a particular category of all rational beings, and is interested in us because of our rationality, and not our humanity. In talking of the principle of duty he warns that it is of the utmost importance that we should not try to derive it 'from the special property of human nature'.[12] He is thus only interested in the demands of reason, which can apply to any rational being in a similar situation. Our natural inclinations and desires may spur us to action. Kant, however, is only concerned with what can be justified rationally. The basic principle of action is called by him the 'categorical imperative' and is that you should 'act only in accordance with that maxim through which you can at the same time will that it become a universal law'.[13] This is not unlike the common ethical demand to think of what would happen if everyone performed a particular action. Kant's point is that if we wish to do something that we could not in consistency envisage everyone doing, that shows that it is absolutely wrong. His is a logical criterion. We cannot do something whilst willing others in the same situation to do something different.

All this provides a highly intellectual approach to moral obligation. It abstracts from our particular nature as human beings, from our particular situation as individuals with family relationships, and from our historical situation. Kant subtracts our rationality from its context in our ordinary lives. Indeed our particular desires are to be put on one side to such an extent that it becomes a positive disadvantage from a moral point of view if we actually want to do something. We must do it because it is right, and not because we are inclined to do it, even, say, because of our love for the beneficiary. Kant remarks that 'the sublimity and inner dignity of the command in a duty is all the more manifest the fewer are the subjective causes in favour of it, and the more there are against it'.[14] In other words, if I desperately want to murder someone in a blind rage, but just manage to resist the temptation, that is somehow more sublime than if I naturally love my fellow human beings, and never have any urge to do them harm.

Kant believes that only a 'good will' can serve morality. Our motive for action is all important. We must do what is right because it is right and not for any other reason. Why we act is more important than what we happen to achieve. He does, however, give examples of principles which he believes can be produced by the categorical imperative. One is of a person who is tempted to commit suicide.[15] Kant's response is that we could never will that suicide become a universal law of nature. I might out of 'self-love', to avoid trouble, will the destruction of my life. Yet it is the function of this same principle of self-love to further life. Kant sees as this as a contradiction. Another example is someone making a promise without any intention of keeping it. Yet again Kant sees that this could never be a universal law of nature since it is inherently contradictory. The idea that everyone can make promises without feeling that they have to be kept would merely undermine the notion of promise-keeping. In these circumstances, 'no one', says Kant, 'would believe what was promised him'.[16]

The structure of Kant's arguments is basically formalistic. They do not depend on particular features of human nature. He reasons a priori (from first principles), and not from particular features of the world. As a result, he believes that his conclusions must hold for anyone rational. Locke derived morality from the particular way God happened to have created us. For Kant, both God and human nature are irrelevant. Otherwise we will be ruled by something other than our own reason, and our autonomy and dignity as human beings is threatened. We must be our own legislators, and cannot push responsibility off somewhere else. Our freedom, as rational beings, and our duty go together. Indeed it is a basic principle for Kant that it must be true that if we ought to do something we can do so. 'Ought' implies 'can'. There cannot be duties that are impossible to fulfil.

Yet all this cloaks a deep ambivalence in Kant's approach. He believes that as rational beings humans can rise above the causal order of the phenomenal world. At the same time, science can reveal the causal connections between things. This depends on the split between the noumenal world and the phenomenal world, the world of reason and our ordinary world. Thus no empirical discovery about human nature can have any bearing on the demands of reason. 'Moral anthropology' is irrelevant to a 'metaphysics of morals'.[17] Nature may be a machine, but as 'noumenal' beings we are not part of the mechanism. Indeed, although Kant placed great emphasis on the self, and the unity of each individual consciousness, he insisted that 'I have no knowledge of myself as I am, but merely as I appear to myself.'[18] We can each know that we are, but can never discover the noumenal self which is the source of all our reasoning. It is a presupposition underlying the very possibility of understanding. By this means, as he says, Kant hoped to secure our thinking self against the danger of materialism.[19]

Kant tried to show that our autonomy and rationality is independent of the constraints of the ordinary world studied by science. Yet even if freedom is a presupposition of reason, that does not remove the doubt that perhaps the possibility of pure rationality could be an illusion. Such scepticism may perhaps be self-contradictory, because it makes use of the very rationality it is undermining. Yet Kant's divorce of the phenomenal and noumenal sits uneasily with a scientific approach. His rejection of the relevance to morality of any substantive notion of human nature merely underlines the formal character of the moral principles he is putting forward. It is amazing that from within the constraints of rationality, the logical need for consistency and the avoidance of contradiction, he can derive major moral prohibitions of a kind acceptable to Lutherans in his own time.

## Human Society

Kant has been highly influential in his view that human beings must always be treated as ends in themselves and never means. He uses his previous examples to argue that by committing suicide I am merely treating my own humanity as a means to maintain 'a tolerable condition to the end of life'. Similarly, making a false promise is to make use of another human being merely as a means. Kant declares: 'A human being is not a thing and hence not something that can be used merely as a means, but must in all his actions always be regarded as an end in itself.'[20] His practical imperative runs as follows: 'So act that you use humanity, whether in your own person or in the person of any other, always at the same time as an end, never merely as a means.' Kant's reasoning is simply that rational nature exists as an end in itself. It is the starting-point for everything, and any attempt to subordinate the rationality of any person to other purposes must deny the absolute worth of our rational will. In this Kant is uncompromising, and puts forward an 'absolutist' view of ethics. For him, a good end cannot justify evil means. He is no utilitarian, counting heads, and looking for the greatest good of the greatest number. He would deny that a minority can be abused for the good of the majority.

Such an attitude is, of course, not only important in personal morality. It is of vital importance in politics, and Kant does not hesitate to extend it to the public sphere. He says, for instance, that 'the right of human beings must be held sacred, however great a sacrifice this may cost the ruling power'.[21] Similarly when he considers the advantages of different types of government, his highest concern is that the government, or executive, should be separated from those empowered to make laws (the legislature).[22] Kant's wish is that whoever is in power should not be able to rule in a despotic way by fixing the laws to suit themselves. Government should not set its own rules. Kant has misgivings about democracy on this point since it establishes an executive in which the majority get their way. The majority are pitted against the minority so that 'all who are nevertheless not all, decide; and this is a contradiction of the general will with itself and with freedom'. This certainly highlights a difficulty about a democratic government which considers it has a mandate from the people to rule, and yet does not adequately respect the rights of a minority in disagreement with it.

Kant's philosophy in fact has major implications for how we live together. His vision of society must begin with the individual worth of each human being, considered as a a rational being. In consequence, his views must tend towards an individualism and a radical egalitarianism. He is concerned with freedom and equality, regardless of rank, power, wealth or any such consideration. As a consequence, Kant has little respect for tradition, to be viewed as a repository of wisdom, or for any authority relying on tradition. His faith in reason is such that he has no fears that it can be fundamentally corrupted. His is the optimism of the Enlightenment. Although he personally believed in gradual change, and perhaps could do no other living under the constraints of an absolute monarchy, he had some enthusiasm for the French Revolution. He did not share the extreme revulsion to its excesses that swept through many in England and led in politics there to a desire to conserve existing institutions for the protection of citizens.

There is always in politics a dispute between those who, like Hume, stress habit and custom, and those who are confident enough to rely on the demands of reasoning without regard to tradition. The one side may believe in cautious reform within the framework of existing institutions. The other is content to sweep away the old entirely in the hope of a more rational future. The latter was much more in the spirit of the French Revolution, and, indeed, the American Declaration of Independence. Those, however, with a less optimistic view of human nature might well feel that the removal of traditional ways would merely give new opportunities to the unscrupulous. Kant can be ranked with the optimists. He said in his essay about Enlightenment: 'One age cannot bind itself and conspire to put the following one in such a condition that it would be impossible for it to enlarge its cognitions, and to purify them of errors, and generally to make further progress in enlightenment.'[23] Significantly, he even goes on to appeal to human nature, calling the control of a subsequent age 'a crime against human nature, whose original vocation lies precisely in such progress'.

Kant in fact shared the general presupposition of the Enlightenment in the capacity for goodness in human nature and in the possibility of continual improvement. He did not take the view that our nature is basically corrupt. His whole stress on our freedom carried with it the presupposition that we can do what is right. We are capable of progress. Whatever set-backs there may be, Kant insists that since the human race is 'constantly advancing with respect to culture'; it is also to be conceived 'as progressing toward what is better with respect to the moral end of its existence.'[24] Whatever evidence history might produce to the contrary, Kant insists that it is essential that we go on believing this as a maxim to guide us. He concludes his essay with an impassioned plea that we cannot take human nature to be so immersed in evil that it cannot finally triumph over it. He even envisages a time when whole nations will recognize a 'right of nations' with an international law based on a power to enforce it. He remarks that 'nowhere does human nature appear less lovable than in the relations of entire peoples to one another'.[25] Yet it is at the heart of Kant's philosophy that human rationality can not only identify problems such as this, it can in the end triumph over them. 'Human nature' may provide obstacles, but it does not describe our essential nature as rational beings. The very fact that we know that we ought to become better shows that this must be within our power. What we ought to do, we can do. Kant believed that as a result not only can individuals be transformed, but through them whole societies, and indeed international relations.

## Contemporary Relevance

With his emphasis on our capacity for improvement and progress, and his basic optimism about human nature, Kant represents a strong line of thinking in the eighteenth century, and throughout the modern world. Indeed it is one that he himself did much to foster. If one has confidence in the power of human reason, it is easy to forget that the institutions and traditions of thought that have been passed down to us are themselves examples of that power. An exaggerated trust in progress or, to use an earlier concept, in 'improvement', can lead to a contempt for earlier generations and customs. It can seem as if contemporary understandings are bound to be superior to those preceding. Certainly this is now taken for granted in much of modern science. Even if our current ideas are built on the achievements of previous generations of scientists, it is taken for granted that the newer ones are better. It is a paradox, however, that if one accepts this view too whole-heartedly, the views of someone such as Kant are bound to seem totally irrelevant two hundred years later. If human reason has the capacity imputed it by Kant, its insights cannot be bound to time and place. Indeed with his emphasis on the discovery of universal truths of reason, Kant himself would have had to agree.

Yet this appeal to pure reason and the disparaging of tradition can itself bring problems. We humans may have the capacity to rise above our particular situation and to make rational judgements which are not historically conditioned. Even so, an appeal to reason which totally neglects the role of history and tradition is making far too sharp a split in the human personality. We may be rational beings, but we also live in a particular context which is bound to colour our thinking. Even science has to recognize that it is not invented anew each generation. Current science is built on the achievements of previous generations. Even revolutions preserve more continuities than are first apparent. America after the Declaration of Independence still owed much to its British inheritance. In the twentieth century, Russia before and after its Revolution showed many continuities. Even after the demise of Communism, Russia shows evidence of the same character (and the same problems) as under previous rulers. No state can continually reinvent itself, but must always start with existing customs and institutions.

In fact the danger that is more apparent at the beginning of a new millennium is not an undue faith in reason, but a total denial of the possibility of a rationality detached from circumstances. Kant's thinking itself will be categorized as typical of its age, and thereby dismissed. The very possibility of a 'universal' human reason will be denied. Yet, if this happens, Kant's whole philosophy is undermined. Although he is interested in rational beings, rather than just human beings, for that very reason any attack on the idea of any rationality rising above historical context denies the central importance of rationality. The very basis of both his epistemology and his ethics goes. If there are no 'rational' beings, they cannot have rights, or be free or moral. They cannot have a common set of concepts structuring the world.

The result will be to make concepts relative to context, so that humans will not necessarily share the same categories of thought. Indeed the very category of the 'human' becomes problematic. When history defines us, we cannot then be thought to share properties in virtue of some common human nature. In particular the idea of human rights becomes difficult to explain. It is one of the paradoxes of the current age that there is much agitation in favour of human rights. Many indeed share Kant's vision of an international order to enforce them. Yet at the same time, as we shall see in the Conclusion, the idea of the 'human' is hotly contested, and the notion of rights seems to have no grounding, in rationality or anything else.

At root of many of the difficulties bequeathed by Kant to his successors is his 'Copernican revolution'. When all concepts are derived from humans, or rational beings, instead of somehow reflecting reality, everything can become fragmented. We only need to lose our grip on the notion of rationality to lose a common basis for our thinking. Kant thought that the major problems of metaphysics centred on the issues of God, freedom and immortality. We are free to make moral choices, and from this fact Kant derived the ideas of God and the immortality of the soul as necessary postulates. He asserts: 'The attempt to prove God and immortality by the merely theoretical route had to fail because by this route (of concepts of nature) no cognition whatever of the supersensible is possible.'[26] He is thus still in thrall to the empiricist outlook bequeathed by Hume. As a result, he turns inwards to human beings and away from the reality they inhabit. He concentrates on their reactions to that world, rather than acknowledging that we all live in the same world. As he says, 'The rationalist, by virtue of his very title, must of his own accord restrict himself within the limits of human insight.'[27] The problems come when this methodology is combined with a lack of confidence either in the possibility of pure reason, or even in the idea of the human.

We have then lost grip on the world, and at the same time have lost any understanding of who 'we' may be. Kant's policy of making concepts anthropocentric carries great dangers. Once we have lost access to 'reality' and have then give up a notion of anything beyond our own context, the result can only be an extreme relativism, according to which the meaning of our concepts, of everything we think, depends wholly on our own particular historical situation. Reality becomes a projection, rather than something to which we can all have a common access. Our thinking determines how we conceive what is otherwise an indeterminate world. As a result it became possible for Kant's successors to uncover alleged (and previously unsuspected) motivations for various types of thinking. His influence on Marx, Nietzsche and Freud was profound.

CHAPTER EIGHT

# Darwin
### *1809–1882*


## Context

Kant was a philosopher's philosopher, whose influence can still be
felt in professional philosophy. Charles Darwin, on the other hand,
laid no claim to being a philosopher at all. Born at Shrewsbury in
1809, he went to Cambridge University with the intention of becoming a clergyman, but this plan died a natural death when on leaving
Cambridge he joined HMS Beagle as a naturalist. This voyage in the
southern hemisphere meant that Darwin was away for five years
and was, he said, 'by far the most important event in my life'.[1] It was
on this voyage that he began to formulate the views on the development of species through natural selection that he made famous in
*The Origin of Species*, published in 1859. He argued against the idea
that each species has been independently created, emphasizing
instead the gradual evolution of one species into another. His idea
was that individuals face a struggle for existence and must compete
with each other for limited resources. Those that are best adapted to
their environment will be the ones that will survive and leave most
descendants. Individuals, even in the same species, will vary slightly
from each other and this gives natural selection a chance to operate.
Darwin writes: 'Owing to this struggle for life, any variation, however slight, and from whatever cause preceding, if it be any degree
profitable to an individual of any species . . . will tend to the preservation of that individual, and will generally be inherited by its offspring.'[2]

As Darwin points out, that means that the offspring will have
a better chance of surviving, so that there will be a gradual
improvement, step by step, in each species' ability to cope with its

circumstances. Given a long enough period, a species could change its nature entirely and a new species come into being. Darwin's emphasis, however, was on the individual members of the species, since it was they, and not the species, which would flourish. Darwin called the process 'natural' selection, to mark it off from the artificial selection of plants and animals by humans so that they could produce more useful varieties.

Darwin stressed that 'our ignorance of the laws of variation is profound' and to a large extent, given the scientific knowledge available in the 1850s, his hypothesis was a leap in the dark.[3] There was no doubt about the controversial nature of what he was proposing. The idea that each species had a fixed nature, given it by the Creator, was deeply rooted. Darwin's emphasis on the struggle for existence suggested that there really were no such things as species, or at least no fixed ones. Darwin admits that he looks at 'the term species as one arbitrarily given for the sake of convenience to a set of individuals closely resembling each other.'[4] He emphasized the gradualness of change, and did not believe in sudden leaps, whereby strange new species popped up. Each change, according to the theory of natural selection, has to occur through a series of fine gradations. Why then, he asks do we not see these linking forms around us, and why are not all organisms 'blended together in an inextricable chaos'?[5] Darwin emphasizes the slowness of change, and the fact that only a few species would be changing at any one period. We ought, however, to be able to see gradual changes recorded in the succession of fossils left us, and he was somewhat embarrassed by apparent gaps in the fossil record.

This view of species challenged philosophical assumptions stemming from Aristotle and even Plato, about the essences of things. Living things could no longer be seen as sharing the universal characteristics of a species. There could not be anything corresponding to 'horseness' or 'doghood'. There were just lots of individual animals, lumped together in groups by the 'opinion of naturalists having sound judgement and wide experience'.[6] Darwin accepts that species are 'tolerably well-defined objects',[7] but the changes brought about through natural selection are always for the good of each organism and not of the species. References to 'the survival of the species' are in fact un-Darwinian. Because, too, of the emphasis on gradual change rather than on fixed characteristics, evolutionary history becomes important. The crucial factor is which are the ancestors of the members of a current species, not the superficial similarities they share with other creatures. What enables us to group different species together is what Darwin refers to as 'the hidden bond of community of descent'.[8]

This was all highly controversial to the naturalists of Darwin's day, although some, such as A. R. Wallace, had been coming to similar conclusions. What, however, made it intellectual dynamite, was the effect of such biological views on our understanding of our own place in the scheme of things. No other scientific theory could have so challenged the most fundamental philosophical and theological assumptions about the importance and uniqueness of the human race. Darwin was reluctant to get involved in the controversy but he understood well enough what he was saying. Only one sentence in *The Origin of Species* refers to the matter but Darwin was in no doubt about the significance of that sentence. After looking to the future and seeing new possibilities for research, particularly in the field of the gradual acquirement of mental powers, he said: 'Light will be thrown on the origin of man and his history.' A. R. Wallace later proved to be much more cautious than Darwin about the relevance of the theory of evolution to human nature. He preferred to make a distinction between the evolutionary development of the human body through natural selection, and the intellectual and moral faculties, which, he maintains, could not have been so developed. As a result of this dualism he was able to hold that there was a side to human nature which could not have been derived from animal ancestors. Since Wallace had arrived at the theory of natural selection independently of Darwin, and since it was the fact of his parallel work which prompted Darwin to publish *The Origin of Species*, the divergence between the two is of some interest. Wallace wanted to uphold the 'spiritual nature' of humans and says:

> Thus alone can we understand the constancy of the martyr, the unselfishness of the philanthropist, the devotion of the patriot, the enthusiasm of the artist and the resolute and persevering search of the scientific worker after nature's secrets. Thus we may perceive that the love of truth, the delight in beauty, the passion for justice, and the thrill of exultation with which we hear of any act of courageous self-sacrifice, are the workings within us of a higher nature which has not been developed by means of the struggle for material existence.[9]

Darwin and his successors tended to reject this dualist vision, and have instead tried to explain all human characteristics in terms of evolution through natural selection.

## Our Place in the World

Darwin was far from being the first thinker to have suggested that the human race was merely one part of the material world, with no special status. Indeed Plato and Aristotle had reacted against the pre-Socratics on this issue precisely because they sought intelligibility and purpose rather than the working of blind chance. Early Greek philosophy, too, had been fascinated by the question of change and flux and had often emphasized it at the expense of any apparent stability. Darwin's stress on variation and evolution, and his consequent attack on fixed categories was not novel, but it did seem to contradict the account in Genesis where it is stated that 'God made wild animals, cattle and all reptiles, each according to its kind.'[10] It seemed that each species had been created from the very beginning as it was meant to be. Above all God 'created man in his own image'.[11] Humans were therefore not so much complicated animals, as reflections of God himself. The special status of humans seemed assured.

Darwin's outlook was influenced itself by Christian theology, and in particular by the works of William Paley, who considered that the apparent order and purpose to be seen around us spoke of a Designer, just as the intricate workings of a watch would indicate a watch-maker. Darwin explained order in the biological world in terms of natural selection rather than the purposes of God. A blind, unconscious and automatic process seems to replace the conscious design of the Creator. The struggle for existence becomes paramount, in which chance variations are selected if beneficial and rejected if harmful to the organism. Purpose has, it appears, been transmuted to chance, and *Homo sapiens* as a result becomes one animal species amongst many, the chance production of an immensely long process of evolution. It is easy for theologians to dismiss Darwinism as a belief in the meaninglessness of existence. The theory of evolution can be portrayed as providing a unified scientific world view at the expense of any sense of human worth or dignity.

Darwin later wrote specifically on *The Descent of Man*, but tremendous interest was aroused by the publication of *The Origin of Species*. It is easy to imagine that the forces of science were arrayed against those of religion, and that the pursuit of knowledge was challenged by entrenched prejudice. It was not quite like that. The debate has become symbolized by one encounter at the Oxford meeting of the British Association for the Advancement of Science in 1860. Legends have grown up about the angry confrontation between Samuel Wilberforce, Bishop of Oxford, and Professor T. H. Huxley, a friend of Darwin. Darwin's health did not allow him to attend. Wilberforce is alleged to have asked Huxley whether he was descended from an ape on his grandmother's or grandfather's side. The story has it that Huxley replied with dignity that he would rather be descended from an ape than a bishop who misused his position and his rhetorical gifts by introducing ridicule into a serious scientific discussion. Accounts vary about who said what, and the legend probably owes much to the later antagonism between religion and science, as perceived by many. Each man appeared to epitomize the opposing sides. Religion seemed to have been defeated by the calm rationality of science in a manner that foreshadowed the ensuing century of intellectual debate.

The Bishop, however, was speaking at the meeting as a scientist. He was a vice-president of the British Association, and an ornithologist. He had just written a searching review of *The Origin of Species*, which Darwin took seriously and called 'uncommonly clever'. He was an amateur, and science would soon become too specialized to be a matter of ordinary intellectual debate. Nevertheless one contemporary report says that his views received the support of 'the most eminent naturalists assembled at Oxford'. They were not willing to give up the notion of the fixity of species without a struggle. Huxley was at the time in a minority. What appeared to be a war between religion and science was a disagreement between scientists.

It is important not to see the situation in black and white, since Darwinism was not as antagonistic to a religious interpretation as might be thought. Evolution has certainly supplanted special Creation, but it is too hasty to assume that purpose has in fact been replaced by chance or even theism by atheism. Darwin certainly accepted that what he said about species in general also applied to *Homo sapiens*. He wrote: 'As soon as I had become, in the year 1837 or 1838, concerned that species were mutable productions, I could not avoid the belief that man must come under the same law.'[12] He also firmly believed that just because, say, the hinge of a shell appeared particularly suited to its circumstances, it did not follow that it had been expressly designed like the hinge of a door. This meant that the argument from design for the existence of God was in Darwin's eyes no longer valid. There was no more design, he held, in the variability of organic beings, and in the action of natural selection, than in the way the wind blows.[13]

All this, though, did not mean that Darwin was an atheist. He himself thought that 'agnostic' would be a more correct description.[14] That term had in fact been coined by T. H. Huxley. This agnosticism was genuine in that Darwin did feel the attraction of religious belief. He wrote in 1873: 'The impossibility of conceiving that this grand and wondrous universe, with our conscious selves, arose through chance, seems to me the chief argument for the existence of God, but whether this is an argument of real value, I have never been able to decide.'[15]

Even Huxley denied that teleological and mechanical views of the universe were necessarily exclusive.[16] He accepted that the phenomena of the universe could have been *intended* to evolve out of what he termed the 'primordial molecular arrangement'. The precise interplay of purpose and chance would clearly be complicated and difficult to demonstrate, but it is intriguing that neither Darwin nor Huxley came down unequivocally on the side of chance.

Darwin mentioned how 'strong and instinctive' the belief in immortality is. He referred to the view of the physicist that the sun would eventually grow too cold to sustain life on earth. He continues: 'Believing as I do that man in the distant future will be a far more perfect creature than he now is, it is an intolerable thought that he and all other sentient beings are doomed to complete annihilation after such long continued slow progress.'[17]

He remarks that the destruction of the world may not appear so dreadful to anyone believing in the immortality of the human soul. His belief, however, in the continued progress of humanity is very significant. Followers of Darwin often deny there is any assumption of progress or improvement built into Darwinian theory. The idea that the fittest of chance variations will survive and leave more descendants does not of itself suggest that the biologically fittest will be in any other sense the best. There need not be any definite direction in the process of natural selection, except in so far as organisms survive because they are suited to their particular ecological niche. Evolving organisms need not be going towards any pre-ordained goal. Some may arrive at a dead end. Words like 'progress' and 'improvement', let alone 'perfection' do not come easily to the lips of neo-Darwinian biologists. The Victorians had no such inhibitions. Herbert Spencer, a philosopher who based his thought on evolution, and who was much admired by Darwin, believed that everything, including human nature and human society, was constantly getting better. He said, for instance, 'Sentient beings have progressed from low to high types, under the law that the superior shall profit by their superiority, and the inferior shall suffer from their inferiority. Conformity to this law has been, and is still, needful, not only for the continuance of life, but for the increase of happiness.'[18]

His idea was that the 'superior' had developed in such a way that they were better suited to their circumstances. This was not so very different from Darwin's own view that 'every step in the natural selection of each species implies improvement in that species in relation to its conditions of life'.[19] Darwin was inclined to associate natural selection with the idea of 'natural improvement'. He was more cautious than Spencer about the possibility of progress but he gives the impression of great optimism about human nature. It has got better and will continue to do so. The rise of science itself seemed to epitomize the improvement of the human race.

## What is it to be Human?

The gradual improvement of humanity was nowhere more clearly shown, in Darwin's view, than in the sphere of morality. He followed Hume, whom he quotes, in regarding morality as the outcome of human nature. It could not be determined by reason, independently of our natural impulses and instincts. Morality arises out of our desires and moral feelings, such as sympathy, are part of our nature. Darwin recognized that our 'social instincts' may sometimes conflict with 'lower' impulses. He says: 'Looking to future generations, there is no cause to fear the social instincts will grow weaker, and we may expect that virtuous habits will grow stronger, becoming perhaps fixed by inheritance. In this case the struggle between our higher and lower impulses will be less severe, and virtue will be triumphant.'[20]

Darwin accepted that 'man is a social being',[21] and that the influence of habit and social pressure will be great, but his reference to inheritance shows that he wanted to account for the transmission of morality in terms of natural selection. It would, though, be a mistake to hold that acquired characteristics can be transmitted genetically. A giraffe that had lengthened its neck through stretching up would not pass on this trait to its offspring any more than people who have learnt virtue can pass it on genetically to their children. A trait has originally to be under genetic control to be inherited. Such traits cannot be learnt. They arise originally through chance mutations and are then subject to natural selection.

Darwin did recognize some basic inherited instincts in humans. He instances self-preservation, sexual love, the love of a mother for her new-born baby, and the baby's desire to suck.[22] These are typically shared with animals. Darwin recognized that morality sets us apart, so that our moral sense is the most important difference between us and the 'lower animals'. The problem is how such a sense can be explained by evolution. Darwin follows Hume in stressing how we care about other people's opinion of us, and he believed that the community would have had an impact on the conduct of each member from very early in human history. He considers that the social instincts would have been acquired 'by man as by the lower animals for the good of the community'.[23] His view was that moral sense was based on these social instincts, and that at first 'primeval man' was only concerned for the welfare of the tribe. Then, he claimed, as small tribes were united, nations gradually came into being, whose members would for the most part be personally unknown to each other.[24] Nevertheless, the 'simplest reason' would encourage them to extend their sympathies to all those who made up the nation, and then after that to all nations and races. Indeed Darwin refers to disinterested love for all living creatures as 'the most noble attribute of man'.[25] Yet he accepts that the social instincts might never by themselves have led us to the heights of morality, as when, for instance, we believe we should do good in return for evil. He says that the social instincts, together with sympathy, had to be extended 'by the aid of reason, instruction, and the love or fear of God'.[26]

This picture of the gradual widening of our sympathies and concern from the tribe, to the nation, to humanity, and then even to animals is attractive and some might argue that it bears some relation to what actually happened. It fits with the idea of the gradual improvement of the human race, though that underlines how theories of improvement and progress are loaded with moral assumptions. Darwin thought that at the base of the social instincts lay the 'parental and filial affections', which had been acquired through natural selection.[27] This though raises the question of the precise way in which evolution could build on them, to produce a moral sense.

Evolution, through natural selection, works through individuals. Darwin pointed out that in early society those who were cleverest and best able to defend themselves would rear most offspring.[28] This would have an effect on their tribe, since the one which had the greatest number of such people would supplant other tribes. It is individuals who are competing for scarce reserves, and morality could prove an obstacle. A member of a tribe, as Darwin points out, who was willing to be altruistic and sacrifice his own life, would often leave no offspring who would inherit 'his noble nature'.[29] How then could moral virtue be transmitted? If only the fittest survive, and morality on occasion hinders survival, natural selection may even be biased *against* morality. Darwin prefers to believe that although morality may not gain an advantage to an individual, it would help the tribe. He says: 'A tribe including many members who, from possessing in a high degree the spirit of patriotism, fidelity, obedience, courage and sympathy were always ready to aid one another, and to sacrifice themselves for the common good, would be victorious over most other tribes, and this would be natural selection.'[30]

Morality certainly does aid the cohesiveness of society, but the problem facing Darwin is that of how virtues can be transmitted through inheritance rather than teaching. Unless it can be shown how individuals will survive in the struggle for existence, despite caring more for others than their selves, morality cannot be inherited. A moral sense cannot then be part of human nature. Darwin had no conception of the mechanisms of inheritance, and knew nothing of modern population genetics. He had no knowledge of genes, the minimum portions of DNA that can be replicated and passed on. This undoubtedly inhibited his attempt to explain the origins of morality.

Genetic variations, influencing behaviour, can soon spread in the right circumstances. An animal prompted to care for its offspring would leave more descendants than one which neglected them. The relevant genes would be likely to be inherited by the young, which were cared for, and they in turn would look after their offspring. Similarly, a human child which sought the care of its parents would be more likely to survive than one which was indifferent. Parental care and the love of a child for its parents could then become part of human nature through natural selection. Darwin's basis for social instincts would be in place. What is much more problematic is how a tendency to altruism could be passed on genetically. Any behaviour which was positively disadvantageous to the agent, could not be under genetic control. Unless I myself gain some reproductive advantage, I am pursuing a course which is unlikely to spread my genes. Unselfishness, except in the interests of those genetically related to me, could not be an inherited trait.

Darwin's reference to the advantages for the tribe is only relevant for genetic transmission in so far as the other members are fairly close relatives of mine. They may then share my genes, so that helping them will enable my genes to spread. Once, however, a tribe grows into a nation, which is not composed of near relatives, it is more difficult for pure altruism to be passed on genetically. Darwinian theory is much better suited to explaining the differential selection of individuals rather than groups. In other words from a neo-Darwinian point of view, individual selection is normally preferable to group selection. It is questionable how far a highly developed 'moral sense' could be under genetic control. His references to habit, reason and even religious belief suggest that Darwin himself recognized the limitations of an appeal to biology in such matters.

## Human Society

The concept of evolution has provided a powerful inspiration for many pictures of human society. In fact the ideas of variation and selection have been put to conflicting uses. Although Darwinian theory can usually only be applied at the level of individual organisms, that has not prevented it from being applied to societies and even races. The crude idea of the survival of the fittest suited fascist notions of a master-race. Even Darwin himself talked sometimes of races. He commented on how the so-called Caucasian races had beaten the Turkish in the struggle for existence. He continued:

'Looking at the world at no very distant date, what an endless number of the lower races will have been eliminated by the higher civilized races throughout the world.'[31]

Races, however, can have no more relevance to natural selection than any other human grouping. Individuals are the vehicles of genes, and nations, and races, can only flourish in as far as they provide the context in which their members will flourish and leave plenty of descendants. Even a technologically advanced civilization will not survive unless it can encourage enough of its members to have enough children. A rich and cultured country with a declining birth-rate is heading for trouble. Individuals reproduce and races, or nations, do not. Obviously, if more members of a particular group, whether class, race or country, are biologically fitter, it will appear as if membership of the group is itself a significant factor. That is, however, an illusion. Certainly it would not follow that a proper biological explanation need make any reference to the group.

Neo-Darwinian theories are still sometimes accused of racism. Since, though, they take the human gene pool as their subject matter, they encourage us to think of the whole of humanity. Many people, however, find the emphasis on individual competition equally repugnant. It has been alleged that evolutionary theory tends to read off the state of affairs in a particular economic system, namely capitalism, and then project it illegitimately on the biological world. The survival of the fittest is thus the counterpart of the acquisitive competitiveness encouraged, it is suggested, by capitalism. An economic system is thus given an ideological justification by apparently being grounded in human nature.

Crude notions of individuals competing for scarce resources have at times been used to underwrite equally crude versions of capitalism. Such views, however, owe as much to Hobbes as to Darwin, who was far from being an egoist. The occurrence of altruism, however, remains a problem for evolutionary theory, and this is a symptom of a more general difficulty. Because its emphasis is so much on the individual, it has difficulty in explaining much that occurs at the social level. Reference to social instincts cannot properly explain why people are willing to co-operate with non-relatives, when it is not directly advantageous for them or their family. It merely pushes the problem back a stage, by raising the question how such instincts were acquired through natural selection. Whatever the benefits of society, those who contributed more than they gained would be at a disadvantage from the point of view of biological fitness. Yet at the same time no society could flourish if its members all tried to ensure that they obtained more benefits than the costs of belonging to it. It is probably mistaken to try to measure all social phenomena in terms of what is genetically advantageous to individuals. To do so is to espouse an extreme individualism. It is also to ignore factors that have nothing to do with measurements of costs and benefit, such as the search for truth. Presumably both Darwin and his followers had been fired by a concern for truth in putting forward their theories, rather than merely reproductive advantage. There is little reason to suppose that the one necessarily leads to the other.

Notions of evolution and selection are often employed at the level of scientific theories or even of social systems. It is easy to refer to the mutation or variation of theories and systems, so that those best adapted to their circumstances can survive. One can use Darwin's terms in fresh contexts. Marxists can, for example, talk of the historical selection of social systems through economic factors. These are, however, analogical uses of Darwinian theory, and evolution is being used as a metaphor. Unless there is a direct effect on the reproductive advantage of individuals, biological evolution through natural selection is not being talked about at all. Social systems can certainly have such effects. Cultures can fail because of the kind of influence they have on their members. Any culture, for example, which enforced rules of celibacy, but failed to recruit new members from outside, is obviously doomed to a swift end.

Social practices within a culture are often far from neutral in their effects on biological fitness. Most societies have rules on sexual matters, and this is hardly surprising in view of the intimate link between sexual behaviour and biological fitness. There are biological limits beyond which human cultural variation cannot go, at least for any length of time. Darwin pointed to the importance of biological nature as the basis of society, although it is more difficult to work out the precise connection between human nature and the different forms of human culture. A strong hold on Darwinian theory certainly acts as an effective antidote to the relativism which suggests that each society must be understood in its own terms, and that there is nothing in common between societies separated by time and space.

## Contemporary Relevance

To do justice to Darwin's insights, they have to be taken out of their nineteenth-century context. His theory of evolution began as not much more than a promissory note. Now that we have knowledge of genetic variation, neo-Darwinian theory can afford to be ambitious in what it attempts to explain. Yet the workings of evolution can still arouse much controversy. Some biologists have appeared to want to describe human behaviour almost exclusively in terms of the influence of genes. They have forgotten the enormous impact society can have on us, let alone the way in which reason can help us to withstand and even re-channel our most basic biological urges. Human sociobiology has tried to apply the insights of Darwin to the workings of society. At its best, it can show the biological constraints on human society, but at its worst it can reduce everything mental and social to the level of the promptings of genes. It can, in fact, change the subject from the contents of our thoughts and the character of our social institutions to what, allegedly, produces them.

One contradiction at the heart of Darwinian theory when applied to humans is that the theory of evolution seems to challenge the very category of the human. There can be little emphasis on the notion of a species, since ultimately it holds that organisms merge into one another without any sharp break. *Human* nature cannot, it seems, be sharply distinguished from other aspects of biological nature. It has even been alleged that an evolutionary explanation of human nature is self-contradictory because it assumes a pre-Darwinian category. Even, however, given evolution, it must be possible to identify general human traits, as they are at present, since from the point of view of recorded history, evolutionary change cannot be a significant factor.

When Darwinism is expressed by aggressive materialists, it can seem a major threat to religious views of human nature. Any view which attempts to reduce complex questions of human personality and human sociability to issues about segments of DNA is going to be accused of leaving out of account all that is most distinctively human. T. H. Huxley, however, asserted originally that 'the doctrine of Evolution is neither theistic nor anti- theistic'.[32] Certainly, despite modern advances in biochemistry, there is also a greater appreciation of the subtlety of the human mind and the complexity of human society. Not everything can be simply translated into physical terms, and the theory of natural selection cannot be used to explain everything we think or do. It can, though, show some of our persistent biases. Modern theories of 'kin selection' show that we are likely to favour relatives, since they will probably share our genes. Genes prompting such favouritism will thus be easily passed on. Sociobiology also stresses the way in which the so-called phenomenon of 'reciprocal altruism' can also become entrenched by biological means. This is a general willingness to co-operate with those who are willing to co-operate in return, coupled with a reluctance to help those who do not reciprocate. This, unlike kin selection, involves an appeal to pure self-interest and is very Hobbesian. The idea behind it is simply that genes will not spread when they encourage behaviour the costs of which outweigh the benefits. My ultimate biological advantage is not assisted when I help others at my own expense.

There seems to be a basic inconsistency between a morality encouraging unselfishness and the theory of evolution when applied rigorously to all human behaviour. Certainly sociobiology can demonstrate why it is sometimes hard to be moral. Our biological inheritance prompts us to seek our own good, or that of our family, while our morality tells us to consider other people's good. Our natural desires prompt us one way, while reason tells us to resist. Darwin, himself, may have accepted this picture but some modern neo-Darwinians are more inclined to explain morality wholly in evolutionary terms. Such an enterprise is misconceived. Human reason, as a capacity, may be the product of evolution, but it is sufficiently flexible and free-ranging to detach itself from the direction of our natural inclinations. It can even sit in judgement on them. Certainly evolutionary theory is more adept at dealing with the origin of our natural sympathies and aversions, our likes and dislikes, than in explaining the operation of human reason. Since it is itself the product of the latter, it is wise not to overreach itself.

One example of a widespread, if not universal, aversion is the repugnance most humans feel to incest. Yet it does occur and most societies have taboos and moral injunctions against it. We try to reinforce at a social level what is already deeply ingrained by nature. This is significant since incest is agreed to be exceedingly dangerous for our biological fitness. Incestuous relationships are more likely than other kinds to produce a child that is in some way defective.

Genes encouraging them would soon die out, while those discouraging them would have a clear advantage. Other apparently natural desires and aversions can be explained in similar ways. A fear of snakes could be biologically advantageous and be under genetic control. Yet the fact that a desire may be 'natural' does not mean that it is always right to indulge it. We should consult our reason as well as the immediate emotional reactions which go towards making up our human nature. It may be natural to try and further our own interests, but it is sometimes better if we do not.

Neo-Darwinian theory can enlarge our understanding of what it is to be human. It can show us the biological advantage of some human characteristics. It is more controversial as a global theory of the place of the human race in the scheme of things. The issues originally raised by Darwin's ideas remain very much alive. The natural selection of random genetic variations seems to leave little room for purpose. The theory of evolution makes it appear difficult to ascribe a unique status to *Homo sapiens*, and to separate us in any convincing way from other animals. It becomes all too easy to disregard the significance of human morality, of human reason and of other signs that, after all, we may be more than the animals from which we have descended. The most powerful of biological theories cannot remove the need for facing up to profound philosophical questions.

# CHAPTER NINE

# Marx
## *1818–1883*

## Context

Like Darwin, Karl Marx has been one of the great moulders of modern thought. Whereas Darwin was a scientist, Marx was much more involved in the political events of his day. He was always contemptuous of divorcing theory and practice. One of his most famous remarks was 'the philosophers have only *interpreted* the world in various ways: the point, however, is to *change* it'.[1] After an upbringing in Germany (he was born in Trier in 1818) and a time at Berlin University, he became embroiled in the revolutionary politics of his time. He was forced in 1849, after a turbulent year in Continental Europe, to seek permanent exile in London, where he was supported financially by his friend and collaborator, Friedrich Engels.

Marx differed from Darwin in paying attention to the social, rather than the biological, context for human life. The more biology is emphasized as a formative influence, the less it seems possible to do anything about it. One reason why conservative thinkers often stress the 'given' aspects of human nature, and radicals the way society shapes us, is that it seems difficult to change our biology, without indulging in hazardous long-term genetic engineering. On the other hand, societies can be and have been changed, as revolutionaries are well aware. The more that wrongs can be ascribed to defects in society, the more hope there is for the future. Doctrines about original sin, or the inherent selfishness of our biological nature, seem to offer a prescription for passivity in politics and for an acceptance, however reluctant, of the way things are.

Just as Darwin knew that humans needed society, so Marx could not ignore the basic facts of human biology. However much society influences us, society, and indeed history, are human creations. There is a dialectical process in which humans create society, which then moulds them, so that they then alter their social surroundings, which in turn have a further influence. It is tempting for Marxists to pay so much attention to the social determinants of action that they forget the human, and hence partly biological, underpinning to the whole historical process. At one point, Marx deliberately quotes Aristotle's reference to a 'political animal'. He says: 'Man is in the most literal sense of the word a *zoon politikon*, not only a social animal, but an animal which can develop into an individual only in society.'[2] Marx points out that one could not imagine production outside the influence of society, any more than language could develop without individuals living and talking together. Yet although this shows the indispensability of society for much that makes us properly human, it is important to remember that we are also *animals*. Many Marxists have taken this simple fact so much for granted, that they appear to have forgotten it.

Marx was a contemporary of Darwin and was undoubtedly interested in his work. A more important influence on Marx came from German philosophy. There are echoes of Hegel and his followers in his work, particularly in his emphasis on the role of consciousness. Nevertheless, Marx wrote to Engels of the *Origin of Species* that 'this is the book which contains the basis in natural history for our view'.[3] He approved of the way, as he saw it, that a death blow had been dealt to the notion of teleology in the natural sciences. He wrote: 'Darwin's book is very important and serves me as a basis in natural science for the class struggle in history.'[4] Marx was using the Darwinian notion of natural selection as an analogy for historical change. He did not think that Darwin shed any direct light on the workings of human society. Economic systems could be overthrown when they were no longer properly adapted to new social circumstances. Changes could not be explained directly in terms of human biological needs. In fact, Darwin was ridiculed by Marx for seeing amongst the beasts and plants a mirror of 'his English society', complete with such things as 'division of labour, competition, opening up of new markets, "inventions", and the Malthusian "struggle for existence" '.[5]

Marx died in 1883 and was buried in Highgate Cemetery in London. At his graveside, Engels tried to sum up his achievements and, significantly, began by comparing Marx to Darwin. He said that

Darwin had discovered the law of development of organic nature, and Marx had discovered the law of development of human history.[6] Engels asserted that mankind must eat, drink, have shelter and clothing, before it can pursue science, art or religion. Therefore the means of subsistence, and consequently economic development, must form the basis on which all social and political institutions rest. It follows, according to Marx, that such institutions must be explained in terms of economic interest, instead of the other way round.

An illustration of the way in which Marx explained everything in terms of economics is given in the preface to the first edition of his major work: *Capital* (1867). He makes it clear that, as a matter of methodology, he would only deal with individuals as 'the personific-ation of economic categories, the bearers of particular class-relations and interests'. He wanted to view the economic formation of society 'as a process of natural history'. He then gives an example of the way in which economic interest is predominant, saying: 'The Established Church will more readily pardon an attack on thirty-eight of its thirty-nine articles than on one thirty-ninth of its income.'[7] This remark about the Church of England may seem cynical but it shows how for Marx economic and class interest govern ideas, whether in the field of politics, religion or anywhere else. Ideas cannot of themselves, he believes, change the path of history, and that is why objective economic circumstances have to be changed by revolution. We cannot change people without chang-ing their circumstances.

A strong form of economic determinism can overreach itself. If ideas are powerless in the face of the demands of economic interest, and are in fact produced by them, how can revolutionary voices be raised effectively in the first place? The history of Marxism itself appears to demonstrate the great power of beliefs to influence human behaviour. Yet if all any of us can do is react to the pressure of economic circumstance, we may yearn for change when exploited, but it seems as if revolutionary agitation is pointless. Either economic factors will bring a society to collapse or they will not. Our desires may seem to play little part in the process, being mere froth on the top of processes occurring independently. Are we powerless in the face of economic circumstances, the creatures of them, or have we the possibility of rising above them? Marx himself seemed in no doubt that consciousness, the way people see their situation, is important. It can become distorted by social factors, and a constant Marxist preoccupation is to expose 'false' consciousness. It is only when we can see our economic situation as it is and not as we have been conditioned to view it, that we can hope to do anything about it. Showing people their true situation is an important step, since revolution has to be brought about by people. Economic circumstances may make it inevitable, but its inevitability comes partly as a result of people being awakened to their true situation. Circumstances certainly make men, but Marx also believed that 'men make circumstances'.[8]

## Our Place in the World

Marx thirsted for change, and wanted to create a better kind of society. He regarded capitalism as a system in which money took on a life of its own, and humans were systematically exploited and degraded. It was, though, merely a stage in historical progress, because just as capitalism had replaced feudalism, it would itself be replaced. Our history may have made us, but we can go on to make history. He did not believe that we are irredeemably selfish. Marx believed that under the right conditions we could all co-operate. He looked to the future and not the past. Some would hold that if we are moulded by the society we live in, we cannot deny that inheritance without denying ourselves. That kind of view is the mainspring of some conservative theory. Marx, however, believed that we are what we might become. He had the difficult task of emphasizing the way society has moulded us and of advocating the overthrow of that society. Human beings, he believed, can only be themselves under the right social conditions, and these can only be provided by communism. As things are, we are not as we should be.

What has sometimes been called the 'humanist' strain in Marx's theory comes out clearly in his earlier writings before he worked with Engels. Controversies rage as to how far the mature Marx changed his own views, or merely developed them. A key concept at the beginning for him was that of alienation. He complained that the worker was alienated from the product of his labour, which seemed to take on a life of its own. The more the worker creates things, the more they seem to become an 'alien, objective world'. The world of commodities takes on a power of its own which is hostile and crushes the worker. Indeed the more commodities are produced, the more labour becomes itself a commodity. Work, instead of being the free and creative expression of individuality, becomes an instrument of degradation and dehumanization. Marx writes: 'The depreciation of the human world progresses in direct proportion to the increase in value of the world of things.'[9] He maintains that the 'species-characteristic' of man is 'free conscious activity'. When labour is alienated it 'degrades man's own free activity to a means'.[10] The conscious, purposeful labour that distinguishes humans from animals is distorted. It is no longer an expression of freedom but the means of creating a world that oppresses its creators. Central to the fact of alienated work, and hence of alienated life, in which people are separated from each other, is, Marx believes, the fact of private property. *The Communist Manifesto* written by Marx and Engels sums up the theory of communism in a single phrase: abolition of private property.

Marx uses the term 'alienation' less frequently in his later writings. In *Capital*, however, the idea of 'commodity-fetishism' is very similar. Marx takes an analogy from what he terms the 'misty realms of religion'. He continues:

> There the products of the human brain appear as autonomous figures endowed with a life of their own which enter into relations both with each other and with the human race. So it is in the world of commodities with the products of men's hands. I call this the fetishism which attaches itself to the products of labour as soon as they are produced as commodities.[11]

In other words, humans could not see their own products for what they were. Marx had no room for religion and was a materialist (although he remarked that Hobbes' brand of materialism 'became hostile to humanity'[12]). His philosophical thought becomes extremely anthropocentric at times. He wanted the recovery by humans of control over their own abilities and the products of those abilities. The early years of the Industrial Revolution had produced many examples of human exploitation, and Marx found it easy in *Capital* to quote examples of appalling suffering. Bad working conditions, long working hours, child labour, and the tyranny of machines all illustrated the way in which human lives were used as a means to further profit. Individuals may ameliorate conditions but Marx

believed that, in the last resort, everyone was a prisoner of the
capitalist system, which depended on the exploitation of one part
of society by another. Only a completely new society could remove
class antagonisms. As it was, he held, the system dictated that
factory labour should be performed in poor conditions. His particular
target was England, as 'the land of machinery'. He admitted that the
British Factory Acts had had a beneficial effect, but he complained
that the factory system in the hands of capitalists resulted in the
'systematic robbery of what is necessary for the life of the worker
while he is at work'.[13] There was a lack of essential space, light and
air.

Marx traced the division between classes in society back to the
division of labour. Indeed he suggested that 'division of labour and
private property are identical expressions'.[14] From that comes the
conflict of interest which arises in society between individuals. From
that, too, comes the fact that 'man's own deed becomes an alien
power opposed to him'. Each person has a role in society, a sphere of
activity from which there is no escape. Someone is a hunter, perhaps, or a fisherman or a shepherd and has to remain as such if he
does not want to lose his livelihood. Marx is always aware, however,
that features of society that seem unalterable can be changed. Our
own understanding of them is itself a product of the society. We have
inherited from previous generations a sum of productive forces
which govern our lives. Marx continues:

> This sum of productive forces, capital funds, and social forms of
> intercourse, which every individual and generation finds in existence
> as something given, is the real basis of what the philosophers have
> conceived as 'substance' and 'essence of man'.[15]

What appears to constitute our very nature, is, in other words,
merely the creation of particular forms of production. If they are
changed, so-called 'human nature' can be too. Marx warns that the
*idea* of revolution is not enough, because ideas cannot change
society on their own. He points out that the material conditions for
revolution must also be present. A few revolutionaries cannot overthrow a State unless a revolutionary mass has been prepared by
social conditions. In this he shows himself a consistent materialist.
Human beings are firmly located as part of the material world. Marx
is not concerned with any 'pure' consciousness, detached from its

surroundings. He is only concerned with the consciousness of 'real living individuals', namely the way people think who are situated in a particular society, with a particular history.[16] Thought is not abstract, he believes, any more than 'mass' is. We think and act because of what happens in the material world.

## What is it to be Human?

Marx recognized that in order to be able to 'make history' we must first of all be in a position to live. Basic human needs have to be catered for, such as eating and drinking, a place to live, clothing and so on. Meeting these needs, however, leads to new needs, he thought, and many of our desires and preferences are in fact moulded by society, and are not part of an unalterable human nature. A modern example might be the way in which advertising creates new demands. This emphasis on our desires and needs being as much an outcome of society as an explanation for society is a typical Marxist one. The danger is of totally excluding the biological basis of human nature from the reckoning.

However much that is apparently unalterable in human nature is traced back to conditions in society which can be altered, this process cannot go on indefinitely, if appeal is made to concepts such as 'dehumanizing'. Marx judges existing capitalist society against a standard. He has a vision of an ideal society in which humans can find their true selves. Yet there is no way in which all existing societies can be found wanting if everything distinctively human has to be the product of a society. There is no external standard for human nature left to which appeal can be made. Marx has to have some concept of human nature as it should be. He has to have an abstract philosophical notion as a basis for the critique of existing society. There is a similar tension to be found in the way Marxist critiques of morality proceed. Morality is often derided as 'bourgeois', as the belief of a particular section of a society at a particular time, which, presumably, merely serves to further the interest of one class. Yet Marx himself denounced the evils of capitalism with convincing fervour. He seemed to be proclaiming what he saw as the truth, and not voicing the prejudices of a class or using empty rhetoric. The inhumanity of factory conditions was such precisely because people were being treated as no human should.

Capitalism, it was alleged, took little account of the way people ought to live.

Marx did have a view of the proper conditions for the human race, and it was bound up with his vision of a future communist society. One famous passage illustrates his vision. He looks forward to a time in which there will no longer be any division of labour, society will be classless and everyone will co-operate, instead of being merely concerned with private interest. Whereas Hume thought that justice was necessary to meet the conditions created by scarcity and too little benevolence, Marx believed that his perfect society would produce abundance and altruism. It would, in a sense, no longer need justice, as Hume thought of it, since it would be perfect. It would be a secular version of the Kingdom of Heaven. In such a society, no one would be constrained by economic considerations, or have one exclusive sphere of activity. Marx therefore thought that so long as 'society regulates the general production' it would then be possible 'for me to do one thing today and another tomorrow, to hunt in the morning, fish in the afternoon, rear cattle in the evening, criticize after dinner, just as I have a mind, without ever becoming hunter, fisherman, shepherd or critic'.[17]

Marx looked forward to a society in which we could all be truly human because none of our potentialities were needlessly frustrated. He emphasized the importance of what he refers to as the individual's 'self-realization'.[18] This is perhaps surprising as socialism has often been portrayed as being more concerned with the mass or the collective than the interests of the individual. No doubt some socialists would hold that to be necessary policy on the path to full communism. In a genuinely communist society, however, Marx believed that each person should have the freedom to become what they truly are through creative activities. He tended to identity individual self-realization', 'freedom' and 'labour'. By 'labour' is meant creative, purposeful work in which humans are genuinely able to express themselves, and not the drudgery established by the Industrial Revolution. Nor did Marx mean by it mere idle amusement, and he gives as an example of 'really free labour' the composing of music, which, as he points out, demands great effort.

The economic determinism, which Marx sometimes appears to espouse, is only a feature of one form of society, and is not an invariant feature. He wanted to remove the coercion which he saw as resulting from capitalism. His goal was true freedom, once the hindrances and shackles restraining us have been taken away. *The Communist Manifesto*, written by Marx and Engels in 1848, proclaims: 'Let the ruling classes tremble at a Communistic revolution. The proletarians have nothing to lose but their chains.'[19]

Yet the picture Marx paints of a society which can release everyone's creativity is a picture of *human* society. To be strictly consistent, he should show how others – not just the proletariat – need that kind of freedom. All classes are equally prisoners of the economic system. The ruling classes may benefit at the expense of others, but even they do not enjoy genuine freedom. Marx does attack what he calls the absurdity of 'considering free competition as being the final development of human liberty'.[20] It all takes place within the context of the dominion of capital, and is in no way an example of free individuality. He continues: 'The assertion that free competition is the final form of the development of productive forces, and thus of human freedom, means only that the domination of the middle class is the end of the world's history.'

As he comments, this might be a pleasant thought for the members of that class. Nevertheless, on his view, however much they profit from their place in the class system, their own human potential cannot be realized. Marxist thought, however, tends to concentrate on the exploitation of the working classes, rather than the alleged inhumanity of the whole system. The effect is to direct hatred from one class to another.

The Utopian vision of a world of plenty, in which greed and selfseeking is eliminated, may seem desirable, but the real question is whether it can be put into practice. The free exercise of human talents, without a division of labour, may result in a world of abundance, but it may not. Perhaps only the prior existence of a world of material bounty could allow such an idyllic state of affairs. Marx himself is not always clear how far human fulfilment comes through labour or whether the realm of freedom begins when basic necessities have been provided for. Is communism concerned with the centrality of work or the importance of leisure? In *Capital*, Marx refers to a 'realm of necessity' which is the precondition for that of freedom. He says: 'The shortening of the working-day is its basic prerequisite'.[21] Any society has, of course, to produce the essentials for life.

Marx also assumed that socialism will produce altruism, so that each person pursues the common interest, instead of their own.

Perhaps he thought that no one needed to be greedy in a world of plenty, but this raises the question as to how deeply ingrained in human nature is selfishness. Those who have enough often want more, and the very rich do not seem to be any less greedy. Marx might blame this on the economic system, but the lurking worry must remain that it might be more deeply ingrained, and even perhaps be part of our biological inheritance. In that case, it would not be eradicated through a transformation of society.

Just as Marx's reference to self-realization is vague, and nowhere is any clear view of the self given, notions of the common interest are far from precise. Merely wanting to uphold the common good is insufficient, as we all have to agree on what constitutes our good. Marx assumes that there will be no conflicts about the nature of a good society under communism. He must also assume that we shall know how to achieve it. The former may be an optimistic assumption, but the latter is a particularly worrying one. What Marx says may possibly be applicable to small groups of craftsmen living in communes, but it is harder to fit it to a highly complex modern society. Central planning by the State, for example, may seem social-ist, but to be successful it must involve a grasp of the complexities of human behaviour, which may be beyond one group of people.

Marx was more concerned with the class struggle than with airy speculation about the nature of a perfect society or of the realization of human potentialities. He was more sure that capitalism is in-human than that he knew all the possibilities open to us. Indeed he could say that he could not predict what humans could become when they were genuinely free. Theirs would be an active process of self-creation. Yet Utopian visions of what might be are disturbing as well as challenging. We are being invited to destroy all we have, without any clear idea of what is going to be put in its place.

## Human Society

Marx regarded all existing social institutions with grave suspicion, referring for instance to 'the slavery latent in the family'.[22] He had a vision of a form of communist society where even appeals to equal rights are suspended. He said in a famous phrase that society should inscribe on its banners: 'From each according to his ability, to each according to his needs.'[23] His point was that mere equal shares for equal labour would be insufficient. One worker would be married, and another not: one would have more children than another. Equal shares would create further inequality, although Marx recognized that this might be inevitable in the first phase of communism as it emerges from capitalism.

The long-term future of the family under communism is far from clear. *The Communist Manifesto* regarded it as primarily a bourgeois institution based on capital. Indeed it is claimed that 'in its completely developed form the family exists only amongst the bourgeoisie'.[24] It points out how industry had torn asunder family ties amongst the proletarians, and children had been 'transformed into simple articles of commerce and instruments of labour'. Thus bourgeois 'clap-trap about the family' is exposed to the satisfaction of the writers as essentially hypocritical, and some salty remarks about the existence of prostitution are thrown in. The manifesto also points out that 'working men have no country' and adds 'we cannot take from them what they have not got'.[25] Its outlook is firmly international, and this underlines how communism wants to remove many of the familiar landmarks of human life.

Marx set no great store by social tradition or personal habit. Nor for him was the stress on custom, as given by Hume, or the development of a virtuous character through habitual action, as with Aristotle. Because he believed that our assumptions and inclinations at a social and an individual level had their source in the workings of a particular economic system, he insisted that people could only be altered on a mass scale and through revolution. Because of the primacy, in Marx's eyes, of social influences, people would never be changed significantly while the same economic factors create the same social effects. Everything would still be tailored to suit the interests of capital. He said of the revolution he advocated: 'This revolution is necessary, therefore, not only because the ruling class cannot be overthrown in any other way, but also because the class overthrowing it can only in a revolution succeed in ridding itself of all the muck of ages and become fitted to found society anew.'[26]

The reference to the 'muck of ages' makes revolution a form of cleansing, and gives a quasi-moral basis to the cause of revolution. Rhetoric linking the shedding of blood with purification uses images with a long history. The danger is always that once the forces of disorder and death are unleashed within a society, it is hard to restrain them once again. Marx's particular twist to the revolutionary theme is his stress on the significance of class membership in a society. A fully communist society would be classless, but citizens of an existing capitalist society can only be viewed in terms of their class. They must act as the economic structure determines it is in their interest to act. The proletariat has to identify its class enemies and act accordingly. Marx does not hold an 'organic' view of society, according to which the different parts of society must function in their separate ways for the good of the whole. His is, at least until the revolution, a creed encouraging conflict rather than harmony, hatred rather than co-operation.

The case for revolution needs the assumption that changing a society fundamentally will change human nature, as it is expressed in present-day society. Yet if natural selection has made us self-centred, we will be the same biological creatures with the same tendencies in a communist society as a capitalist one. If, on the other hand, we are potentially immortal souls with the power of rational free choice, but with a bias towards evil, a perfect society on earth is already doomed. There is, too, the very real question why anyone should prefer to seek actively the uncertainties of revolution rather than the comforting familiarity of their present state. There is some evidence that people are naturally conservative. That, at least, was Hume's view. Marx, indeed, recognized that the proletariat may not always realize where their real interests lie, and revolutionary leaders often feel entitled to ignore what ordinary people consciously want, on the grounds that they do not realize the truth of the situation they are in. The complication, though, is that even if they do, they might still not want to change. Many people are very attached to their family and their nation, even if from an economic point of view they are near the bottom of the heap. Darwin certainly argued that such attachment was, in the strict sense, natural. Once again the issue is whether the social determinants of our character are the main ones.

A further problem about the quest for revolution centres on motivation. I may be poor and exploited, realize it *and* want to change my circumstances, but it still does not follow that I will become an ardent revolutionary. A lot of blood may be spilt in the creation of a communist society, and some of it will probably be mine. I may not survive to taste the fruits of my sacrifice. The average member of the proletariat, however downtrodden, is being asked to give up everything so that others will live a better life. A clear-sighted revolutionary has to be very altruistic. Yet Marx's emphasis on the role of class reflects his attempt to get away from the vision of a society of atomic individuals, each self-sufficient and paying no regard to others, but making decisions in the light of its own interests. Questioning how far individuals would be willing to make even necessary sacrifices perhaps trades on a model of human society which Marx would never have held. He envisaged the whole revolutionary process as inevitable. Capitalism had set up such strains and stresses, and had produced so many internal contradictions that the proletariat had no choice in the matter. Their historic destiny was waiting for them.

## Contemporary Relevance

No thinker has had a more profound effect on the political structure of the modern world than Karl Marx. His ideas have spawned many revolutions in the twentieth century, although they have not occurred in the most advanced industrialized countries, as Marx predicted. No society, however, has succeeded in reaching an advanced state of communism. Certainly the romantic individualism that seemed to be Marx's aim once the State has withered away is nowhere in evidence. Even apparently communist societies are derided by some of his followers as examples of 'state capitalism'.

Centralized planning, together with public ownership of all significant sectors of a national economy, has given vastly increased powers to the State in many instances. Yet the rigidities and inflexibilities of such a system worry even dedicated Marxists. The complexities of modern society do not lend themselves easily to total bureaucratic control. One does not need to be cynical to see the emergence of managers and bureaucrats as a new class, with its own special interests, in control of the apparatus of State. It could be argued from a Marxist point of view that such a class is bound to arise as a result of the development of productive forces. The danger is that once it is in place its prime purpose will be to perpetuate itself. Attempts have been made to make socialism more flexible, with less control from the centre. 'Market socialism' advocates the collective ownership of the means of production while ensuring some form of market mechanism to guide the allocation of resources. Whether the enterprise is self-contradictory remains to be seen, but it is pre-eminently a problem for economics. Marx raises issues at a deeper philosophical level about what is wrong with the human condition and what can be done to put it right. All economic theories must themselves rest on assumptions about human nature.

Above all, Marx put his trust in human perfectibility. He believed that we are all hindered and frustrated from living as we should by the structures of capitalist society. Once these are swept away, there will be an opportunity for the proper flowering of all that is truly human. Yet it is perhaps not irrelevant to examine the state of affairs in post-revolutionary societies and to ask whether self-styled Marxist countries provide examples of how human nature can properly flourish. This may seem unfair, particularly as no society has yet achieved what Marx saw as the final phase of communism. It is a commonplace that human beings very often fail to practise what they preach, and that of itself does not undermine the validity of what they urge. Judged by the standards of Christianity itself, the history of the Christian Church has at times been deplorable. Why should anything different be expected of Marxism? The Christian emphasis on the power of sin, however, does suggest that any human institution will find it difficult to drag itself clear of the effects of human selfishness. The question is whether Marxism can also explain why it is so difficult to achieve its objectives. Once the economic base of a society has been organized on Marxist principles, there seems no reason why communism should not appear, as Marx envisaged.

The underlying question must be whether there are insuperable obstacles in human nature to the production of pure communism. Does Marx's Utopian dream about the possibilities open to the new humanity contradict basic and unalterable facts about our make-up? Can we be so certain that greed and selfishness will disappear when the external conditions of a society are altered? Will people become more co-operative simply because economic facts in a society have been changed? Will all conflict have been genuinely eradicated in a communist society? These are not easy questions to answer.

The fact of conflict is particularly important for any theory of human nature. It can occur within an individual or between people. Some theories, like Hobbes', show how we must live with it, and, control it, while others may try to find a cure. Marx blames all conflict on the class struggle, so that there would be none in a classless society. Because all human problems are social in origin, once society is put right, there will be no problems. Yet even if Marx were right in his diagnosis of the tensions of a capitalist society, he does not deal with wide areas of human experience. In particular, he ignores the difficulties that stem from our individual psychology and biology, and may be pre-social in origin. For instance, the kind of inner conflict, described by Plato, and later to be researched by Freud, is never taken into account. The power of dispassionate human reason should not be easily dismissed, either, by being made to appear merely the inevitable reflection of class-interest. Marxists have, indeed, sometimes found it difficult to show why they can see things so clearly, whereas everyone else's judgement is systematically warped.

Marx's achievement was to highlight the power of society on our thinking and on the kind of people we become. He coupled this with an emphasis on the way in which societies are moulded by economic factors. In the end, however, we are left with the recurring question as to how far one can change people by changing the economic structures of the society to which they belong. The roots of human nature may grow deeper than human society. If they do, society may be as much the expression of that nature as its cause.

# CHAPTER TEN

# Nietzsche

## 1844–1900

## Context

Greek philosophy and the Christian religion have been the major influences on the development of the western world. Thought in the nineteenth and twentieth centuries owes more to them than is often realized. More obvious, however, is the way they have been attacked over that period. The possibility of metaphysics, and of the disinterested use of human reason, has been challenged. Marx, Nietzsche and Freud have all been described as using the weapons of suspicion. Each in his own way has taught that people's reasons and intentions should not be taken at face value. The real motives and interests which lie behind their words and actions may not even be appreciated by the individuals concerned. Marx tried to show how ideologies are put forward not because of their claim to truth but because they help to sustain the economic interests of a particular class. Freud was to show the great importance of the unconscious elements of our minds in controlling what we become aware of. No one, however, more than Nietzsche, has ever attacked so whole-heartedly the possibility of human rationality, or condemned so absolutely the Christianity of his forbears. He attempted to demonstrate the interests at work in the erection of our moral and metaphysical systems. By showing their 'genealogy' or origins, he began the process of undermining our faith in them.

Friedrich Nietzsche was born in 1844 near Leipzig, the son, and grandson, of Lutheran clergymen. His father died when he was 5 and he was brought up solely by women, a fact which may have influenced his view of Christianity. He was trained in classical philosophy and obtained the chair in the subject at Basle University. He was more interested in the question of the sources of the New Testament than its theology and was much influenced by the type of German biblical criticism which 'demythologized' the life of Jesus and removed all supernatural elements. In particular, the notorious writings of D. F. Strauss on the question of the historical Jesus helped him as a young man to turn from his childhood beliefs to a virulent atheism. Yet, however thorough it may be, it is an atheism that depends for its force on the prior existence of Christianity. It is essentially a reaction against the tenets of a particular religion.

Nietzsche's attacks on Christianity were unparallelled in their ferocity. He described it as 'the most fatal seductive lie that has yet existed, as the great unholy lie'.[1] Plato, however, also came in for abuse, because of his dualist view of reality and the consequent devaluing of the ordinary physical world. He was dismissed as 'the great viaduct of corruption'.[2] For Nietzsche, Plato's view of reality was too static, and he was more attracted by Heraclitus' notion that everything was in a constant state of change. Nothing was fixed, even in the phenomenal world, and there was no second world as the source of fixed standards. True to his background as a philologist, Nietzsche often chose to view the world as a text, open to varying interpretations. He says: 'Facts are precisely what there are not, only interpretations.' Just how radical he was prepared to be in his attack on the most basic assumptions in philosophy can be gauged from the fact that he denied that the concept of an interpretation implied there must be an interpreter. Even that, he maintained, was invention. One of his main aims was to show how the world that is taken for granted is merely the result of one possible interpretation amongst many. He argued that it has been produced by a Christian understanding which has suited the particular interests of one type of person, but which has been against the interests of others. Even its insistence that only one interpretation can be right is geared to preserve its own status. Claims to truth lose their power, when it is accepted that truth is an illusion.

Nietzsche's detestation of Christianity led to the ending of his friendship with Wagner, when he felt that the great composer was being influenced too much by it. In particular he was disgusted by the Christian symbolism which permeates the mystical opera, *Parsifal*. Yet his own fate is not reassuring for those who would wish to live, as he did, by opposing the possibility of human rationality. His health progressively broke down; he had to retire at the age of thirty-five; and he eventually died in 1900 after a period of insanity lasting eleven years. His views gained in influence after his death, although he should perhaps not be held responsible for some of the uses made of them. He was not himself a German nationalist, but it is hard to read much of what he wrote without being aware of the way in which his philosophy was eagerly embraced in the German Third Reich under Hitler. The latter was at pains to publicize his veneration of Nietzsche, visiting the Nietzsche Museum in Weimar and posing for photographs by the bust of the philosopher. There are strong echoes in Hitler's *Mein Kampf* of some of Nietzsche's views and there is no doubt that he eventually conceived himself as what Nietzsche termed 'Superman'. This is perhaps no more relevant to the study of Nietzsche than are Stalin's excesses to the study of Marx. The disquieting question must remain, however, as to what there is in Nietzsche's thought which could have curbed the atrocities of the Nazi era. It is all too probable that a Nazi would have found only encouragement in Nietzsche's utterances, since all moral restraints had been swept aside.

## Our Place in the World

No one has drawn out more relentlessly than Nietzsche the consequences of a rejection of belief in God. It is tempting for anyone brought up as a Christian to reject the metaphysical foundations of religious belief, while imagining that life can be lived in much the same way as before. Life, it seems, can have meaning, and moral claims can still exist, even when God is rejected. Nietzsche would have none of this. He was remorseless in his attack on metaphysics, but was not afraid to draw out the consequences of his position with great honesty. Metaphysics might seem an abtruse and dispensable discipline, but in fact it comprises everything that underpins the assumptions we bring to the world. Not only is 'God' a metaphysical notion, but so is the concept of a continuing physical world existing independently of our conceptions of it. Even the idea of a physical object persisting as the same entity through various changes is metaphysical, as, more particularly, is the idea of a human person as a self continuing as the same person while his or her body alters. We may all have a clear idea of ourselves as distinct individuals, remaining essentially the same up to and perhaps beyond death, but that cannot be the result of empirical investigation, as Hume noted.

Nietzsche ruled out the possibility of fixed categories applied to a static reality. All judgements had to be made from different perspectives about a world that was constantly changing. Any attempt to impart a belief in order or purpose was misguided. We find in 'things' what we bring to them. Everything is linked to everything else, and nothing is determinate. He says: 'Truth is the kind of error without which a certain species of life could not live.'[4] He also says about the human thinker: 'There exists neither "spirit" nor reason, nor thinking, nor consciousness, nor soul, nor will, nor truth: all are fictions that are of no use. There is no question of "subject and object".'[5]

Our whole language is imbued with the distinction between subjects and objects, between the world and the way we think of it or act towards it. Removing the distinction renders unstable not only the idea of a world 'out there' that has its own characteristics, but also the idea of a particular subject, or self, who is perceiving, understanding, thinking about and acting on the world. It is difficult for anyone such as Nietzsche, who wishes to challenge the metaphysics taken for granted in our language to do so without apparently using language in contradictory ways. The question is not as to whether one can get beyond the categories of language without doing violence to language, but whether such a programme is rationally defensible. It is hard to make sense of much of what Nietzsche says except as a way of telling us something of the character of reality. It is impossible to deny everything. An attack on previous metaphysics must itself depend on certain assumptions about what is the case. If everything is fiction and invention, and nothing is real, we lose our grip on the concepts of fact and fiction, truth and falsity, and reality and unreality. There comes a point at which the attack on the presuppositions of *our* language becomes an attack on the presuppositions of *any* language. If any interpretation is as good as any other, nothing can ever be ruled out.

Any attack on reason, particularly from a philosophical standpoint, is bound to be at constant risk of refuting itself. How can I argue against the possibility of argument? How can I give reasons for distrusting the power of human reason? Nietzsche has to face the fact that he expects us to accept *his* views while denying there could be a good reason for doing so. Like all attacks on the possibility of metaphysics, his seems a classic case of sawing off the branch on which one is sitting. Nietzsche is even apparently left without any ground for criticizing Christianity. Without truth, there is no error, and Christianity cannot then be mistaken. Nietzsche seems to imagine that Christian beliefs do not match the character of the world. This is hardly surprising, as the dichotomy between the world and what is said and believed about it can never finally be transcended. Otherwise anything can be said and believed with impunity, and then there can be no point in saying or believing anything. Nihilism is reached at this point, and the consistent nihilist has to be silent. Anything said assumes a difference between something being or not being the case. Assertion always involves claims to truth, however trivial, while nihilism allows commitment to nothing.

Few philosophers have confronted the possibility of nihilism as honestly as Nietzsche. His starting-point was the repudiation of the Christian God and of a world beyond this one. The dismissal of any idea of a soul, or of a life after death, meant that any meaning and purpose for life had to be given within the confines of this life. No loving Creator could be thought of as the source of meaning, and there was no cosmic purpose. This earth marks the boundary of our concerns. Nietzsche makes his hero Zarathustra (or Zoroaster), named after the founder of the ancient Persian religion, say: 'I entreat you, my brothers, *remain true to the earth*, and do not believe those who speak to you of superterrestrial hopes! They are poisoners, whether they know it or not. They are despisers of life.'[6]

Zarathustra goes on to say that once the greatest blasphemy was that against God, 'but God died', and now the greatest offence was to blaspheme the earth. This notion of the death of God has echoed down the years. Nietzsche announced it in a well-known passage about a madman who lit a lantern in 'the bright morning hours' and ran to the market-place shouting, 'I am looking for God'. People who did not believe in God laughed at him and taunted him. Nietzsche continues: 'The madman sprang into their midst and pierced them with his glances. "Where has God gone?" he cried. "I shall tell you. *We have killed him* – you and I. We are all his murderers.'[7] Later in the day, the madman entered various churches and on his way out remarked, 'What are these churches now if they are not the tombs and sepulchres of God?'

This startling vision is easy to dismiss in a superficial manner. How could an eternal God die? Either he never existed, or he cannot die. Yet the image is a haunting one and has been used by theologians in more recent times. It can be a graphic way of describing the onset of atheism after the long rule of Christianity. Without a firm grasp of the notions of truth, and of objective reality, there could seem a close connection between the loss of faith and the death of God. Nietzsche's use of the image could be further evidence of how far he was from accepting any reality independent of belief, and how easily he could slip into thinking that people's beliefs make their world. Christians, however, could never believe that God existed simply as a result of their belief, or that He could go out of existence because they gave up their belief. Such a God would be merely the projection of one's own wishes. What matters, though, is not what I conceive to be true but what is true.

Nietzsche recognized that a world without God would be emptied of all meaning and that humans would lose the importance they had seemingly possessed. Darwin had influenced him and Nietzsche felt the full impact of evolutionary theories about human origins. He wrote: 'Formerly one sought the feeling of the grandeur of man by pointing to his divine *origin*: this has now become a forbidden way, for at its portal stands the ape.'[8] He wonders whether one should try the opposite direction and hope that 'the way mankind is *going* shall serve as proof of its grandeur and kinship with God'. Nietzsche's response is that at the end of this way 'stands the funeral urn of the *last* man'. We can never pass into a higher realm. There is nothing beyond for which we can strive, any more, we are told, than the ant and earwig can rise up to kinship with God and eternal life.

The bleakness of Nietzsche's philosophy is perhaps accentuated by the explicit contrast with Christian claims about human importance in the eyes of God. A faith which held that God so loved the world that he sent His son to redeem it could not value humans more highly. Repudiating it could make them seem worthless. Nietzsche wrestled with this problem, teetering on the edge of nihilism and despair. He solved it to his own satisfaction by postulating the idea of 'eternal recurrence'. He squarely faced up to the ultimate meaninglessness and purposelessness of life because he thought there was no final destination, but instead of decrying life, he still wished to affirm it. He considered it was the Platonists and the Christians who denigrated ordinary human life by contrasting it with a superior form of eternal life. The idea of an eternal recurrence is a way of accepting life. By countenancing the same events occurring again and again, instead of considering life imperfect because of some metaphysical standard, we thereby show, he thought, that we are affirmers of the value of life, rather than deniers of it. He says: 'Let us think this thought in its most terrible form, existence as it is, without meaning or aim, yet recurring, inevitable without any finale of nothingness, "the eternal recurrence". This is the most extreme form of nihilism: the nothing ("the meaningless") eternally.'[9]

We must, it seems, be willing to accept everything as it is. There can be no question of improvement or progress, no notion of redemption or salvation, no reason for guilt or regret. Zarathrustra is made to say: 'I shall return, with this sun, with this earth, with this eagle, with this serpent – *not* to a new life or a better life or a similar life: I shall return eternally to this identical and self-same life, in the greatest things and in the smallest, to teach once more the eternal recurrence of all things.'[10]

This is Nietzsche's response to nihilism, and in fact he would say that Christianity is nihilistic in failing to accept life and affirm it in its present form. Its strong sense of human imperfection and sin, and its view that nothing is as it should be, makes it antagonistic to many prevalent characteristics of human life. Marxism, too, would come under Nietzsche's condemnation, because of its search for a better life on earth. He says: 'It is a disgrace for all socialist systematizers that they suppose there could be circumstances – social combinations – in which vice, disease, prostitution, distress would no longer grow – but that means condemning life.'[11]

Nietzsche's affirmation of life comes from within himself. It can have no rational justification, but is an attitude comparable to the impulse of an artist to create a work of art. The idea of cosmic cycles, of everything always coming back to the same state of affairs, is itself not original, but is an idea that has itself regularly recurred in the history of human thought. Yet in the end it only serves to underline the pointlessness of human existence. There is no direction. Even if we are able to endure the thought of everything happening in the same way again and again, we have to recognize that it means that nothing can ever improve.

## What is it to be Human?

Because of his opposition to any constancy underlying change, Nietzsche could not accept there was any continuing self. His influence on Freud is undoubted but the two diverged in this. Nietzsche did not believe in any reality underlying appearances. The 'real' self could not be separated from its manifestations, so that there is no way I could be systematically deceiving myself. Notions such as false consciousness and self-deception trade on a distinction between appearance and reality. Yet Nietzsche was at one with Freud in stressing the importance of sub-personal forces, or instincts, governing human behaviour. He believed that it is possible to explain, as he put it, 'our entire institutional life as the development and ramification of *one* basic form of will – as will to power'.[11]

This idea of a 'will to power' is fundamental for Nietzsche, and yet it is very sketchily described. It is a somewhat vague amalgam of biological drives, and what it may not be too unkind to describe as a metaphysical principle. Above all, the individual should not be subordinated to the interests of others. Nietzsche's ideal is the heroic individual who refuses to be bound by the restraints of society or by traditional morality. One's purposes are not presented from outside but must be imposed by one's own will. We have to exert ourselves to create our own standards, because there can be no objective source for moral standards. For Nietzsche there was no question of the will being free or unfree, but rather of it being strong or weak. He was thus able to claim that 'life itself is *essentially* appropriation, injury, overpowering of the strange and weaker, suppression, severity... and at the least and mildest, exploitation.'[12] He went on to deny that exploitation was a sign of a corrupt, imperfect or primitive society, but said: 'It pertains to the *essence* of the living thing as a fundamental organic function, it is a consequence of the intrinsic will to power, which is precisely the will of life.'

Life, Nietzsche believed, needed a will to power to stamp some direction on it. Since we cannot discover any meaning for life, we have to create it. Thus the will to power is a wider notion than the mere zeal to dominate others. It involves, too, the recognition that we cannot afford to let all our impulses have a free reign. The strong person is sufficiently integrated to be in full self-control. Nevertheless, the idea of the quest for power over others is an unsettling one. Without the restraints of traditional morality, the prospect of strong individuals, however heroic, exerting themselves at the expense of the weak can only be horrifying.

In the ancient world, there was a saying that one should 'know thyself'. Because, according to Nietzsche, we have no fixed self to know, it is not surprising that he replaced it with the commandment, 'Will a self and thou shalt *become* a self.'[13] Everything, therefore, is possible to us. We create our own law and, in a real sense, we make ourselves. To what end do we do this? Nietzsche prohibits us from asking this question, but even he cannot finally deprive life of all purpose. He makes Zarathustra teach 'the Superman' (*Ubermensch*). As a species, human beings should strive to transcend their present conditions. Nietzsche thought that only a select number of individuals would be able to do this, but they would be the justification for the existence of the masses. He says: 'What is the ape to men? A laughing-stock or a painful embarrassment. And just so shall man be to the Superman: a laughing-stock or a painful embarrassment.'[14]

Zarathustra continues by saying that the Superman is the meaning of the earth. He orders: 'Let your will say: The Superman *shall be* the meaning of the earth.' Man is, we are told, 'a rope, fastened between animal and Superman – a rope over an abyss'. The influence of the theory of evolution in all this is clear. Although Nietzsche criticized Darwin from time to time, the whole course of his thought would be impossible outside a Darwinian framework. Above all his vision of the human race is of an animal species with animal instincts. Yet he believed that 'man as a species is not progressing'.[15] For him, the Superman would be the glorious exception, not one of the herd. There is, he believes, a greater difference between the individual who has the strength to take control of his or her own destiny and the rest of humanity, than between the latter and other animals.

For Nietzsche the best type of human was the exceptional one, beholden to no one. He extols the idea of the 'sovereign individual, like only to himself, liberated again from morality of custom, autonomous and supramoral'.[16] He points out that the notions of morality and autonomy are mutually exclusive, and he goes on to praise 'this emancipated individual'. It is a vision that has influenced many, including later 'existentialist' philosophers. Like an artist brushing aside stultifying conventions, Nietzsche's Superman could rise above the confining claims of others. Religious and moral restraints could be repudiated. The exhilaration of throwing aside the traditions and customs of centuries is obvious, and yet the prospect of unbridled creativity can soon lose its appeal. When everything is permitted, it can soon appear that it does not matter what one does, and that can mean there is little point in doing anything. The exultation of the Superman can easily lapse into the despair and hopelessness of one who sees that everything is meaningless.

## Human Society

Nietzsche championed the individual and decried the needs of society as a whole, but he still had a lively respect for social influences. He argued that consciousness itself arose only because of the need to communicate. Because our ancestors needed help and protection they had to learn to make themselves understood. This meant that they first had to know what they themselves felt and thought. Nietzsche says therefore that 'the development of language and the development of consciousness go hand in hand.'[17] His conclusion is that 'it was only as a social animal that man acquired self-consciousness'. As a result, he is none too impressed by the manner in which we know ourselves. Such knowledge, he holds, is not a product of our individual existence, but of our social and 'herd' nature. Thus we become aware not of what is truly individual but only what is average. We are governed by the perspective of the herd.

This is in fact a strikingly modern emphasis on the way in which language can shape our thought and in which the private world of the individual can depend very much on the standards of the public, and social, world. It is a theme that was to be taken up more than sixty years later by Wittgenstein. The difference is that in Nietzsche it was taken to be not a fact of human existence, but a 'corruption, falsification, reduction to superficialities'.[18] The traditional values and concerns of society were not to be accepted but rejected.

Nietzsche was always concerned that the individual should not be swallowed up by the demands of the masses, and he was vehemently opposed to anything that restrained the exceptional individual in the interests of the majority. He was contemptuous of 'the pleasure in large-scale associations found in all herd animals' and had no time for appeals to 'community spirit' or invocation of the 'Fatherland' because of their lack of emphasis on the individual.[19] Anything which urged the strong to sacrifice themselves for the weak was anathema. Socialism negated life while 'religion has debased the concept man'.[20] His theme was that everything was always reduced to the level of the average. He described the concept of the 'equality of souls before God' as crazy, and was totally opposed to the idea that anyone could be so important as not to be sacrificed.[21] He writes: 'This universal love of men is in practice the preference for the suffering, underprivileged, degenerate: it has in fact lowered and weakened the strength, the responsibility, the lofty duty to sacrifice men... What is Christian altruism if not the mass-egoism of the weak?'[22]

Nietzsche's aim was not so much to abolish all morality as to reinterpret it. He was passionately concerned with the question 'how should one live?' but he denied the Christian answer. It is in this area, above all, that he uses his technique of investigating the 'genealogy' of ideas, by trying to show how Christian morality arose as a defence by the weak against the strong. He argues that praise of those who do not exert all their strength and power for their own ends is not itself disinterested. Nietzsche says pithily, that 'one's neighbour praises selflessness because *he derives advantage from it.*'[23] In other words, it is often in my interest that you do not pursue your own interest. The more I extol morality, the more, in a subtle way, am I furthering my own ends. Morality, therefore, as traditionally understood is a powerful weapon for one group against another. It restrains the strong in the interests of the weak. Anyone who believes in the fundamental equality of all people would applaud this. What is wrong in protecting some members of society from the depredations of others, of compensating some for their infirmities, or in favouring the needy? Most modern societies are run on precisely these principles. Nietzsche, however, challenges much of what is nowadays taken for granted.

The way in which the individual's interests and those of the group should be balanced is always difficult, but the difficulty is that Nietzsche is only concerned for *some* individuals, and has no room for talk of equal rights and no sympathy with those who suffer. He scorns the Christian fear of self-assertion and pride. For him the preservation of the sick and suffering meant 'the deterioration of the European race'.[24] He believed that 'elevation of the type "man"' will always be the work of a society which upheld 'gradations of rank and differences of worth among human beings'.[25]

Nietzsche thought that the very existence of society was the result of how the 'sickly' strive after a 'herd organization' to compensate for their weakness. He said that 'the strong are as naturally inclined to *separate* as the weak are to *congregate*'.[26] The former might need to unite with the aim of collectively satisfying their will to power, but it would be against their inclination. The weak, on the other hand, positively enjoy the life of the herd, with the protection it brings. Nietzsche was, not surprisingly, opposed to parliamentary government, because it was one of the means 'by which the herd animal becomes master'.[27]

It is, however, in his unwillingness to talk of any form of equality, and his eagerness to divide people into 'higher and lower men' that Nietzsche's vision is most disquieting in its consequences. He was prepared to say that a single individual could justify the existence of whole millennia. Modern types of mass society may stifle genius and bring everyone to the level of the mediocre, but Nietzsche is saying more. He appears to believe that some matter more than others. Perhaps it is more accurate to say that since no one matters at all, because there is no God, it is within the power only of the exceptional few to master themselves and their environment. Apparently liberated from the bondage of sin and guilt, the self-sufficient hero can obtain control of his destiny. Social bonds and conventions are regarded as stifling, the product of an outmoded religion. Custom is seen as oppressive. Pity is despised.

## Contemporary Relevance

Nietzsche is an enigmatic writer, using a literary style for the most part instead of the rigorous arguments of the philosopher. His views developed over time, the idea of the eternal recurrence, for example, coming to fruition comparatively late, as he tried to cope with the prospect of nihilism. Just as he was much given to emphasizing the role of interpretation, so his own work can be interpreted in different ways. Many disparate thinkers can still claim Nietzsche as an influence.

There are many important strands in his thoughts. His emphasis on the role of our instincts rather than our reason, his insistence that the soul is only a word for something about the body, his recognition of humans as the originators of their own values, are all significant. Most crucial of all, however, is his attack on Christianity and the Christian God, although he is not the only influential atheist of modern times. Marx and Freud have played their parts in undermining religion. Nietzsche, however, was remorseless in drawing out the consequences of the so-called 'death of God'. He saw how meaningless human life could be without God. His solution, of affirming rather than denying life, even to the point of willing to return eternally, has appealed to those who approach life as an artist coming to an empty canvas, glorying in their freedom to create as they will. His thought has in fact a great attraction for the modern age. As human control over the environment has increased, and science and technology give us greater power, it has been easy to assume that we can indeed become 'lords of the earth' (a phrase of Nietzsche which has often been quoted). We have, it appears, 'come of age'.

Perhaps we humans can be self-sufficient, not needing a grovelling dependence on some higher Being. Certainly when this feeling was coupled with a belief in progress, which it was easy to derive from Darwinism, the result could be an unbridled optimism. Anything could appear possible if we have the will. Yet the history of the twentieth century, since the death of Nietzsche, is far from reassuring. The greater power given us by science can be used for terrible purposes as well as noble ones. The rejection of the traditional categories of good and evil, and the discarding of the concepts of sin and guilt, have not increased the sum of human happiness. Indeed, it could be argued that they have helped us ignore the dangers always lurking because of basic facts about human nature.

Above all, the simple questions about the meaning and purpose of human life keep reoccurring. If life only has the meaning we each choose to give it, there seems little to prevent us falling into the despair induced by nihilism. Everything can seem totally arbitrary, if there is no purpose built into the very nature of things, with any choice as good as any other. Total paralysis might be the only response to such a belief. Nietzsche believed that without the existence of the Christian God, and without a substantial self able to survive the death of the body, the spectre of nihilism grew ever more real. Indeed his nihilism was so far-reaching that it not only highlighted the lack of purpose in human life and undermined prevailing conceptions of morality. It also questioned the objectivity of the world. He removed the constraint which a firm belief in reality places on our thoughts and beliefs, and together with it the possibility of truth and falsehood. Instead his stress was on the perspective from which we make judgements, and the flux in which things 'become' rather than statically 'are'. Yet paradoxically he still valued truthfulness, and points out that it is a Christian virtue, eventually serving to demolish Christianity. He also seemed to have some faith in science. If, however, he is to be consistent, *nothing* can be rejected as false or accepted as true, unless he is willing to hold that our interpretations are always *of something*.

Genuine nihilism is so self-defeating that it can never be consistently stated. A more restricted type, undermining religious and moral truth might seem possible. Nietzsche might, however, be right in considering that the assumption of order and stability in the world is at root theistic. He did have a conception of human nature, or at least of sub-personal forces influencing us all. He could not avoid believing that, in some respects at least, the world has a definite character, in that humans are creatures of a particular sort. What, however, his thought most clearly illustrates is not just the impossibility of stating nihilism coherently. It is the challenge to each of us to find a rationale for living our lives. The problem Nietzsche posed was whether it is possible to have one, if it cannot be derived from religion.

The denunciation of Platonism and Christianity as denigrators of life as it is raises questions at the heart of human existence. Can we accept our present life, or must we be ultimately dissatisfied with it? Do we feel that we ourselves often fall short of the best of which we are capable? Are we all in some way flawed? The idea that there is a goal we never quite reach can expand into a moral revulsion at the way things are, together with a yearning that they be put right. This need not involve a denial of life so much as its enhancement. It is *because* we feel it is precious that we feel it ought not to be like this. From urges like this come the quest for salvation, whether of a personal kind, as in Christianity, or at the political level, as in Marxism. Certainly the Christian doctrine of the Incarnation suggests an affirmation of the importance of human life rather than the reverse, while suggesting that we are not now as God intended us to be. The conviction that life has a direction goes quite naturally with the view that there is something wrong with it now. Nietzsche's idea of the eternal return effectively disposes of both views. We are on an eternal treadmill, going nowhere and accomplishing nothing. It is a bleak description of the human predicament and Nietzsche can offer no cure. Indeed his advocacy of the urge for domination in his 'will to power' may merely be adding to our problems.

# CHAPTER ELEVEN

# Freud

## 1856–1939

## Context

Scientific advances may have given us greater control of our environment, but it has become steadily more apparent that many of our real problems lie in ourselves. We are often swept along by forces within us of which we are only dimly aware. We find it difficult sometimes to deal with other people. The main obstacles to human happiness can lie within human nature itself. It is not surprising, therefore, that the thinker who has made one of the greatest impacts on the twentieth century has been someone who tried to offer a scientific diagnosis of what has gone wrong in human personality. As such, it offered a modern version of salvation to the individual. Through a fuller understanding of ourselves and the urges within us, we could, it seemed, each gain greater autonomy.

Sigmund Freud was born of a Jewish family in Moravia in 1856. He spent nearly all his life in Vienna, until he was finally forced into exile in London by the Nazi takeover of Austria. He died there in 1939. As he pointed out, his creation of psychoanalysis coincided with the birth of the twentieth century, since his major work on *The Interpretation of Dreams* was published in 1900. In it he argued that all dreams really have a secret meaning, which represents the fulfilment of a wish. As Freud put it, 'the interpretation of dreams is the royal road to a knowledge of the unconscious activities of the mind.'[1] This idea, that much and perhaps most of what takes place in the mind is unconscious, was of major importance. Freud regarded it as the fundamental premise of psychoanalysis. It meant however, that the images humans hold of themselves are likely to be only partially true. The human personality has depths, if Freud is right, which the conscious mind can never plumb.

There are instincts, it seems, within us of which we are unaware, and which we often do not want to acknowledge. This makes human rationality seem less important. If what we do is the result of powerful instinctual drives, which are unconscious, rather than of deliberate and rational decision, many traditional views of the human personality may seem at risk. In particular it may be questionable whether we are sufficiently in control of ourselves to be morally responsible. All this has clear links with the outlook of Nietzsche. The threat to human reason sounds familiar, together with the potential for unmasking the 'real motives' for an action in the place of professed ones. Freud claimed that he avoided Nietzsche's writings for a long time so as to keep his mind 'unembarrassed'. He was well aware of how much he was likely to agree with them and perhaps be influenced by them. He said of Nietzsche that his 'guesses and intuitions often agree in the most astonishing way with the laborious findings of psychoanalysis'.[2] It is likely, however, that Nietzsche's influence was more direct than Freud cared to admit.

A more certain influence was that of Darwin, whose theories strongly attracted Freud. The latter wrote that even as a schoolboy he had thought that 'they held out hopes of an extraordinary advance in our understanding of the world'.[3] He was in no doubt about the significance of Darwin in the development of our understanding of ourselves. He considered that science had dealt three principal blows to 'the naive self-love of men'. First, it was discovered that the earth was not the centre of the universe. The second was produced by Darwin and Wallace, when biology took away the privileged place we thought we had in creation and showed our animal nature. Freud continues as follows, perhaps with a certain lack of modesty:

> Human megalomania will have suffered its third and most wounding blow from the psychological research of the present time, which seeks to prove to the ego that it is not even master in its own house, but must content itself with scanty information of what is going on unconsciously in its mind.[4]

Freud recognized that powerful human feelings were hurt by this onslaught on the seeming importance and self-possession of our species, and so he was not surprised when he encountered fierce opposition. He pointed out that Darwin met the same problem, and he attributed the virulence of the attacks made to the 'resistance' of people to learning the truth about themselves. Opposition, for Freud, was merely further confirmation of the accuracy of what he was saying.

The most characteristic feature of psychoanalysis is its refusal to identify our mental life with what we are conscious of. It is often assumed that a dualist distinction between mind and body must identify mind and consciousness but this need not be so. There are dualists who would regard Freud's view of the unconscious as a valuable contribution to our understanding of mind. The theory purports to be an essential aid to the medical diagnosis of neuroses. Patients with nervous disorders hope to be cured through being psychoanalysed. Unfortunately the fact that psychoanalysis, as a theory, stands somewhere between medicine and philosophy, makes it vulnerable to attack from both directions. The unconscious is supposed to be the seat of the instinctual motives and emotions which drive us on to action, while at the same time it includes the 'meanings' and significance with which our mental processes are vested. Anything analogous to animal instinct, which is innate in us, would form 'the nucleus' of the unconscious,[5] but the repressed wishes which Freud believes surface in dreams are also held there. It is, in other words, the cause of much of our behaviour, but also includes the reasons for many of our experiences.

The distinction between reasons and causes is an important, but contentious, one. We can be ignorant of the causes operating on us, and be surprised when they are pointed out to us. Our reasons, however, are intimately connected with how we conceive what we are doing. A reason cannot be detached from how we understand our action. Freud's talk of the unconscious demonstrates the possibility that we may not always be aware of our reasons, and even refuse to admit them as our reasons. Self-deception is always a puzzling phenomenon but it represents a genuine part of human experience. We must, however, at some point be willing to accept our real reasons if they are presented to us. Unless we do, whatever our emotional resistance, it remains very questionable as to whether our reasons are as alleged.

Our understanding of the purpose of psychoanalysis is bound up with the possibility of contrasting reasons and causes. If someone underwent a traumatic experience in early childhood, and suffers a neurosis as a result, that seems a clear case of cause and effect. The more emphasis, however, which is put on unconscious memory, and the part it plays in the patient's life, the less relevant does the original cause of the memory become. One can maintain that psychoanalysis has to deal with the patient's reasoning alone, and that it is irrelevant whether the original event happened as remembered. What matters instead is what the patient is now making of the 'memory'. In other words, psychoanalysis can be made to appear a question of the interpretation of a patient's mental state. It investigates meanings and reasons, it might seem, rather than giving a scientific explanation of the original causes. Yet it does hanker after providing the latter. It hovers uneasily between being like the interpretation of a literary text, trying to produce its meaning, and being a genuine scientific theory, showing the interplay of cause and effect.

## Our Place in the World

Freud believed that science was the only path to genuine knowledge, so that any explanation of human nature had to be put in a setting acceptable to it. He considered the existence of the unconscious could be proved experimentally. He gives the example of post-hypnotic suggestion and tells of a case in which a doctor hypnotizes a patient and tells him that he is going to leave the ward but that, when he returns, the patient is to fetch the doctor's umbrella which had been left in a corner and hold it open over his head.[6] The doctor then brings the patient out of hypnosis and leaves. When he returns, the patient does exactly as he had been told and is asked what he is doing. He is embarrassed and gives some lame reason, such as that he thought the doctor would want his umbrella open before he left, as it was raining outside. This is clearly a rationalization, and the example suggests that we can be unaware of what is really prompting us to action. A corollary of this, not explicitly mentioned by Freud, is that we can imagine we are acting freely when we are not. The mere fact that we feel free does not mean we are. This has important implications for the question of free will.

Another example, given by Freud, of the possible working of the unconscious comes from slips of the tongue. They may, of course, be merely that, but Freud was inclined to read unconscious purpose and meaning into them. It was the same with the method of free association, which Freud made much of, in which a patient is asked to say the first thing he or she thinks of in a particular context. The idea was that unconscious thoughts can sometimes slip through into consciousness. The simple example of a slip of the tongue he gives is that of the president of the Lower House of the Austrian Parliament who opened a sitting by saying: 'I take notice that a full quorum of members is present and herewith declare the sitting *closed*.'[7] Freud considers that the president, having endured some stormy sessions, was really expressing his wish that it was all over.

Once it is accepted that beliefs and desires can be unconscious, a theory is required as to why this should be so. Freud was in no doubt that the experiences of childhood were crucial. He maintained that 'the child is psychologically father of the adult' and he looked particularly to any sexual experiences by the child as explanations for neurotic symptoms in adult life.[8] While there was evidence for the existence of the unconscious in ordinarily healthy people, it became an important factor in those who were mentally disturbed in some way. Freud believed that the trouble could be traced back to thought and wishes that had been deliberately pushed down or 'repressed' into the unconscious mind. Although not consciously accepted, for that very reason they had considerable power and were able to manifest themselves in unexpected ways, and even attach themselves to different objects through 'displacement'. What I consciously want may not be what I really want.

The place where our emotional life was formed, according to Freud, was the family. Our relationships with our mother and father are, he believed, of central importance. Because of his emphasis on the fact of infantile sexuality, understood in a wider sense, it is not surprising that he believed the relationships were sexual in origin. A child's wishes have, he considered, a strong sexual content. The first object of a boy's love is his mother, and of a girl's her father, while the other parent is viewed as a rival and often arouses strong hostility. Freud gave the name of the 'Oedipus Complex' to this state of affairs, after the Greek myth in which Oedipus killed his father and married his mother. He claimed that 'incestuous wishes are a primordial human heritage and have never been fully over-come'.[9] In normal development such wishes are given up, he believed, after the end of a child's early sexual period, at about 5 years of age. They then are transformed, but sometimes the revival of the complex could have serious consequences.

A constant theme in Freud's work was that the psychological development of the individual parallelled the history of the human race. He wrote that 'the deepest and eternal nature of man . . . lies in those impulses of the mind which have their roots in a childhood that has since become prehistoric.'[10] Our relationships with our parents mirror events prior to the formation of social institutions. In his work *Totem and Taboo*, Freud speculated that the father of the 'primal horde' kept all the women for himself and drove his sons away. They eventually, however, combined to kill, and devour, their father, but were so overwhelmed by guilt that they agreed to forgo possession of the women, and were driven to find unknown ones. Incest taboos arose, social organization was introduced, and here too, Freud thought, lay the origins of social and religious institutions. The consequences of an original sin rolled on through the generations, and appear in each individual life, as we struggle to replace our infantile longings with a more mature outlook.

Freud was inclined to treat this fanciful story as fact, but of greater significance is the problem of the connection between prehistory and the psychology of an individual. The only way that events of thousands of years ago could be thought to influence us is through a theory, such as that held by Lamarck, that acquired characteristics can be inherited. Darwin himself was occasionally tempted by it. If a giraffe makes its neck longer through stretching up for food, it might, it seems, pass this on to its offspring. Similarly a neurosis acquired in appalling circumstances in prehistory could perhaps influence the human race. Yet the theory goes against the neo-Darwinian belief that characteristics can only be passed on through genetic variation and natural selection. According to modern genetics, therefore, the effect of an experience on an individual cannot echo through succeeding generations.

Freud is also at odds with evolutionary theory in another respect, since he believed that the existence of incest taboos showed that they were there to restrain a powerful human instinct. There would be no need for them if we did not secretly nurse incestuous wishes. He says crisply that 'the view which explains the horror of incest as an innate instinct must be abandoned'.[11] Yet according to neo-Darwinian theory, there could be no genetic basis for incestuous desires. Despite his scientific bias, Freud is at odds with important aspects of biological theory. Nevertheless, much of what he says about the importance of a child's early upbringing and of his family relationship in the formation of character, remains illuminating. The way we each make our way in the world, when we have grown up, is undoubtedly influenced by our childhood experiences, and by the kind of family we were born into. The significance of family life for a child's psychological development is undoubted.

## What is it to be Human?

The most striking and controversial aspect of Freud's view of human nature is his emphasis on sexuality, whether repressed or not, as a motive for human action. It was such a marked feature of psychoanalysis that Freud had to deny strenuously the charge of 'pansexualism', which, he conceded, was often levelled at him.[12] He did not believe that sexual motives were the only ones however much they masqueraded in other clothing. He did believe they were the most potent forces in human life, and that sexual factors were the main causes of neurotic illness. He comments that he used to warn his pupils not to pre-judge the issue by introducing the sexual factor before the patient did. He did not want to spoil the chance of finding a case where it played no part. He wryly remarks that 'so far none of us has had that good fortune'.[13]

Typical of the way in which Freud tries to show that adult emotions are transmuted childish ones is his treatment of the fear of death.[14] He likens the situation to the infantile one in which a child fears desertion by the forces protecting him or her. Freud refers to the 'anxiety-state of birth', and the anxiety induced by separation from the protecting mother. He then talks of 'the fear of death, like the fear of conscience, as a development of the fear of castration'. This well illustrates how Freud looks to early experiences, linked to sexuality, such as threats of castration, as the source of many adult emotions. Yet the fear of death would seem sufficiently natural not to stand in need of further explanation. From an evolutionary point of view, indeed, it is clear that anyone not afraid of death would be less likely to survive and have descendants.

Another issue facing psychoanalysis, as it delves back to our earliest experiences as far as birth, is how relevant for its purposes it should regard events which occurred before an infant could be expected to remember. It does not seem likely that psychoanalysis could help a patient to recall repressed memories from the earliest months of life, even though it is possible that very early experiences may contribute to the contents of the unconscious mind. Certainly, though, a prime function of psychoanalysis is to control the power of the unconscious by bringing repressed wishes and thoughts into consciousness. Freud believed that it was easier to control them if we faced them for what they were. He said: 'Therapeutic success, however, is not our primary aim: we endeavour rather to enable the patient to obtain a conscious grasp of his unconscious wishes.'[15] His idea was that repression did not reduce the energy behind a desire, but that the energy would have to find another outlet. He had a rather materialist view of nervous energy contained within a system and tended to think in hydraulic terms of its being dammed up, channelled, or discharged. The power of sexual instincts came, he believed, because they were insufficiently tamed, and were dealt with in a manner which Freud considered was psychologically wrong.

Freud recognized that desire, and particularly sexual desire, could not remain unchecked, and that because of this there was considerable scope for conflict within each individual. He wanted us to reach an internal harmony, recognizing and accepting the nature of our impulses, but he was fully aware of the different influences fighting together in the human personality. His original distinction between the 'unconscious' and the 'conscious' proved too simple a model, and in 1923 he proposed a three-fold dissection of the human personality into what he termed the 'ego', the 'super-ego' and the 'id'. The distinction between conscious and unconscious was still important. The 'id', as the seat of our passions, was unconscious. The 'ego', which was 'a bodily ego', rather than a separated 'soul', represents 'what may be called reason and common sense'.[16] The judging activity of conscience, on the other hand, resides in the so-called 'super-ego'.

Freud was not the first thinker to propose a tripartite division of the human personality, and there are striking analogies between the distinctions made by Plato and those of Freud. Plato, too, had inferred division from the fact of internal conflict, and, across the Darwinian divide, Plato and Freud are strangely akin. There may have been some direct influence, although Freud remarked in 1933 that his knowledge of Plato was very fragmentary. Certainly Freud's id corresponds to Plato's view of the appetitive part of the soul, except that the latter was largely conscious. A comparison can be made between the super-ego and the spirited element, particularly in so far as each can be a source of guilt, and are non-rational influences. Finally, the rational element of the soul for Plato, has its counterpart in Freud's ego, which is the part of the personality open to the influences of the external world. Both aim for what is real and try to direct the passions, although Plato's conception of what was real differed markedly from that of Freud's. The latter was content with the world shown us by science, and held a less grand view of the role of reason than Plato did.

Freud's particular concern was the way in which inner conflict can give rise eventually to mental illness. The super-ego, for instance, inherits the role of parents in its threat to the ego. Freud says that 'it represents the claims of morality, and we realize all at once that our moral sense of guilt is the expression of the tension between the ego and super-ego.'[17] He regards the super-ego as the heir of childhood's Oedipus Complex.[18] In linking the force of morality with the child's relationship with parents, Freud was in danger of following Nietzsche and undercutting its authority. Displaying its alleged psychological origins makes morality seem merely the demands of our parents, which go on echoing through adult life.

The fundamental theme of the division between conscious and unconscious remains a complicated one. Freud could not assume reason and conscience were always conscious, since he knew that repression could be a product of a sense of guilt, and that was a matter for the super-ego. Patients often showed 'resistance' in analysis, not wanting to admit certain truths, and not even being conscious of such resistance. Freud accepted that 'large portions of the ego and super-ego can remain unconscious and are normally unconscious'.[19] Yet this means that the ego, perhaps under orders from the super-ego, is essentially hiding something *from itself* if it represses it. Why, though, should the ego and super-ego try both to be aware and unaware of the same thing at the same time? If they already know what it is that they are repressing, what does repression accomplish? This is the paradox of self-deception and Freud's tripartite division does nothing to meet the problem. Whether the self is regarded as deliberately deceiving itself, or the super-ego and ego keep elements of themselves ignorant, the self, or its parts, still seem to have to be aware of what they are simultaneously

unconscious. Nevertheless, whatever its explanation, the phenomenon is real enough. There can be a deep level of irrationality in
our inner selves, if reality becomes too uncomfortable to face.

Freud saw that the ego can be put under intolerable strain by
many conflicting pressures. He says it has 'three tyrannical masters,
the external world, the super-ego, and the id'.[20] The ego has to admit
its weakness, and the result is anxiety. Freud regarded the purpose of
psychoanalysis to strengthen the ego, so that it was in greater
control of the influences swaying it. He wanted it to be more independent from the super-ego, and to be so organized as to make more
positive use of the subterranean forces of the id. He resoundingly
says: 'Where id was, there ego shall be.'[21] He believed that the ego's
weakest point lay in its attitude to sexuality, and he speculated as to
whether this was the psychological expression of a tension between
the 'biological antithesis between self-preservation and the preservation of the species'.[22] The instincts of the id demand satisfaction,
being geared to obtaining pleasure and avoiding 'unpleasure'. Freud
calls this 'the pleasure principle', but he recognized that the ego had
to face what was real even if it were disagreeable. This was the
'reality principle'. Thus the ego had a basic instinct of self-preservation, with an associated need to recognize the difficulties of the
external world. The search for pleasure has often to be subordinated
to the demands of life, and Freud talks of 'the temporary toleration of
unpleasure as a step on the long indirect road to pleasure'.[23]

For Freud, as for Hume, the power in human life comes from our
instinctual life. Reason can control, but never finally dominate, our
passions. The whole message of his work is that refusal to recognize
the power and influence of our sexuality is going to produce tension,
anxiety and mental disorder. Echoing Plato's image of the charioteer, he writes of the ego: 'In its relation to the id it is like a man on
horseback, who has to hold in check the superior strength of the
horse: with the difference, that the rider tries to do so with his own
strength, while the ego uses borrowed forces.'[24] Reason, for Freud,
can never be truly sovereign.

## Human Society

The concentration in psychoanalysis on the individual might seem
to leave little scope for reflection on the nature of society. That is its

attraction for many. Marxist theory, on the other hand, leaves untouched many of the most pressing concerns and anxieties that beset individuals. Yet the emphasis on instinct in human life, and the stress on sexuality poses a question for any society. Any combination of people living together demands some restraint on individuals. No one can have what they want whenever they want it, since the wishes of others have to be taken into account. Freud appears to teach that repression is bad, but civilization for its very survival does need something like the repression of instincts, because, if unchecked, they would surely destroy it.

Freud accepts this, regarding morality and the demands of civilization as imposing essential constraints on human nature. They are not an outworking of that nature, but are unnatural curbs on it. This portrays human society as fundamentally unstable, trying to contain forces hostile to its very existence. Such an image may not be reassuring, but it may be true to life. Freud believes the battle between primordial human instinct and civilization to be inevitable, but he, partly at least, regrets the necessity for not being able to give our basic desires free rein. Thus he says that 'civilization is built upon a renunciation of instinct'[25] and that it has 'to be defended against the individual'.[26] Nevertheless he remarks that 'the sexual life of civilized man is notwithstanding severely impaired'.[27]

The situation is complicated by the notion of a duality of instincts, which Freud elaborated in his later life. Beside that of Eros, the sexual instinct, he came to believe there was also an 'instinct of death', Thanatos.[28] Civilization was the scene of a basic struggle between the forces of life and those of death. Whereas Eros could provide a way of combining individuals and forming the basis of society, Freud also believed there was an aggressive instinct, set apart from any sexual promptings, which aimed at destruction. This could be turned in on the ego as its source and is particularly expressed in the form of a harsh conscience. Above all, however, the inclination to aggression, which Freud described as an 'original, self-subsisting instinctual disposition in man' constituted a major threat to civilization.[29]

A tendency to self-destruction in an individual may seem fanciful, and there is the question how natural selection could ever have allowed such an instinct to gain a foothold. Nevertheless Freud was developing this theory after the First World War, and modern history has certainly provided plenty of evidence of the human urge to destruction. He was convinced that the roots of aggressiveness lay deep in the human psyche. He argued against the communist view that it could have been created by the institution of private property. He said that if personal rights over material wealth were abolished, the area of sexual relationships would still provide opportunities for aggression. Allowing complete sexual freedom without any of the restrictions imposed by the fact of family life would not help. Calling the family 'the germ-cell of civilization' he said that its removal would not affect the aggressiveness which, he believed, was an 'indestructible feature of human nature'.[30]

Primitive people, said Freud, were in one way better off in having no restrictions, so that they could achieve happiness through giving free rein to their deepest and strongest desires.[31] They would not survive, however, to enjoy much happiness for very long. Freud explicitly adopts an Hobbesian notion of a 'state of nature' from which civilization must rescue us. His concentration on the problems of individuals inevitably leads him to conceive of society as the result of their combination under a social contract. He knew that we would all be in serious trouble without the renunciation of instinct demanded by civilization. Yet even though we need protection, Freud is more than a little attracted by the state of nature. Envisaging the possibility of having sexual relations with whom one pleased, killing whoever gets in one's way, and making off with other people's possessions, he remarks 'how splendid, what a string of satisfactions one's life would be'.[32] The impossibility of such a state of affairs, with its inherent dangers, cannot altogether remove some of its desirability. Freud does believe in civilization just as he accepts the crucial role of family life, but he knows how both bring problems in their wake. Indeed the two are indivisibly linked, since the demands of civilization make their appearance in the context of the family, as children are brought up. Freud still reflects, though, that 'it is easy for a barbarian to be healthy, for a civilized man the task is hard'.[33]

One major aspect of civilization was dismissed by Freud. He did not think a religious impulse was an integral part of human nature or a necessary part of the structure of society. He believed that science provided the 'only road' to a knowledge of reality outside ourselves.[34] Like Nietzsche he looked for the origins of religion and discovered them within human beings. Freud held that religion was derived from human wishes. Just as a child is helpless and needs to be dependent on its parents, so, he thought, an adult's reaction to helplessness is to look for dependence on a heavenly Father. Freud classified religion as an illusion. This did not mean it was necessarily false, since sometimes wishes can come true. He felt, though, that his explanation discredited religion. It was 'so patently infantile, so foreign to reality', a product of the immature side of human reality.[35] This view, coupled with the idea that conscience can only be the product of the influence of our family and society, removes the possibility, it seems, of religion and morality having any independent authority. Freud's views on these matters are, in essence, not so very different from those of Nietzsche.

## Contemporary Relevance

The urge to accept and to understand our basic impulses, rather than to judge and condemn them runs deep in modern consciousness. Yet, as Freud himself recognized when he talked of a 'death-instinct', human nature is not always very lovable. The desire for self-knowledge, followed by self-acceptance, runs up against the fact that society cannot tolerate some human impulses. Repression, in the sense of running away from one's impulses and not admitting their existence, may be undesirable, but control is undoubtedly necessary. Freud demonstrated the fact of conflict within human personality, but emphasized the importance of instinct, a concept on the borders of the physiological and the mental, at the expense of human reason. The more we are unconscious of our impulses, the less authority reason can have. Even when brought to consciousness, Freud believed that they can be channelled but never totally changed. For him, as for Hume, reason must be the slave of our passions. Yet the corollary of this, that we shall not cherish guilt but accept ourselves as we are, is highly appealing to many who would otherwise be nearly paralysed by guilt and regret for past actions. The prospect of freedom from guilt is indeed a liberating one.

Attacking reason, however, can be hazardous as we saw in the case of Nietzsche. Freud himself recognized that science laid claim to rationality and truth. After commenting on how a scientific view reduces human importance, as compared with a religious outlook, he continues: 'None the less, some of the primitive belief in omnipotence still survives in man's faith in the power of the human mind, which grapples with the laws of reality.'[36] Yet the paradox remains that, in the name of science, psychoanalysis has shown how the apparent power of the mind is all too often derived from non-rational factors such as a desire for the fulfilment of one's wishes. Freud said that science was no illusion, but once rationality is unmasked in one area as being something other than it appears, it is difficult to stop the process.

The problem is most acute with reference to psychoanalysis in particular. We all want to be liberated in some way from the darker side of our nature and freed from guilt. Religion has traditionally tried to meet these needs, and psychoanalysis self-evidently does too. Yet why should the one be dismissed as illusion while the other is accepted as science? What grounds are there for thinking that psychoanalytic theory is actually correct? Arguments even rage as to how effective it is in producing medical cures. Many people are helped merely by talking over their troubles with someone, whether it is an analyst, a clergyman or someone else. Others are aided by being given a coherent theory or 'story' with which to view their life. Some illnesses undergo spontaneous remission and are cured without outside help. Once these factors are discounted, it is enormously difficult to judge how much psycho-analysis achieves.

The position is complicated by the question of what happens during the process of analysis. The theory assumes that a patient is unlikely to accept immediately the motives and intentions attributed to him or her. There will be 'resistance' and the role of the analyst is to induce the patient to abandon this. At this point, the notion of 'transference' is introduced, according to which the patient develops an emotional attachment to the analyst and accepts the analyst's authority. Yet when any refusal to accept a particular interpretation or diagnosis of one's psychological condition is dismissed as resis-tance, and when the analyst is in a position to impose theories, the fact that patients finally agree to the accounts given them of their lives is hardly surprising. The more they disagree, the more analysts will believe they are correct. Yet, as many philosophers have argued, how in that case could it be shown that the psychoanalyst is in error? It seems hard to distinguish between someone being given a narrative with which to see life as a coherent whole, with a meaning running through it, and actually being given a scientific account of the cause of a distressing illness.

The philosopher Wittgenstein epitomized a certain reaction to Freud when he said that Freud had propounded a 'new myth'. He went further and claimed that analysis would be likely to do harm. He continued:

> Because although one may discover in the course of it various things about oneself, one must have a very strong and keen and persistent criticism in order to recognize and see through the mythology that is offered or imposed on one. There is an inducement to say, "Yes, of course, it must be like that." A powerful mythology.'[37]

What is at issue is how far Freudian theory can claim truth. It is itself the product of the very human rationality which Freud has led us to distrust. His own theories may be subject to the same doubts about the motives behind them that he raises concerning other products of human consciousness. For his views to be given the attention they claim, they must purport to be true, and hence, if possible, complement other scientific theories about human nature. It is relevant that in some areas, for instance about incest, psychoanalytic theory is seriously at odds with neo-Darwinian biology. They both cannot be completely right. Freud was writing before the advent of modern genetics and did not recognize the tension. There are ways in which the insights of Freud and Darwin might be combined, but not without some modification of Freudian theory. Yet one thing is certain. No thinker in the twentieth century has had such an effect on how we all perceive ourselves and each other. Some of the technical terms of psychoanalysis are now part of our everyday vocabulary. After Freud, human nature can never seem quite the same again.

# CHAPTER TWELVE

# Wittgenstein

## *1889–1951*

## Context

Ludwig Wittgenstein would probably have denied that he had any ideas of human nature. His approach to philosophy was directly opposed to making generalizations or building systems of belief. He did not put forward a unified theory, and his writings are in every sense of the word fragmentary. Most have been published posthumously, and mainly consist of numbered sections, often containing only one sentence and as often asking a question as answering it. To understand his points, one has to be gripped by the same problems and be willing to think with him. Usually his writings are translated from the German, although some of his work appeared first in English. This gives a clue to the complexity of his background, since he straddles several distinct tendencies in twentieth-century philosophy.

Wittgenstein did his main philosophic work in Cambridge, working, to begin with, under Betrand Russell. As a result, he published in 1921 his *Tractatus Logico-Philosophicus*, a difficult work in which he argued that the function of language was to picture reality. Words gain their meaning through naming. His work was sometimes associated with that of the Vienna Circle, an influential group of philosophers meeting in Vienna in the 1920s and early 1930s, who advocated a 'scientific world-conception'. Their work was popularized in English by A. J. Ayer in his *Language, Truth and Logic*. For them, the sole standard of meaning was that provided by the empirical researches of science. Apart from what was true by definition, the only test of truth is what is verifiable or falsifiable in science. This meant that, for example, the assertions of religion, or

philosophers, it is difficult to put him in any category. His connections with the science-based philosophy of the English-speaking
world are apparent, but he was also a German philosopher. He
came from the same intellectual and cultural milieu as Freud, and
was aware of the writings of Nietzsche. The most marked characteristic of his work, however, is the way in which his philosophical
outlook underwent a cataclysmic change. From the 1930s onwards
he repudiated the opinions of the author of the *Tractatus*. He turned
from viewing language as the mirror of reality, and instead stressed
its many different functions. He came to believe that the meaning of
words was not given through their association with particular
objects but from the way they were used. Language could not be
torn apart from its social context. With the publication in 1953 of
the *Philosophical Investigations*, the 'later' Wittgenstein's influence
has grown progressively. There are continuities with the earlier
work. The importance of language is still stressed, to such an extent
that Wittgenstein was associated in people's minds with the whole
movement of so-called 'linguistic philosophy'. He was not, however,
talking *only* of language or worried about the meanings of words for
their own sake. It is, he believed, through language and its place in
our lives that we discover all that is distinctively human.

## Our Place in the World

According to Wittgenstein's later philosophy, language must always
be understood in its context. It cannot be torn out of the human life
and practices in which it is taught and used. He was fond of using
the term 'language-game', to emphasize how language cannot be
peeled away from the activities 'into which it is woven'.[3] He writes
that 'the term "language-*game*" is meant to bring into prominence
the fact that the *speaking* of language is part of an activity, or of a
form of life.'[4] In fact, Wittgenstein's idea of philosophy was to
investigate the various ways language is used, on the grounds that
language is such an integral part of human life, moulding it and
making it what it is. For him philosophy was primarily descriptive,
freeing us of misconceptions and misunderstandings created by a
wrong view of how language is actually functioning. It is all too
easy, he thought, for us to assume that language always works in
the same way, and to imagine, for example, that the word 'pain'

the statements of aesthetics and ethics, could have no claim to trut
Along with all metaphysics, or what is not within the scope
physics, they were to be consigned to the category of the mear
ingless, unless they could be given some harmless function a
expressions of emotion, or of intentions to live in a particular way.

It is now generally recognized that the *Tractatus* is a much mor
subtle work than the members of the Vienna Circle recognized
Wittgenstein ends the work with the enigmatic utterance tha
'what we cannot speak about, we must pass over in silence.'[1] Ye
he did not think that what we passed over was unimportant. He had
a strong sense of what he termed the 'mystical' and took very
seriously the questions he associated with it of value and the meaning
of life. Just because language had limits did not mean, he thought,
that what lay beyond them could be dismissed as of no account.
Typical of his attitude is his remark that 'it is not how things are in
the world that is mystical, but that it exists'.[2] There are clearly
resonances in the work that go beyond the emerging world of the
twentieth-century professional philosopher, who has always wanted
to abstract the so-called 'technical' problems of philosophy from their
wider cultural background. The result has often been a concentration
on logic and the philosophy of language, to the exclusion of issues of
more general human concern. The influence of his *Tractatus* helped
this process, but its own origins were not so clear-cut.

Those who primarily think of Wittgenstein as a pupil of Russell in
Cambridge from 1912 forget that he came from a very different
background. He was born in 1889 in Vienna, then the cultural
and political hub of the Austro-Hungarian empire. His family was
wealthy, and the composer, Brahms, was one of their friends. Wittgenstein's own career was chequered. His first academic interests lay
in engineering and he studied aeronautics, but he eventually turned
to philosophy, giving away his wealth. He served in the Austrian
army in the First World War, and spent some years after as an
ordinary schoolteacher. He returned to Cambridge in 1929, becom
ing Professor of Philosophy in 1939. Even then, however, he pre
ferred to work as a hospital porter and then in a medical laborator
during the war. He resigned his chair in 1947 and died in 1951. H
gave every appearance of being a tormented man, but when he die
he said that it had been a wonderful life.

Because his background and life were so unusual and his wo
strikingly original, with little obvious dependence on oth

refers to pains in the same way that 'house' picks out houses. We then think of pain as a private object, on analogy with public objects. He wishes to cure us of the ways in which we are misled by the superficial features of language. Instead, we should attend to the 'grammar' or logic of what is said, and that means looking to see how a word is used, and in what circumstances it is taught to others. To take 'pain' again, Wittgenstein wished to stress that we do not learn the word through introspection. If we did, we might each mean something different by it. Instead, the use of the word, including the way it is originally taught, has to be linked to public events and behaviour, so that we can all see if anyone is misusing it. Wittgenstein says: 'A child has hurt himself and he cries, and then adults talk to him and teach exclamations and later sentences. They teach the child new pain-behaviour.'[5]

In trying to free us from the illusions into which we are sometimes led by language, Wittgenstein regarded his work as a kind of therapy. He did not aim to provide a rational foundation for our beliefs since 'philosophy leaves everything as it is.'[6] He tried to bring 'words back from their metaphysical to their everyday use' and was totally opposed to the grand system-building indulged in sometimes by metaphysics. Philosophy's task was not constructive in the sense that it could aspire to giving us reasons for living or grounds for our knowledge. Wittgenstein said crisply: 'The philosopher's treatment of a question is like the treatment of an illness.'[7] In fact, there are surprising affinities between the work of Freud and that of Wittgenstein. Both believed that people were not necessarily aware of the true state of affairs and evolved methods to unmask what is really the case. While Freud's concern was the psychology of the individual, Wittgenstein's was the collective use of language. Wittgenstein did sometimes accept the analogy, recognizing that when, for example, we try to understand the nature of mathematics, we tend to repress certain doubts.[8] His response is: 'I say to those repressed doubts: you are quite correct, go on asking, demand clarification.' Overall, however, he took exception to the suggestion that his philosophy was like psychoanalysis, saying that the techniques were quite different.

If the most significant feature about us is that we are language-users, what is our nature apart from the use of language? The traditional idea of the self assumed that I existed before I learnt language, and that deaf-mutes and infants are persons, despite their lack of language. The assumption was that we are each separate entities, perhaps even distinct from our bodies and that our existence is an all or nothing affair. The mind, or soul, which gives us our individuality, is somehow locked inside us. That view has been derided by Gilbert Ryle, the Oxford philosopher and younger contemporary of Wittgenstein. Ryle summed it up as holding that there is a ghost in the machine. In essentials, the position is that of Descartes, who in the seventeenth century recognized that he could be mistaken about everything but the fact that he was thinking. His famous conclusion was 'I think, therefore I am' (*Cogito, ergo sum*). He could imagine himself even without a body, but, he says, 'I could not for all that conceive that I was not.' He held that he was a substance whose whole nature was to think, not needing any place, nor depending on any material thing. He continued: 'So that this "me", that is to say the soul by which I am what I am, is entirely distinct from body, and is even more easy to know than the latter: and even if body were not, the soul would not cease to be what it is.'[9]

The self, which is the subject of all thought and experience, is what 'I' really am, according to this view. Language, in that case, is something I use, and not the major formative influence on me, making me what I am. The individuality of each of us is assured because it is fixed and determinate *before* we enter a community.

The more the importance of language is stressed, the more the dualist view of Descartes comes under attack. Language is of its nature public and shareable, and not private and secret. This at least was what Wittgenstein attempted to establish. It is easy to have a picture of each of us trying to come into contact with a pre-existing reality and using language as a tool with which to describe it. Our understanding of that reality may be independent of language. If language, however, is given priority, the contrast between the private beliefs of individuals and the objective world becomes harder to sustain. A public language, with rules that everyone must follow, sets the norms. The world is limited by the possibilities of language, and our own concepts, the way we make sense of the world, have to be understood in linguistic terms. Analysing language then shows the way we think since we cannot think in any focused or determinate way without language.

Does this mean that infants cannot think, merely because they have not mastered language? Does it mean that I cannot feel pain until I have been taught how to use the word 'pain'? These are difficult questions for Wittgenstein. He says, for instance: 'You learned the *concept* "pain" when you learned language.'[10] He believed that an 'inner process' stands in need of outward criteria. Everything we think is private in fact gains its sense from its surroundings. Intending something is not, according to Wittgenstein, a private feeling, but is linked to the use of a word, which in turn gains its sense from its context. He says: 'An intention is embedded in its situation, in human customs and institutions.'[11]

Wittgenstein quotes from William James the recollections of a nineteenth-century deaf-mute, Mr Ballard, who wrote that before he acquired language, he had had thoughts about God and the world.[12] A Cartesian view of the self would find no difficulty in this, but any emphasis on language makes it difficult to understand how there could be wordless thoughts. Wittgenstein is unhappy about the example, finds the man's recollection a 'queer memory phenomenon' and does not know what conclusions to draw. It is clear enough that he is suspicious of the possibility of any coherent mental life, let alone a rich one, without language. The human world has to be a linguistic one. It is the possession of language that makes us distinctively human and it is language which gives us the categories with which we can conceive of the world we inhabit.

## What is it to be Human?

The attack on the Cartesian notion of the self is implicit rather than explicit in what Wittgenstein says. He certainly wishes to cast doubts on the assumption that we can understand others by comparison with ourselves. Philosophers have often taken it for granted that we can be sure of what goes on in our own minds even if we have to guess what happens in other people's. The argument from analogy has held that we can assume that other people are like ourselves. If we feel a pain, we can reasonably assume that others will do so as well in a similar situation.

Yet Wittgenstein's emphasis on public shared criteria make it doubtful whether we can always properly apply the correct criteria to ourselves. What becomes problematic is not our grasp of the contents of other people's minds but of those of our own. Wittgenstein was horrified that one should 'so irresponsibly' generalize from only one case (that of our own feelings), as the argument from analogy makes us do.[13] Instead he argued that we could not be sure of identifying the contents of our minds properly, if we thought of them as 'private objects'.

The example of pain was a favourite one of Wittgenstein, and it is a particularly striking one when we think of the private contents of our minds, which seem impossible to share. We all know how difficult it is to describe pain even when it is medically important to do so. Pain, above all, seems to be a distinctive kind of sensation, different from itches, electric shocks, nausea or other types of unpleasant sensation. Wittgenstein, however, argued that there cannot be a private language, known only to one individual and referring to his or her private sensations. It is perhaps significant that he could only think of determinate private experience in terms of language, and he set out to show that a language which could not be taught to others was impossible.

If I kept a diary about the recurrence of a certain sensation, Wittgenstein wondered how I could be sure that if I wrote down 'S' whenever I have it, I would always be right. How could I concentrate on the sensation in such a way that I would always recognize it correctly as the same one again? There is no external check, and, in fact, whatever seems right to me will be right, even if my memory is faulty and it is no longer the same type of sensation. There is no criterion of correctness. Wittgenstein concludes that this only means that here we can't talk about 'right'.[14] It is not enough to have one's own private rule. Wittgenstein believes that rules like that are no rules at all. Anyone who plays a game in which what-ever seems a good rule to an individual at any moment is acceptable, will soon find there is no game left. It would be impossible to break the rules and that means it is impossible to play the game properly. Wittgenstein held that obeying a rule must be a public and social practice, with independent checks on whether the rule are kept. He continues: 'And to *think* one is obeying a rule is not to obey a rule. Hence it is not possible to obey a rule "privately", otherwise thinking one was obeying a rule would be the same as obeying it.'[15]

Someone might argue that we can always check our judgements by means of memory. I know that this pain is the same as I had last week and that I used a particular word to describe it, because I remember. Yet this is not an independent justification for Wittgen-stein, since I am describing the contents of my mind with an appeal to other beliefs I have. He comments that this kind of process is like buying several copies of the same morning paper to check that what it said was true.[16] He offered the following as advice: 'Always get rid of the idea of the private object in this way: assume that it constantly changes, but that you do not notice the change because your memory constantly deceives you.'[17]

We must not think of our private experiences as if they were objects in the public world. Yet this means, Wittgenstein believes, that there is no basis for thinking that *any* description is correct. The distinction between correctness and error is removed, he held, when error cannot, in principle, be detected.

Wittgenstein was certain that language has many different functions apart from the description of objects. He uses as an analogy to the language of sensations, the example of people having boxes and giving the name of 'beetle' to whatever was in them.[18] 'No one can look into anyone else's box', suggests Wittgenstein, 'and everyone says he knows what a beetle is only by looking at *his* beetle'. In those circumstances, everyone could have something different in their boxes, and it could even be constantly changing. The contents play no part in the use of the word 'beetle'. The box could be empty, and 'beetle' still mean 'whatever, if anything, is in the box'. Wittgenstein therefore argues that 'if we construe the grammar of the expression of sensation on the model of "object and designation" the object drops out of consideration as irrelevant.' The words we use for our sensations are not the names of things to which we each have private access. Such a basis is too flimsy for even our private understanding of what we mean. The use of a word like 'pain' has to be linked to public behaviour, so that I can be corrected if I misuse it.

We learn the word 'pain' in a public context and that anchors its meaning. Wittgenstein uses the concept of pain as a model for all other concepts, which appear to refer to private experience. He is adamant that meaning cannot be a private matter, and that what goes on in my mind is secondary to the public criteria formed in a particular way of life, which serve to fix the meaning of any word. Yet it is easy to feel that somehow the importance of one's mental life and its characteristically 'inward' nature is being denied. Wittgenstein says that 'the human body is the best picture of the human soul'.[19] It may sometimes seem as if his stress on the importance of behaviour in the learning of concepts which apparently apply to our mental life results from a lingering desire to accept only what is accessible to science. Some have suggested that the force of the argument against a private language rests on the assumption that linguistic meaning can only be given to what is publicly checkable. They have pointed out that in essence that is the verification principle of the Vienna Circle. Matters are, though, more complicated. Wittgenstein accepted that there could be no greater difference than pain-behaviour accompanied by pain and that without any.[20] He denied he was saying that a sensation was a 'nothing'. In typically paradoxical manner, he said: 'It is not a *something*, but not a *nothing* either.' He does not wish to deny the existence of pains or pretend that we are numb. He is just insisting that the feeling can play no part in the application of the concept.

At this point, however, doubts must arise. We do not just have inner experiences in the case of pain. We also rely on our senses to identify and re-identify objects in the public world. Concepts cannot be taught unless we can independently recognize things. It is all very well, for instance, saying a child learns the concept of dog when he or she learns language. The meaning of the word could not be grasped in the first place, unless it is possible to identify independently instances of the same kind of animal, and, in particular, see it as a separate animal, detached from its background. Blind children are handicapped in learning language. Words for colour are particularly difficult for them. Experience of the world is an indispensable precondition for learning which words apply to which bits. We have to pick out the bits first. The teaching and learning of language, together with translation between languages, presupposes that all languages refer to one common world, and that we can each experience the world in roughly similar ways. Wittgenstein, however, would disagree. For him, the world is merely the world as revealed in language. The later Wittgenstein would not accept the metaphysical notion of a world, not seen through language but conceived apart from it. Similarly, he would not detach private experience from the use of language, or regard it as making language possible in the first place. For my experience to be talked about, it has itself to be anchored in the public world and linked conceptually to my behaviour. The constraints of language themselves shape experience, instead of private experience providing the foundation for language.

Language takes priority, and Wittgenstein did not think it possible to look beyond it or outside it. The main human characteristic is the use of language. The human world is a linguistic one, and must differ markedly from that of animals. Wittgenstein says that a dog may believe that his master is at the door, but asks whether 'he can also believe his master will come the day after tomorrow.'[21] In the end, as humans, we must rest content with being shown the working of language. All we can say, he thinks, is that 'this language-game is played'.[22] The workings of language set the limits of our world, and there is no way we can get outside all language to demonstrate its inadequacies. The only means we have of understanding ourselves are linguistic, and, because of this, the self can be seen as the creation of language. The private world depends on the public one. Our humanity is both expressed in, and created by, language. In a real sense, according to Wittgenstein, society determines what it is to be human, since it is in society that language is learnt.

## Human Society

Human life is grounded in the social practices of which language is a part, according to Wittgenstein. Each 'form of life' provides the context in which language is taught and used. The meaning of a language, therefore, is inextricably bound up with the way of life of which it is a part. It becomes very crucial, therefore, to know what counts as a particular form of life, since it looks as if the meaning of its language could be known only to its participants.

At times, Wittgenstein seems to base language on *human* practices, such as human pain-behaviour. He recognizes that there could be difficulties in understanding a strange language in an unknown country, but says quite firmly that 'the common behaviour of mankind is the system of reference by means of which we interpret an unknown language'.[23] The same idea, linking language and human nature, probably lies behind his quaint saying that 'if a lion could talk, we could not understand him'.[24] Animals do not share our mode of life. Yet at other times, another strand of thought becomes prominent. Humans speak many different languages, and even users of the same language may be involved in many different ways of life, with different assumptions being made. At the beginning of the argument against private languages, Wittgenstein points out that there must be general agreement in judgements between people if they are to share the same concepts. He says: 'That is not agreement in opinions but in form of life.' This, though, means that profound disagreement is a sign of a difference in form of life, and hence of a divergence in the use of concepts. An example that has caused much argument is that of religion. Does the atheist contradict the religious person, or are they really talking past each other because they are members of utterly different forms of life? Wittgenstein's notion of meaning growing out of the way people behave leads him to think of concepts not so much being *about* something as playing a role in activities. He would not be interested in abstract reasoning about the possible existence of God, nor would he simply dismiss religious language as meaningless. He would want to know the role it played in people's lives.

This raises the spectre of different societies with ways of life so different that there are no points of contact between them, of different ways of life, which are mutually incomprehensible, even within what is apparently the same linguistic community. Perhaps Wittgenstein is driven to a type of relativism, according to which the existence of different concepts means that there are different self-contained conceptual systems, each of which applies its own criteria of truth and falsity. In that case, the standards of science could not be applied in religion, or the concepts of one society criticized from the standpoint of another. Wittgenstein admits that 'an education quite different from ours might also be the foundation for quite different concepts'.[25] He remarks that life would then run on quite differently. Elsewhere he makes it clear that we cannot use one language-game as a base from which to combat another.[26] Neither can really engage with the other as each has its own standards. Any interchange can only take the form of slogan-chanting or name-calling. The example he gives is that of people who prefer to consult an oracle rather than trust physics. Wittgenstein will not accept that they are wrong to do so or that physics shows us the truth. Reasoning has to come to an end somewhere. Language-games cannot be based on grounds, but are 'there – like our life'.[27] They cannot be compared or criticized, and reason is given little place except within the assumptions of a particular form of life.

The stress on agreement as a precondition for sharing in a way of life pushes Wittgenstein towards relativism. Yet there is still the connection he sees between our concepts and 'very general facts of nature'.[28] An appeal to a universal human nature expressed in different societies could provide a bridge for understanding one culture from the standpoint of another. The seeds of this approach exist in the work of the later Wittgenstein, but his emphasis on the connection between concepts and forms of life makes the possibility of understanding alien societies very problematic. It is not surprising that Wittgenstein's influence has made the practice of social anthropology seem exceedingly difficult.

The attack on the possibility of a private language carries greatest significance for the understanding of human society. Wittgenstein is opposed to any atomistic view of individuals, like that of Hobbes, according to which the members of a society have no great dependence on it, but merely use it as a vehicle for their own self-interest. Wittgenstein's is a *holistic* view, looking at society as a whole, and seeing individuals merely as its parts.

We gain our identity through our participation in a society, however its boundaries are drawn. Marxists, who hold a similar view of the priority a society has over the individuals, are often drawn to Wittgenstein's later philosophy. Both stress our social character, since only in human society, they believe, do we become ourselves. Wittgenstein arrives at his position for philosophical reasons concerning the nature of language, and the similarity of position may be coincidental. Indeed he has sometimes been hailed as a conservative thinker, and the fact that language-games have to be accepted as they are (though they can change over time) hardly chimes with Marxist views of the need for revolution.

## Contemporary Relevance

Wittgenstein has been one of the most influential philosophers of the twentieth century and his thinking still permeates much philosophy. Yet he had a very negative conception of the scope of philosophy. It could merely cure us of our misconceptions and is powerless to provide us with a rational foundation for our most basic beliefs. This has no doubt helped to encourage modern philosophers to give up the search for any grand theory of the world and of our place in it. Not for them has there been any wide vision of reality of the kind favoured by Plato. Wittgenstein himself, however, was not so impervious to wider issues concerning human destiny.

In his distrust of generalization and of metaphysics, he shows affinities with Nietzsche. Yet he was certainly not so dismissive of the Christian faith, recognizing that religious belief stemmed from its own way of life. He could even perhaps feel its attraction, and questions about guilt and judgement were always of great concern to him. Nevertheless he could not allow free rein to human reason and hence could allow no room for rational criticism or justification of religion. Like all social practices, it was just there. In this he was more tolerant than Nietzsche, but like him and like Freud, he acknowledged the primacy of instinct over reason. He said: 'Instinct comes first, reasoning second. Not until there is a language-game are there reasons.'[29]

This links with his wish to regard humans in somewhat biological terms, with a natural history. Concepts grow up out of very general facts of human nature, and language is thus not the result of any kind of reasoning. He remarks: 'I want to regard man here as an animal: as a primitive being to which one grants instinct but not ratiocination.'[30] He does not pick out a particular instinct as important, but he certainly subordinates human reason to instinct as such. It is inevitable, therefore, that the scope of philosophy has to be reduced with metaphysical speculation ruled out. Everything depends on the social practices to which we are introduced.

Certain definite theses are apparent in what Wittgenstein says. He is opposed to dualism or to any admission of as he puts it, 'the existence of a soul *alongside* the body, a ghostly mental nature.'[31] His emphasis on instinct and on the body as the best picture of the human soul suggests that he could be espousing a form of materialism. Yet at the same time he is stressing the distinct nature of the human social world and its separation from the animal world. He shows the importance of membership of a community, and of a public context for the teaching of language. The personal experience of individuals is made irrelevant to our understanding of the world. Any idea of the self, abstracted from society, becomes highly problematic. All that is private and subjective becomes mysterious. Our view of ourselves has been turned inside out. Instead of finding other minds inaccessible, our own seems to slide out of sight. Instead of the private world of the mind, we have to be preoccupied with the public world of language. Much contemporary philosophy is in fact more concerned with the philosophy of language than with the philosophy of mind. Our true nature seems to many to be revealed more by the impersonal operations of language than by the innermost contents of our minds.

If I am who I am not because of some metaphysical fact, but because of the social and linguistic practices I have been introduced to, I cannot abstract myself from my language and see the world without the aid of linguistic categories. Language forms the self and moulds reality. We need no longer agonize over matters that seem beyond our reason. All we have to do is understand the working of language, since we cannot ultimately break out of its confining embrace. In this, at least, there may be more contact between Wittgenstein's earlier and later thought than is sometimes thought.

Yet the unsatisfactory nature of this position is well illustrated by Wittgenstein's own example, the concept of pain. It has to be taught, and this obviously means relying on public criteria such as behaviour. Does this entail, however, that it is irrelevant what pain feels like? Wittgenstein thought it did, but it is also possible that when we are taught the word in particular circumstances, we come to realize that we normally feel a distinctive kind of sensation in those situations. If we are injured, we usually feel a sensation that cannot be ignored. There are good evolutionary reasons why we should receive such an unmistakable warning signal, and it is strange to think that the quality of pain sensations must be unimportant for the concept. It is significant that people who cannot feel any pain, who are congenitally insensitive to it, find it very difficult to apply the word properly. They sometimes even assume they are feeling pain, merely because they have learnt to avoid damaging themselves, when it is clear they are not. Wittgenstein tended to assume that a pain was any sensation evoking distress and typical 'pain-behaviour'. Not all pains, however, need be disliked, and there are many unpleasant sensations that are noticeably different from pains. The kind of sensation we feel must be distinguished from our emotional reaction to it.[32]

Wittgenstein rests a great deal on the fact that we may be mistaken in identifying our inner experiences such as sensations. Yet it is highly controversial that, without the possibility of a public check, a judgement cannot claim truth. We certainly need to show evidence that we understand the meaning of a concept, but it does not follow that each subsequent judgement involving the concept must also be open to verification. That is merely to assume the priority of the public over the private.

The argument is not just about pain. That is just a test-case. The argument is over whether the individual can make any judgements, without the assistance of the norms of language. Can we think without language? The question is how far the possession of language is central to our existence as individuals and essential to our nature as humans. The more language is emphasized, the more the public and social aspects of human life are stressed. Wittgenstein's philosophy makes it a real question as to how far any of us could have existed apart from a community and still be persons.

ose the ontological question 'What are we?' because we have come
see that the main lesson of both history and anthropology is our
traordinary malleability.[3]

s idea is that, instead of worrying about irrelevant metaphysical
tions, we should instead face up to the pragmatic issue of what
can make of ourselves. He goes on, too, to base the idea of
an rights on historical facts rather than on some metaphysical
ication. His claim is that 'nothing relevant to moral choice
rates human beings from animals except historically contingent
of the world, cultural facts'.[4] There is no universal human
re. There are just different histories, moulding us in different
s. Rorty bolsters his position by pointing out that 'between
's time and ours, Darwin argued most intellectuals out of the
that human beings contained a special added ingredient'.[5]
t, if Rorty is to be consistent, this observation can only have the
s of cultural commentary. As a matter of social fact, intellect-
have been impressed by Darwin. What Rorty cannot even imply
t Darwin has been seen to be correct. According to his position,
narch of scientific progress cannot have produced a deeper
rstanding of what it is to be human, because there is no such
as scientific progress. There is ultimately no truth. There is no
an rationality transcending cultural boundaries. There is only a
ng cavalcade of beliefs, appearing and disappearing as cultures
ge. Just as there can be no such thing as human nature, and
ing to investigate, so there can be no scientific reasoning. There
only the prejudices of particular cultures. The prejudice of
ern thought since the seventeenth century has centred on a
in the power of empirical science. It is the task of postmodern
ght to show how this is as much a cultural creation as anything
cientific. 'Western' science is no better and no worse than any
set of cultural beliefs. It is simply the product of a historically
tioned view of reason.

rty accepts that his views could be portrayed as a species of
ral relativism, although he does not embrace the label. Never-
ss, postmodernism runs the risk of sinking into the quagmire of
vism. It begins by insisting that the 'Enlightenment' view of
n is earthed in a particular time and place, but ends by repu-
ng the very possibility of rationality. The dangers of this
ach are illustrated by Rorty's reference to Darwin. The issue

# Conclusion to the Second Edition

## Postmodernism and Human Nature

Who, then, is right? This was the question the 'Conclusion to the
First Edition' posed, and it remains a burning issue. When faced with
so many differing views about the nature of human beings, how can
we decide which is right and which is wrong? It seems as if people
have been arguing for centuries about the same issues without
coming to any settled opinion. Indeed at the start of a new millennium, it becomes all the more poignant that we seem to have
reached no greater agreement about our own place in the world
than the Athenians did when they argued about these matters in the
time of Socrates and Plato.

It is perhaps not surprising that one of the major philosophical
influences in the contemporary world is that of so-called 'postmodernism'. This is above all a reaction against the modern world as
exemplified in the Enlightenment. It opposes the view of reason
which was upheld in particular by people such as Locke in the
seventeenth century and Kant in the eighteenth. For such philosophers reason was the most important characteristic of human
beings, and it could discover truths that held for everyone. The
view had religious beginnings, with rationality seen as a reflection
of the nature of God (or, as Locke and others such as John Wesley,
put it, as 'the candle of the Lord'). Human reason, however, soon
demanded its autonomy, and developed into an expression of human
dignity and self-sufficiency. Its greatest flowering was perhaps in the
rise of modern science, where the empirical method, encouraged by
the philosophy of people such as Locke, seemed to produce an ever-
growing body of knowledge.

At first this enabled us to manipulate the world better, but in the nineteenth century, particularly under the influence of Darwin, it seemed as if humans would even be able to use science to understand the origin and character of humanity. The work of Marx, and then in the twentieth century, Freud, appeared to enable us to use our reason to see that we are as humans often in the grip of forces of which we are not always aware. A scientific approach seemed to give us the key for future progress and even liberation. It was perhaps slightly worrying that there were competing scientific analyses of what was wrong with the human condition and different scientific prescriptions as to how it could all be put right. Marx concentrated on economic and political influences, while Freud, in a more individualist way, looked at psychological ones. Nevertheless in both there was an optimism that suggested that the knowledge that science acquired could somehow set us free.

Indeed a characteristic of the Enlightenment, as we saw in Kant, was an optimism that knowledge would bring improvement, and progress. Even Darwin found it very difficult not to be caught up in the assumption that evolution was somehow not just a matter of chance variations. It was a matter of progressive development to something better. Certainly many of his followers found it easy to equate evolution and progress. The Victorian age was one of great optimism. Human reason was the tool that would raise human beings to greater heights of civilization. The twentieth century has seen those hopes dashed. All too often has it been obvious that science has not brought moral improvement. It may have given us the power to make better gadgets, and to kill each other more efficiently. Whether, though, the world is a better place at the end of the twentieth century than it was at the beginning is a very moot point. Indeed such is the rise of scepticism about the role and nature of human reason, that many would assert that there is no way an assessment could be made about whether it is 'better'. There can be no agreed standards with which to judge. There can be no neutral place on which to take our position in order to make a reasoned judgment. At this point the very nature of 'reason' is put in question.

Alasdair MacIntyre is one of the influential contemporary philosophers who has expressed scepticism about the Enlightenment project of displacing authority and tradition with reason. Indeed he maintains that 'rationality itself, whether theoretical or practical, is a concept with a history'.[1] He goes on to point out since there is a

diversity of traditions of enquiry, with different [ . . . ] fact different kinds of rationality. He says: "[ . . . ] ground, no place for enquiry, no way to enga[ . . . ] advancing, evaluating, accepting, and rejectin[ . . . ] apart from that which is provided by some p[ . . . ] other.'[2] In other words, the Enlightenment a[ . . . ] itself be seen in its historical context, and vi[ . . . ] historical phase. Reason divorced from the con[ . . . ] life must lose its power and relevance. So far fr[ . . . ] mining human tradition and authority, it is see[ . . . ] such tradition. Many thinkers appeal to Niet[ . . . ] power and see appeals to a supposedly objec[ . . . ] selves merely attempts to wield more effective[ . . . ] course is then seen as a form of rhetorical per[ . . . ]

As a consequence of this type of thinking, th[ . . . ] of any attempt to step outside one's own h[ . . . ] generalize about human nature. We are, it w[ . . . ] of our time and place. There are no 'grand [ . . . ] about the nature of human beings and our p[ . . . ] things. Our views are conditioned by who we [ . . . ] We cannot transcend our own particular vie[ . . . ] tures of context and history. Indeed the very [ . . . ] anything specific about 'human' nature is deri[ . . . ] claimed, no cross-cultural or trans-historical [ . . . ] Thus not only are we imprisoned by the ass[ . . . ] There is nothing to appeal to across cultures[ . . . ] transcend local conditions.

The contemporary American philosopher[ . . . ] been in the forefront of those who question[ . . . ] ahistorical human nature. He notes the 'quar[ . . . ] Nietzsche about what we are really like'. Rorty[ . . . ] as an argument over whether humans have [ . . . ] dient (such as rationality or the soul) that [ . . . ] ontological category' from animals. Rorty, [ . . . ] there has been a decline of interest in the c[ . . . ] nature?' He continues:

We are much less inclined than our ancestor[ . . . ] human nature' seriously, much less inclined [ . . . ] history or ethology as a guide to life. We are [ . . . ]

cannot be whether Darwin has gained acceptance amongst intellectuals. At the moment, his views are indeed very fashionable, but that surely must be beside the point. The issue is whether Darwin is right. Are humans merely complicated animals, or does their ability to reason place them in a different category? Of course, it is hardly surprising that those who decry the power of reason do not see it as an important possession of humanity. Nevertheless, the mere fact that humans are malleable in a cultural sense, and have the ability to choose their way of life immediately marks them off from animals. The more that relativism is put forward as a consequence of great cultural variation, the more an important difference from animals is exposed.

## The Indispensability of the Idea of the Human

Animals do not have cultures that develop through history in any significant way. They do not have language. It is indeed striking that many postmodernists (Rorty included) are very influenced by the view of the later Wittgenstein on the priority of language. Yet the picture of a language-user immersed in the historical flux of human existence is about as far from a neo-Darwinian picture of human life being constrained by our genetic inheritance as one can imagine. The postmodern stress on the importance of language is merely a contemporary version of the view of the centrality of rationality. There is still a fundamental distinction being made between humans as speakers of languages, living in an environment that has been linguistically constructed, and animals in a 'natural' environment. The relativism that is typical of postmodernism may wish to deny that there is any essence of humanity. There is no human nature. Yet its very starting-point is language, which is being implicitly regarded as a product of humans. We may not be marked out by our rationality, but it soon appears that we are essentially language users and hence producers of culture. Human nature reappears in a new guise.

Rorty is willing to face the issue of how 'we' think of 'ourselves'. Yet this kind of question can never be posed without some assumption surfacing about who 'we' are in the first place. If he is doing anything more than talking of like-minded Americans of a liberal disposition, he must start with some idea of human beings. He cannot take biological notions at face value, since that would be to attribute a status to science which postmodernism is reluctant to grant. He must begin with some theory about who is to count as human and who does not. His reply may be that he is indeed merely working within the contingent presuppositions of a particular culture. If that is so, his views can be easily dismissed by those who do not share his background.

It may be an interesting cultural phenomenon that many intellectuals, particularly in the United States, feel impelled to reject the possibility of rationality, and the possibility of any universal human nature. By their own admission, however, that is all it is. They could never be seen as presenting a rational argument.

It was not just the idea of reason that played such an important part in the Enlightenment. We have seen that the idea of natural rights also arose. It is a fascinating paradox that the very philosophers (Rorty included) who deny cross-cultural ideas such as that of human nature, are also concerned to uphold the idea of human rights. Yet it cannot be said too often that any conception of human rights without any conception of human beings is incoherent. It is no more enlightening that a campaign for 'heffalump rights' would be in the absence of any explanation of what a heffalump might be. We cannot respect each other in virtue of our common humanity, if it is denied that we share any such thing. Ideas of human nature, in other words, have more than a philosophical significance. They provide the grounding for some of our most important moral and political views. How we treat each other depends on how we regard each other. Too easy a use of the rhetoric of human rights cloaks the fact that without a rational basis, belief in them has no more status than any other passing fashion.

Whether in politics or elsewhere the issue of human nature cannot easily be brushed aside. Once it is assumed that there is no such thing, any connection between different cultures or historical epochs is destroyed. The philosophies of ages other than our own become irrelevant to us, and indeed inaccessible. I said in the Introduction that Plato and Aristotle are recognizably concerned with the same problems as we are in an age of science. Even Rorty refers to 'the quarrel between Plato and Nietzsche'. Yet if we are in fact each thinking only within the assumptions and concepts of our own age, this kind of trans-historical debate is impossible. Postmodernists must hold not just that there is no permanent human nature, and that who 'we' are changes. They must maintain that the under-standing of each generation is constituted by the thought forms of the age. There are no facts, only interpretations. We saw that Nietzsche held this view, and postmodernism is heavily influenced by him. Yet if this is so, different ages talk past each other. We who are at the start of a new millennium cannot engage with Plato or Nietzsche, any more than Nietzsche could engage with Plato. We can only project our understanding on to a text that may once have been understood very differently.

As with all radical theories, there is a half-truth buried here. It is all too easy to produce, say, a Shakespeare play as if it was written in the contemporary age. The result may be fascinating but is not going to be true to Shakespeare and his understanding of human nature. There are theatrical producers who are so imbued with the presup-positions of their own age that they find the attitude to women, say, shown in *The Taming of the Shrew*, or to Jews in *The Merchant of Venice*, impossible to portray. Yet if Shakespeare was dealing in the Elizabethan age with timeless truths about human nature, it may be that we can learn from him much about human passions and needs. We can still recognize important political and cultural differences, but without the concept of human nature, the literature of past ages will quickly be discarded. It is no accident that in some educational circles this has been happening in recent years. There is a cultural parochialism and arrogance in such attitudes that leaves us content with the prejudices of the moment. We are led to believe that we can learn nothing from past generations because there is nothing to learn. We are fundamentally different.

A postmodern suspicion of reason as the mere rationalization of the prejudices of a particular culture is self-defeating. Like all such global positions, it destroys itself when applied to itself. It can claim neither rational grounding nor truth for itself, since it denies that such things are possible. Yet there are features of the postmodern approach that provide a salutary antidote to an excessive faith in rationality as understood in the Enlightenment. Kant had little faith in the role of tradition in shaping our views. He thought that 'Enlightenment' meant that we could with confidence appeal to a reason that needed no heritage, and would have universal appeal and application. This was significantly different from Hume's stress on the central importance of habit and custom. There is no doubt that an emphasis on reason instead of tradition can lead us to underestimate the power of our most settled assumptions. Anyone reading Kant can see that his Lutheran upbringing had at least as much influence as any 'pure reason'. Since, indeed, human beings are born into continuing societies, it is nonsensical to think that we do not make use of the wisdom and accumulated knowledge of previous generations. Indeed a great paradox about postmodernist attacks on reason is that they simultaneously show the role of tradition and wish to ignore history, because of its apparent irrelevance. We are, it seems, historically constituted, and yet we are cut off from the thinkers of previous generations.

## Ideas and Truth

A particular vice of much current controversy is that, because of a distrust of reason, we are led to look at who holds certain views and not what views are being held. It could, for instance, be a criticism of this book that the thinkers chosen come from a narrow spectrum of human thought. They are all, it will be said, dead, white males, and worse than that, they seem to come from a limited range of European thinking. The nine thinkers taken from the modern world were either English or German speaking. What, it will be said, have they to do with the those from other cultures and civilizations? Should there not be a fair representation of different viewpoints? No doubt, those who quite sincerely put forward such an objection would also object to a view of music that made Bach and Beethoven in some way centrally important. We should expand our musical taste, they would say, so as to value in an indiscriminate way the products of different cultures. Indeed it is significant how the very word 'discrimination' has acquired sinister overtones.

Again, however, we must recognize a truth embedded in such objections. Reflections on human nature have certainly not been confined to one civilization or one type of person. Anyone who holds that the idea of human nature is of something transcending cultures must recognize that who one is and where one is must be irrelevant to the question of the truth of the views being expressed. Being European or American does not necessarily give one any greater insight into who we are. Everyone can learn from others. That same argument, however, means that views cannot be dismissed merely because of who puts them forward. The question of their universal validity is not the same as a discussion of the circumstances which produced them. However interesting the history of ideas may be, what produced the ideas does not resolve the issue of their correctness. Embedding all reasoning in 'traditions' must involve a slide back into the relativism that denies objective truth. The nonsensical result will be that different generations and cultures can never talk about the same issues.

The ideas discussed in this book may have mainly arisen in part of Europe. That does not mean they only have validity for Europeans. Indeed, because they have been explicitly about the human condition, the reverse has always been intended to be the case. One should not, of course, exaggerate the issue of European origin. Plato was influenced by ideas emanating from the East, and in the last two thousand years the predominant influence on philosophic thought has been that of the Christian religion, which certainly had its own origins beyond Europe. Other religions and philosophies, particularly in India and China, must be taken seriously, but it is significant that even in those countries, western views have had great influence. It is undoubtedly true that the views that have held sway in the modern world in any continent have sprung from the thought of many of the thinkers discussed in this book. Modern China would be very different if it had not been for the influence of Marx. The language of human rights, coming from such thinkers as Locke and his successors, dominates modern international relations.

Those who meditate and write on the human condition, whether in philosophy or literature, can aspire to a world-wide audience. Anyone who has visited Stratford-upon-Avon, the birthplace of Shakespeare, will recognize the appeal his plays have for the people of every nationality, who throng its streets. The reason is clearly that he was not writing predominantly about the inhabitants of Elizabethan England. He was exposing permanent tendencies in human nature. Something similar can be said about the thinkers examined in this book. Right or wrong, they are talking about human beings and their relationship to the rest of reality. Because of this, what Plato said can be as relevant as the fashionable views of the latest postmodern thinker.

Even if, though, it is granted that views cannot be dismissed because they were written in a different age or by a certain kind of person, that does not settle the question of how we can judge between the different views. It is impossible that all the views discussed can be right. For example, a continuing theme, implicit and explicit, is whether we have been created by a God. Christianity has set the agenda for discussion. Even an atheist like Nietzsche is reacting against it, and his thought his conditioned very largely by his repudiation of Christianity. Others, such as Aquinas, the Catholic, and Locke, the Protestant, are above all Christian philosophers. However much they respect reason, their thought is centred on their belief in divine revelation through Christ. This may surprise some who think of Locke as above all an empiricist philosopher, following the discoveries of science. Yet his position suggests that we should be wary of taking it too easily for granted that a scientific view of human nature must oppose a religious one. The Enlightenment produced a view of human reason which ultimately saw it as autonomous and self-sufficient. This encouraged an idea of science as not only having no need of religion, but even as being opposed to it. Yet the postmodern attacks on the possibility of a detached and unprejudiced rationality raises once more the issue of the grounding of human rationality. If, as philosophers such as Aristotle thought, it is what distinguishes us from animals, what produced it and what grounds it? It is hardly surprising that some would see it as a God-given faculty, which is somehow in tune with the Reason (or, in Greek, the *Logos*) present in the physical structures of the world and reflecting the mind of the Creator.

Portraying human nature in this kind of way makes it look as if there are different parts of human nature: our animal inheritance, for instance, as opposed to a rational, or even 'spiritual' part that is wholly separate. Divisions of human beings can mark off the mental and the physical, denying that either can be reduced to the other. This is all linked to the crucial question as to whether human beings, or any part of them, can survive death. We have seen how this was a central question for many philosophers from Plato on. It is still of major importance in any judgement about human nature. Are we merely complicated animals or something more? Have we an eternal destiny? 'Dualism' is to some extent an unfashionable philosophy in the contemporary age. It is suggested that we do not have different parts, a body and a soul. We are essentially embodied beings. This is partly because, despite the corrosive attacks on reason by postmodernism, scientific reasoning can still command great respect. The result is an unwillingness on the part of many to accept that there are components of the human person which are beyond scientific scrutiny. It is all too easy for everyone to forget that science is itself a product of that very human reason, which, many have claimed, sets us apart from the rest of the animal kingdom. The more that it is claimed that we are only animals, the more the status of human reason is again put into question.

## Science and Human Nature

In this kind of debate about human reason and the role of science, the figure of Darwin looms large. In recent years, progress in the human genome project has brought closer the possibility of our understanding the genetic basis of disease and much else. While postmodernism has stressed the fact of human malleability, and of cultural variation, modern sciences such as sociobiology, and more recently, evolutionary psychology, have stressed the opposite. Greater understanding of the role of genes has led many to the view that the key to human nature lies in our biology. In particular, neo-Darwinian theory has shown how genes can be transmitted through the generations. The mechanism of evolution through natural selection at the genetic level can favour the spread of some characteristics and the suppression of others. The tools provided by Darwinian theory can, it seems, enable us to understand ourselves in a way which even holds out the possibility of our being able to change our nature by manipulating our genes. Such a prospect, of course, depends on a view of human nature as being primarily the creation of our biology rather than our cultural environment. It also suggests that scientific research can somehow supplant the philosophical and metaphysical speculation of earlier generations.

Both of these views are firmly in the tradition of Enlightenment thinking. E. O. Wilson, the founder of sociobiology, has referred to the postmodernist and Enlightenment extremes, and sums up the difference by alleging that 'Enlightenment thinkers believe we can know everything and radical postmodernists believe we can know nothing'.[6] Certainly there is an arrogance in those who think that science can supplant religion and philosophy, which takes little account of human fallibility. Ironically, however, postmodernists also ignore the fact that we can be mistaken, since their relativism cannot take seriously the possibility of error. Different traditions exist, and we cannot say that any of them could be mistaken.

Wilson himself is very firmly on the side of the Enlightenment. His faith in science in general, and biology in particular, is based on a view that everything, including human social and mental phenomena, is based on material processes that are ultimately reducible to the laws of physics. A main thrust of this view is, as he puts it, that 'culture and hence the unique qualities of the human species will make complete sense only when linked in causal explanation to the natural sciences'.[7] Humans are wholly parts of the physical world, to be understood by the same methods of the physical sciences that are appropriate for the investigation of both other animals and of inanimate matter. Wilson thus places himself on one side of the great battle about materialism which has been fought since the time of Plato. Is the material world all that there is? Are humans merely physical beings? The evidence of evolution, and of human genetic similarity to apes makes many biologists think that human nature has a completely physical basis. We are merely another animal species.

It is important to recognize that positions such as this may rely on scientific understanding, but they are also importing philosophical assumptions into their science. The idea, for instance, that the only real processes are material ones is certainly not a scientific discovery. Science may be able to uncover physical processes, but that does not mean that only physical processes are real. The debate between those who are 'naturalists' and believe that the only reality is that accessible to natural science, and those who are unwilling to reduce everything to physical processes will go on. Part of the naturalist position must be a reluctance to allow philosophy any status independent of science. It cannot have access to some independent body of knowledge that cannot be accounted for in scientific terms. It is significant that Wilson says that 'philosophy, the contemplation of the unknown, is a shrinking dominion'.[8] He himself says that the goal should be to turn as much philosophy as possible into science. In other words, science is the only proper source of genuine knowledge. Yet that is itself a philosophical assumption of the first order. Why should empirical discovery be considered the only form of knowledge? What indeed makes scientific knowledge possible in the first place? Is the order discovered in the world by science actually a necessary precondition for science? It is remarkable that Locke, the empiricist philosopher, who appeared to underwrite the possibility of positions such as that of Wilson, also accepted the reality of the supernatural.

The issue is not just whether we are merely physical beings or whether parts of our nature cannot be reduced to physical terms. The question is also the relevance of philosophical ideas about human nature. Do the kind of philosophical views put forward by many of the thinkers discussed in this book have any real relevance? Postmodernists deny that there is any proper subject matter for philosophy. There is merely a historical succession of different views, each only really meaningful in its own context. Their arch opponents would also decry metaphysics and philosophical reasoning, looking instead to the discoveries of empirical science. In a sense the heirs of Nietzsche confront the followers of Darwin. Yet these are not the only possibilities. There should not be a choice between relativism or a blind worship of contemporary science. Both fail to take seriously the fact that ideas can live on through different periods of history. Right or wrong, such ideas are themselves major influences on human behaviour.

The most potent ideas of all are those that we form about ourselves. In one sense, it is not surprising that we find it so difficult to agree about the kind of beings we are. It is a truism that if you want to avoid controversy, it is always best to avoid the subjects of religion and politics. Both are intimately bound up with questions both about how we individually should live our lives, and about how society should be organized. Our own personal interests are closely bound up with the responses we make to these problems. Yet, as is abundantly clear from our discussion of twelve major thinkers, religion and politics are both themselves intimately connected with understandings of human nature. Relativists in effect give up when faced with alternative positions. They are content to accept that different people think and behave differently. Those who are committed to modern science are, on the other hand, saying in effect that the latest views are the true ones. Previous generations did not have the knowledge we now possess. Reason can start afresh. We now know more than our predecessors.

In some areas we do know more at the beginning of the third millennium than our predecessors did at the beginning of the first or the second. We are clever at manipulating and to some extent controlling the phyical world, though all too often we set in train events that we totally fail to foresee. The problem is that with all our new knowledge, it does not seem as if the humans in charge of it are very different from our predecessors. We make mistakes, we are selfish, arrogant, and short-sighted. In fact it often seems as if we are not very different from those flawed human beings who figure in Greek tragedies. Despite their great talents, they only succeed in engineering disaster for themselves. The comparison is instructive, since it suggests that across the centuries we see the similarities between them and us. Fashions may change, but people do not. As Hume pointed out, if you want to know about the Greeks and Romans, study the French and English. Yet that remark was itself made in a very different society from ours. The fact that it can still seem apposite only serves to illustrate the fact that ideas of human nature can leap from epoch to epoch, and culture to culture. Yet because they concern something which persists, their relevance remains. No doubt the biologist would wish to point to the stability of our genetic inheritance. Our genetic constitution cannot change very rapidly, judged in terms of recorded history. Yet this is to lapse into science, and it should be clear that even science itself must be fired by a philosophical vision of the nature of the world and our place in it. A view of humans as complex physical objects, even animate ones, is very different from one of us as beings endowed with a reason that can transcend local circumstances and formulate claims to truth. It is indeed ironic that contemporary science often tends to the former view, whilst simultaneously taking for granted the ability of its practitioners to recognize truth themselves.

Unless in fact there is an unchanging core to human nature, it will have been fruitless paying attention to the opinions of those living nearly two and a half thousand years ago. Unless the same ideas can be potent even in different circumstances, an examination of the views of past thinkers must be irrelevant. Above all, however, unless truth is at stake, there is little point in discussing the varying beliefs that have been held. Many of them have been, and are, influential. Aquinas is still a major influence on Roman Catholic thinking. The legacy of those purveyors of suspicion of our real motives, Nietzsche, Marx and Freud, permeates modern thinking, even when their views have been apparently discarded. The Enlightenment, particularly as seen by Kant, continues to influence our attitudes, even when we are reacting against it. In politics, Marx's name may not be invoked as often as it used to be, but other ideas cast their spell. Hobbes' individualism, and Locke's liberalism, permeate the thinking of the contemporary world. We should, though, be wary of allowing ourselves to become the slaves of fashion. In the end, however potent an idea may be, the point is not how many people accept it. The crucial issue must always be whether it is true. Since the most dangerous ideas are always those that are accepted uncritically, it is always crucial that we be aware not just of the views that are currently influential. We should be aware of the alternatives, and be prepared to weigh them in the balance. It is only through discussion and comparison, and willingness to engage with those who disagree with us, that we ourselves may come to a better understanding of which ideas may be true.

# Notes

## Chapter 1    Plato c.429–347 BC

1   Book 3, p. 38.
2   Plato, *Meno*, 71e.
3   Plato, *Republic*, 508d.
4   *Meno*, 82b ff.
5   *Meno*, 286b.
6   *Republic*, 479d.
7   Plato, *Phaedo*, 415c.
8   Plato, *Phaedrus*, 253c ff.
9   *Republic*, 611b.
10   Ibid., 475c.
11   Ibid., 435e.   .
12   Ibid., 415a ff.
13   Ibid., 495c.
14   Ibid., 443d.
15   Ibid., 444d.

## Chapter 2    Aristotle 384–322 BC

1   Aristotle, *Physics*, 194b.
2   Aristotle, *Metaphysics*, 1073a.
3   Aristotle, *Nicomachean Ethics*, 1096b.
4   *Politics*, 1252b.
5   Ibid., 1332a.
6   *Nicomachean Ethics*, 1180a.
7   Ibid., 1134b.
8   *Politics*, 1254b.
9   *Nicomachean Ethics*, 1098a.
10   Aristotle, *De Anima*, 412b.

11 *De Anima*, 403a.
12 Ibid., 412b.
13 *Nicomachean Ethics*, 1178a.
14 *Politics*, 1264b.
15 Ibid., 1262b.
16 Ibid., 1263a.
17 *Nicomachean Ethics*, 1168b.
18 *Politics*, 1262b.
19 Ibid., 1337a.
20 *Nicomachean Ethics*, 1141a.

## Chapter 3    Aquinas 1225–1274 AD

1 Aquinas *Summa Theologiae*, 76.1.
2 I Corinthians 15: 19 (NEB).
3 *Summa Theologiae*, 1a, 75.4.
4 Ibid., 1a, 76.1.
5 Ibid., 1a, 76.3.
6 Ibid., 1a, 76.3.
7 Ibid., 1a, 76.2.
8 Aquinas, *Summa Contra Gentiles*, 4.79.
9 *Summa Theologiae*, 1a, 81.
10 Ibid., 1a, 83.1.
11 Ibid., 1a, 83.2.
12 Ibid., 1a, 2, 85, 1.
13 Ibid., 1a, 2.82.
14 Ibid., 1a, 2.96.2.
15 Ibid., 1a, 2.95.1.
16 Ibid., 1a, 2a.91.6.
17 Ibid.
18 Ibid., 1a, 2a, 94.2.
19 Ibid., 1a, 2a, 94, 6.
20 Ibid., 1a, 2a, 94, 6.

## Chapter 4    Hobbes 1588–1679

1 W. Molesworth (ed.) *English Works*, vol. 1, *The Elements of Philosophy*, p. 11.
2 Ibid., vol. 3, frontispiece.
3 Ibid., vol. 4, *Human Nature*, p. 22.
4 *English Works*, vol. 3, *Leviathan*, part 4, ch. 46, p. 669.
5 Ibid., p. 674.
6 Ibid., p. 687.

7  Ibid., part 1, ch. 26, p. 41.
8  Ibid., p. ix.
9  Ibid., vol. 1, *Elements of Philosophy*, p. 409.
10  Ibid., vol. 4, *Of Liberty and Necessity*, p. 253.
11  *Leviathan*, part 1, ch. 15, p. 13.
12  Ibid., ch. 13, p. 114.
13  *English Works*, vol. 4, *Human Nature*, p. 53.
14  *Leviathan*, part 1, ch. 14, p. 117.
15  *Human Nature*, p. 49.
16  Ibid., p. 44.
17  Ibid., p. 49.
18  *Leviathan*, part 1, ch. 14, p. 116.
19  *English Works*, vol. 2, *De Cive*, p. 21.
20  *Leviathan*, part 2, ch. 17, p. 154.
21  Ibid., ch. 18, p. 163.
22  Ibid., ch. 21, p. 208.
23  *Leviathan*, part 1, ch. 15, p. 132.

## Chapter 5    Locke 1632–1704

1  *An Essay Concerning Human Understanding*, ed. P. H. Nidditch, 1975, p. 668.
2  Ibid., p. 696.
3  Ibid., p. 698.
4  *The Reasonableness of Christianity*, reprint of the 1794 edition, 1997, p. 104.
5  Ibid., p. 140.
6  Ibid., p. 104.
7  Ibid., p. 10.
8  *Reasonableness*, p. 133.
9  *Essay*, p. 45.
10  Ibid., p. 87.
11  *Some Thoughts Concerning Education*, ed. J. W. and J. S. Yolton, 1989, p. 325.
12  *Essay*, p. 143.
13  *Essay*, p. 540.
14  Ibid., p. 336.
15  Ibid., p. 95.
16  Ibid., 627.
17  *Political Essays*, ed. M. Goldie, 1997, p. 126.
18  Ibid., p. 127.
19  Ibid., p. 126.
20  Ibid., p. 281.

21  Ibid., p. 126.
22  Ibid., p. 300.
23  Ibid., p. 301.
24  Ibid., p. 119.
25  *Reasonableness*, p. 139.
26  *Political Essays*, p. 82.
27  Ibid., p. 93.
28  *Two Treatises of Government*, ed. P. Laslett, 1960, p. 271.
29  Ibid., p. 280.
30  Ibid., p. 291.
31  Ibid., p. 417.
32  Ibid., p. 419.
33  Ibid., p. 301.
34  Ibid., p. 279.
35  *Essay*, p. 560.
36  See my *Rationality and Science: Can Science Explain Everything?* (Oxford, Blackwell Publishers, 1993) (particularly chapter 10) for a discussion of the metaphysical assumptions science might need.

## Chapter 6    Hume 1711–1776

1  L. A. Selby-Bigge (ed.) *A Treatise of Human Nature*, revised by P. H. Nidditch, 1978, p. 183.
 2  Ibid., p. 187.
 3  English Works, vol. 4, p. 125–6.
 4  *Treatise*, p. xx.
 5  Ibid., p. 402.
 6  Ibid., p. 402.
 7  Ibid., p. 400.
 8  Ibid., p. 407.
 9  L. A. Selby-Bigge (ed.) *Enquiry Concerning Human Understanding*, 3rd edn, 1975, p. 75.
10  Ibid., p. 83.
11  *Treatise*, p. 252.
12  'Of the immortality of the soul', in T. H. Green and T. Grose (eds) *Philosophical Works*, vol. 4, Darmstadt Scientia Verlag Aalen, reprinted 1964, p. 406.
13  *Treatise*, p. 415.
14  *Enquiry*, p. 46.
15  Ibid., p. 48.
16  *Treatise*, p. 179.
17  Ibid., p. 416.
18  Ibid., p. 481.

19  Ibid., p. 483.
20  Ibid., p. 487.
21  Ibid., p. 618.
22  Hume, *Enquiry Concerning the Principles of Morals*, p. 286.
23  'Of the origin of government', in T. H. Green and T. Grose (eds) *Philosophical Works*, vol. 3, p. 114.
24  *Treatise*, p. 493.
25  Ibid., p. 485.
26  Ibid., p. 494.
27  Ibid., p. 539.
28  Ibid., p. 537.
29  Ibid., p. 551.
30  Ibid., p. 490.
31  *Enquiry*, p. 108.

### Chapter 7   Kant 1724–1804

1   *Critique of Pure Reason*, trans. Norman Kemp Smith, 1993, p. 668.
2   *Critique of Practical Reason* in *Practical Philosophy*, Cambridge Edition of the Works of Immanuel Kant, ed. Mary Gregor, 1996, p. 181.
3   Ibid., p. 180.
4   Ibid., p. 269.
5   'What is Enlightenment?', in *Practical Philosophy*, p. 17.
6   *Critique of Pure Reason*, p. 59.
7   Ibid., p. 56.
8   Ibid., p. 20.
9   Ibid., p. 268.
10  Ibid., p. 22.
11  *Critique of Judgment*, trans. Werner S. Pluhar, 1987, p. 323.
12  *Groundwork of the Metaphysics of Morals*, in *Practical Philosophy*, p. 76.
13  Ibid., p. 73.
14  Ibid., p. 77.
15  Ibid., p. 74.
16  Ibid.
17  Ibid., p. 64.
18  *Critique of Pure Reason*, p. 169.
19  Ibid., p. 354.
20  *Groundwork*, in *Practical Philosophy*, p. 80.
21  'Toward perpetual peace', in *Practical Philosophy*, p. 347.
22  Ibid., p. 324.
23  'What is Enlightenment?', in *Practical Philosophy*, p. 20.
24  'On the common saying: That may be correct in theory', in *Practical Philosophy*, p. 306.

25  Ibid., p. 309.
26  *Critique of Judgment*, p. 368.
27  *Religion Within the Limits of Reason Alone*, trans. T. M. Greene and H. H. Hudson, 1960, p. 143.

## Chapter 8    Darwin 1809–1882

1   Francis Darwin (ed.) *Life and Letters of Charles Darwin*, vol. 1, London, 1887, p. 61.
2   Darwin, *The Origin of Species*, ed. J. W. Burrow, 1968, p. 115.
3   Ibid., p. 202.
4   Ibid., p. 108.
5   Ibid., p. 438.
6   Ibid., p. 104.
7   Ibid., p. 210.
8   Ibid., p. 409.
9   'Darwinism as applied to man', in H. R. Steeves and E. H. Ristine (eds) *Representative Essays in Modern Thought*, New York, 1913 (also includes concluding chapter of Wallace's *Darwinism*, 1889).
10  Genesis, 1: 25 (NEB).
11  Ibid., 1: 27.
12  *Letters*, vol. 1, p. 93.
13  Ibid., p. 309.
14  Ibid., p. 304.
15  Ibid., p. 306.
16  *Letters*, vol. 2, p. 201.
17  Ibid., vol. 1, p. 312.
18  Spencer, *The Data of Ethics*, London, 1907, p. 170.
19  *Letters*, vol. 2, p. 177.
20  Darwin, *The Descent of Man*, 1888, p. 125.
21  Ibid., p. 108.
22  Ibid., p. 66.
23  Ibid., p. 124.
24  Ibid., p. 122.
25  Ibid., p. 126.
26  Ibid., p. 113.
27  Ibid., p. 105.
28  Ibid., p. 128.
29  Ibid., p. 130.
30  Ibid., p. 132.
31  *Letters*, vol. 1, p. 316.
32  *Letters*, vol. 2, p. 202.

## Chapter 9    Marx 1818–1883

1   'Theses on Feuerbach', in D. McLellan (ed.) *Selected Writings*, p. 158.
2   D. McLellan (ed.) *Marx's Grundrisse*, 1971.
3   K. Marx and F. Engels, *Selected Correspondence*, London, 1934, p. 125.
4   Ibid.
5   Ibid. (also McLellan (ed.) *Selected Writings*, p. 525).
6   K. Marx and F. Engels, *Selected Works*, vol. 3, Moscow, Foreign Languages Publishing House, 1970, p. 162.
7   K. Marx, *Capital*, vol. 1, 1976, p. 92.
8   K. Marx and F. Engels, *German Ideology*, ed. C. J. Arthur, p. 59.
9   'Economic and Philosophical manuscripts', in D. McLellan (ed.) *Karl Marx, Early Texts*, p. 134.
10  Ibid., p. 140.
11  *Capital*, vol. 1, p. 165, 1.4.
12  'The Holy Family', in McLellan (ed.) *Selected Writings*, p. 152.
13  *Capital*, p. 552.
14  *German Ideology*, p. 53.
15  Ibid., p. 59.
16  Ibid., p. 47.
17  Ibid., p. 53.
18  McLennan (ed.) *Marx's Grundrisse*, p. 124.
19  McLennan (ed.) *Selected Writings*, p. 246.
20  McLennan (ed.) *Marx's Grundrisse*, p. 131.
21  McLennan (ed.) *Selected Writings*, p. 497.
22  *German Ideology*, p. 44.
23  *Critique of the Gotha Programme*, in McLellan (ed.) *Selected Writings*, p. 569.
24  Ibid., p. 235.
25  Ibid.
26  *German Ideology*, p. 95.

## Chapter 10    Nietzsche 1844–1900

1   Nietzsche, *Will to Power*, section 200.
2   Ibid., section 202.
3   Ibid., section 481.
4   Ibid., section 493.
5   Ibid., section 480.
6   Nietzsche, *Thus Spoke Zarathustra*, p. 42.
7   Nietzsche, *Gay Science*, section 125.
8   Nietzsche, *Daybreak*, section 49.

9   *Will to Power*, section 55.
10  *Thus Spoke Zarathustra*, p. 237.
11  *Will to Power*, section 25.
12  Nietzsche, *Beyond Good and Evil*, section 36.
13  Ibid.
14  Nietzsche, *Assorted Opinions and Maxims*, section 366.
15  *Thus Spoke Zarathustra*, section 3.
16  *Will to Power*, section 684.
17  Nietzsche, *On the Genealogy of Morals*, p. 59, 2.2.
18  *The Gay Science*, section 354.
19  Ibid.
20  *Will to Power*, section 41.
21  Ibid., section 136.
22  Ibid., section 765.
23  Ibid., section 246.
24  *Gay Science*, section 21.
25  *Beyond Good and Evil*, section 83.
26  Ibid., section 223.
27  *On the Genealogy of Morals*, p. 136.
28  *Will to Power*, section 753.

## Chapter 11   Freud 1856–1939

1   Freud, *The interpretation of dreams*, in *Collected Works*, vol. V, 1900, p. 608.
2   Freud, 'An autobiographical study', in vol. XX, 1925, p. 60.
3   Ibid. p. 8.
4   Freud, 'Introductory lectures in psychoanalysis', in vol. XVI, 1917, p. 285.
5   Freud, 'The unconscious', in vol. XIV, 1915, p. 95.
6   Freud, 'Some elementary lessons in psychoanalysis', in vol. XXIII, 1940, p. 285.
7   'Some elementary lessons', p. 284.
8   Freud, 'An outline of psychoanalysis', in vol. XXIII, 1940, p. 187.
9   Freud, 'The question of lay analysis', in vol. XX, 1926, p. 214.
10  'The interpretation of dreams', p. 247.
11  Freud, 'Totem and taboo', in vol. XIII, 1913, p. 124.
12  Freud, 'A short account of psychoanalysis', in vol. XIX, 1924, p. 204.
13  'The question of lay analysis', p. 207.
14  Freud, 'The ego and the id', in vol. XIX, 1923, p. 58.
15  Freud, 'Analysis of a phobia in a five- year-old Boy', in vol. X, 1969, p. 140.
16  'The ego and the id', p. 25.

17  Freud, 'New introductory lectures on psychoanalysis', in vol. XXII, 1933, p. 61.
18  'New introductory lectures', p. 64.
19  Ibid., p. 69.
20  Ibid., p. 77.
21  Ibid., p. 80.
22  'An outline of psychoanalysis', p. 186.
23  Freud, 'Beyond the pleasure principle', in vol. XVIII, 1920, p. 10.
24  'Ego and id', p. 25.
25  Freud, 'Civilization and its discontents', in vol. XXI, 1930, p. 97.
26  Freud, 'The future of an illusion', in vol. XXI, 1927, p. 6.
27  'Civilization and its discontents', p. 105.
28  Ibid., p. 119.
29  Ibid., p. 122.
30  Ibid., p. 113.
31  Ibid., p. 115.
32  'The future of an illusion', p. 15.
33  'An outline of psychoanalysis', p. 185.
34  'The future of an illusion', p. 31.
35  'Civilisation and its discontents', p. 74.
36  'Totem and Taboo', p. 88.
37  C. Barrett (ed.) *Lectures and Conversations*, Oxford, Blackwell Publishers, 1966, p. 51.

### Chapter 12   Wittgenstein 1889–1951

1   Wittgenstein, *Tractatus Logico-Philosophicus*, 1921, para. 7.
2   Ibid., para. 6.44.
3   Wittgenstein, *Philosophical Investigations*, 1953, para. 7.
4   Ibid., para., 23.
5   Ibid., para. 244.
6   Ibid., para., 124.
7   Ibid., para. 225.
8   Wittgenstein, *Philosophical Grammar*, 1974, p. 382.
9   E. Haldane and G. R. Ross (trans.) *Philosophical Works of Descartes*, vol. 1, Cambridge, Cambridge University Press, 1931, p. 101.
10  *Philosophical Investigations*, para. 384.
11  Ibid., para. 337.
12  Ibid., para. 342.
13  Ibid., para. 293.
14  Ibid., para. 258.
15  Ibid., para. 202.
16  Ibid., para. 205.

17   Ibid., para. 207.
18   Ibid., para. 293.
19   Ibid., p. 178.
20   Ibid., para. 304.
21   Ibid., p. 174.
22   Ibid., para. 654.
23   Ibid., para. 206.
24   Ibid., para. 241.
25   Wittgenstein, *Zettel*, 1967, p. 387.
26   Wittgenstein, *On Certainty*, 1975, para. 609.
27   Ibid., para. 609.
28   *Philosophical Investigations*, p. 230.
29   Wittgenstein, *Remarks on the Philosophy of Psychology*, vol. 2, ed. G. H. Von Wright and H. Nyman, 1980, para. 689.
30   *On Certainty*, para. 475.
31   *Remarks on the Philosophy of Psychology*, vol. 1, ed. G. E. M. Anscombe and G. H. Von Wright, 1980, para. 901.
32   For a full discussion of these complex issues see R. Trigg, *Pain and Emotion*, Oxford, Oxford University Press, 1970.

### Conclusion to the Second Edition

1   Alasdair MacIntyre, *Whose Justice? Which Rationality?*, London, Duckworth, 1988, p. 9.
2   Ibid., p. 350.
3   Richard Rorty, *Truth and Progress*, Philosophical Papers 3, Cambridge, Cambridge University Press, 1998, p. 169.
4   Ibid., p. 170.
5   Ibid., p. 174.
6   Edward O. Wilson, *Consilience: The Unity of Knowledge*, New York, Alfred A. Knopf, 1998, p. 40.
7   Ibid., p. 267.
8   Ibid., p. 12.

# Bibliography

Many of the books from which I have quoted are available in different translations and editions. Where possible I have given references to a standard edition, although I have sometimes used versions that are more readily available.

## *Plato*

I have used the famous translation by Benjamin Jowett of *The Dialogues of Plato* (Oxford, 1871). Plato's best-known work is *The Republic* (available in Penguin Classics, Harmondsworth, Penguin Books, 2nd edn, 1974). Important dialogues such as the *Meno* on the nature of virtue, and the *Phaedo* on the immortality of the soul, give a good indication of Socratic method. Section numbers (e.g. *Republic* 479d) are standard and given in most editions.

## *Aristotle*

I have quoted from Sir David Ross's translation of *The Works of Aristotle*. Volume III (1931) includes the *De Anima* (About the Soul), volume IX (1925) the *Nicomachean Ethics* and volume X (1921) the *Politics*. The *Nicomachean Ethics* and the *Politics* are of central importance, and are both available in Penguin Classics, amongst many other translations. As in Plato, the numeration (e.g. *Ethics*, 1097a) is standard.

## *Aquinas*

I have referred to the *Summa Theologiae*, Latin text and English translation, London and New York, 1963. This edition appears in sixty volumes but I have given standard references to 'questions'. For instance, volume XI of this edition includes Part *1a*, Questions 75–83, dealing with Man. Question 75 discusses the soul's nature and 76, the soul's union with the body. Question 83 is on free will. Volume XXVIII includes Part 1a, 2ae (the first part of the second part) and Question 94 on natural law. I have on occasion given my own translation. The *Summa Contra Gentiles* appears in four volumes, translated by the English Dominican fathers, London, 1924.

## Hobbes

The standard edition has been *English Works* collected and edited by Sir William Molesworth, London, 1839, in eleven volumes. Volume II includes *De Cive* (Of a Citizen), volume III *Leviathan* and volume IV *Human Nature*. *Leviathan* is his most famous work and appears in many editions (including Penguin Classics).

## Locke

Locke's main philosophic work is his *Essay Concerning Human Understanding*. I have quoted from the edition first published in 1975 by Oxford University Press and edited with an Introduction by Peter H. Nidditch. Another influential work is his *Two Treatises of Government*, and I have used the edition edited by Peter Laslett (first appearing in 1960) and published in the series 'Cambridge Texts in the History of Political Thought'. Also in this series is Locke's *Political Essays* edited by Mark Goldie (Cambridge, Cambridge University Press, 1997). Two other relevant works are Locke's *Some Thoughts Concerning Education*, ed. J. W. and J. S. Yolton (Oxford, 1989) and *The Reasonableness of Christianity*. I have used the 1997 reprint of the 1794 edition (Bristol, Thoemmes Press, 1997).

## Hume

References are given to *A Treatise of Human Nature* edited by L. A. Selby-Bigge and revised by P. H. Nidditch, Oxford, Oxford University Press, 1978, and to *Enquiries* edited by L. A. Selby-Bigge and revised by P. H. Nidditch, Oxford, Oxford University Press, 1975. This includes Hume's *An Enquiry Concerning Human Understanding* and *An Enquiry Concerning the Principles of Morals*. The latter were written to introduce the ideas of the *Treatise* to a wider audience.

## Kant

Kant's major philosophical works are his three Critiques. I have quoted from the translation by Norman Kemp Smith of his *Critique of Pure Reason*

(London, Macmillan, first published in 1929, reprinted 1993). The *Critique of Practical Reason* is now available in the new Cambridge edition of Kant's works. The volume *Practical Philosophy* was translated and edited by Mary J. Gregor (Cambridge, Cambridge University Press, 1996) and includes other important writings such as the essay 'What is Enlightenment?', and the *Groundwork of the Metaphysics of Morals*. The latter is also available separately in the series 'Cambridge Texts in the History of Philosophy' (Cambridge, Cambridge University Press, 1997). I have quoted from *The Critique of Judgment*, using the translation by Werner S. Puhar (Indianapolis, Hackett, 1987). *Religion Within the Limits of Reason Alone*, translated by T. M. Greene and H. H. Hudson, is available in Harper Torchbooks (New York, Harper, 1960).

### Darwin

*The Origin of Species* was first published in 1859, but I have given references to the Penguin edition, ed. J. W. Burrow (Harmondsworth, 1968). I have used the second edition of his *The Descent of Man* (London, 1888).

### Marx

Some of his early writings (for instance the *Economic and Philosophical Manuscripts* of 1844) appear in *Karl Marx Early Texts* edited by D. McLellan, Oxford, Blackwell Publishers, 1971. *Marx's Grundrisse* is also edited by D. McLellan, London, Macmillan 1971. Extracts from many of Marx's most famous works, including the *Theses on Feuerbach*, the *Communist Manifesto*, *Critique of the Gotha Programme* and *The German Ideology* appear in *Selected Writings*, ed. D. McLellan Oxford, Oxford University Press, 1977). I have given references to the edition of *The German Ideology* edited by C. J. Arthur (London, Lawrence and Wishart, 1970). I have used the Penguin edition of *Capital* (Harmondsworth, 1976).

### Nietzsche

I have referred to *On the Genealogy of Morals*, translated by W. Kaufmann and R. J. Hollingdale (New York, *Vintage Books*, 1968). *The Will to Power*, translated by Kaufmann and Hollingdale (New York, Vintage Books, 1968), and *Thus Spoke Zarathustra*, translated by Hollingdale in Penguin Classics, (Harmondsworth, 1961). A useful collection of short extracts from a variety of works is *A Nietzsche Reader*, edited and translated by R. J. Hollingdale, Penguin Classics (Harmondsworth, 1977).

## *Freud*

The Standard Edition of *The Complete Psychological Works* is in twenty-four volumes, published in London from 1953, and was translated from the German under the editorship of James Strachey. I have given volume and page numbers together with the title and date of the relevant work. A definitive collection of some of the most important works is *The Essentials of Psychoanalysis*, selected by Anna Freud (Harmondsworth, Penguin, 1986). Two relevant works not included in it are *The Future of an Illusion* (1927) and *Civilization and its Discontents* (1930).

## *Wittgenstein*

An edition of *Tractatus Logico-Philosophicus* translated by D. F. Pears and B. F. McGuinness was published in London, Routledge and Kegan Paul, 1961. All his other works are published by Basil Blackwell, Oxford, and references are given to these. Wittgenstein's most influential work is *Philosophical Investigations*, ed. G. E. M. Anscombe, Oxford, 1958 (New York, 1973). Part I is divided into sections and the famous argument against the possibility of a private language begins at paragraph 241. References to Part 2 are by page numbers. References to other works are normally by sections.

# Index